Renata Singer is a writer who conceived the idea of *Older & Bolder* when she realised how much she loved talking to old people. Her other books include *True Stories from the Land of Divorce*, *Goodbye and Hello* (on the experience of emigration) and a novel, *The Front of the Family*. With her husband, the philosopher Peter Singer, she co-edited *The Moral of the Story: Ethics Through Literature*.

Renata likes to get things done. After working with disadvantaged women in New York, she co-founded Fitted for Work, the Australian non-profit that helps women back into the workforce. In earlier lives she was a high school teacher, a community worker, a publications officer for Oxfam Australia and a member of the Workcare Appeals Tribunal.

Renata and Peter have three children and four grandchildren. They divide their time between New York and Melbourne.

Older
&
Bolder

Renata Singer

MELBOURNE
UNIVERSITY
PRESS

MELBOURNE UNIVERSITY PRESS
An imprint of Melbourne University Publishing Limited
11–15 Argyle Place South, Carlton, Victoria 3053, Australia
mup-info@unimelb.edu.au
www.mup.com.au

First published 2015
Text © Renata Singer, 2015
Design and typography © Melbourne University Publishing Limited, 2015

Cover design by Nada Backovic
Typeset by Typeskill
Printed in Australia by McPherson's Printing Group

National Library of Australia Cataloguing-in-Publication entry

Singer, Renata, author.
Older and bolder: life after sixty/Renata Singer.

9780522865950 (paperback)
9780522865967 (ebook)

Older people—Life skills guides.
Older women—Psychology.

646.79

Contents

Introduction

It all started when I fell in love. With Bel Kaufman. And it was love at first sight. Here's what I wrote in my notebook on that fateful day in September 2011:

> Only my sense of duty brings me to the 'Grand Opening' of the new Workmen's Circle Building in New York City, where I fidget through three management speaks about the passion for 'renewal', 'restructure', and 'being true to our mission'. Yawn!
>
> And then Bel Kaufman is introduced. Completely unexpected. The legendary, the one and only. I've never seen her in real life before. Of course I know who she is—the granddaughter of the famous Yiddish writer Sholem Aleichem, and author of the 1965 bestseller, *Up the Down Staircase*, about an idealistic young teacher's first year in the New York City Public School system.
>
> We're told she's 100 years old—it can't be true. She looks fantastic: hair in an elegant upsweep of curls, enormous glamorous sunglasses, a red scarf draped over her shoulder. Even better, she's smart, funny, charming. Last year she taught a course at her alma mater, Hunter College, on Jewish humour. What a thrill, she says, in these days of education cuts to be offered a college teaching job at the age of 100.

Speaking without notes for twenty minutes—yes, she has a stick to balance on her red stilettos but hey she's 100—she tells stories about her famous grandfather. By his wish he is buried among the 'workers and poor folk'. At one stage she momentarily loses her thread and quips, 'I would never have forgotten what I wanted to say at ninety-nine.'

She loves being old, she says, because, 'All my life I had to do what I had to do—like we all did. To study, to work, to raise children. And now I don't *have* to do anything. It's liberating. Whenever anyone asks me to do something I don't want to do I say, "No thank you", and when they ask "Why?" I answer, "I'm 100 years old." It's the most marvellous excuse.'

We're completely in her power—and right there in the front row is her husband looking at her adoringly. He may be a mite younger—say early to mid nineties.

I love her. Now that I have such a role model I want to live to be 100.

Isn't it always a surprise when love strikes? It was unexpected and not planned but when I look back on it I could have predicted it. I wolfed down *Up the Down Staircase* when I first read it, hoping the heroine would make it through that school year as I was wondering if I'd make it through mine. Her experiences mirrored my struggles teaching at Williamstown Technical School, where the boys were punished for walking the wrong way down the one-way corridors.

Lovers often have similar backgrounds and Bel, like me, is Jewish from Eastern Europe, although she's from the Ukraine and I'm from Poland. Both of us arrived in our new countries unable to speak a word of English. Her first languages were Russian and

Yiddish and mine Polish and Yiddish. My mother, if she'd lived as long, would have looked like Bel, although she would not have had the confidence to wear those giant Emilio Pucci sunglasses.

I'm still in love with Bel, even though I've never met her and now never will. She died in July 2014 at the age of 103 at home in Manhattan. The last time I saw her, on stage at the celebration of folk singer Theodore Bikel's ninetieth birthday in 2013, she was wearing flat shoes and had to be helped onstage. But she gave a wonderfully warm and witty speech, and still no notes.

If I had seen Bel a few years earlier, I probably wouldn't have fallen for her so hard. I was ready and open to her message because a week after I turned sixty my first grandchild was born. Suddenly I wanted to live long enough to see him grow up, to see what sort of a person he'll become. With this unexpected surge of desire to become a nonagenarian, I began to imagine his wedding, his graduation—why not be optimistic when the kid's still a few months old—and becoming a great grandmother. Hey, wait a minute, hadn't I just become a grandmother?

Although I now wanted to get old, before Bel Kaufman my view of ageing was like most people's. We'll creak more and move less as our bodies and brains deteriorate and our horizons shrink. We'll get rigid and crabby and people will not want to be around us. Our politics will become more conservative as we resent the young who are pushing us out. And so on ... But Bel said, 'Retirement means death. I will never retire from life while I'm alive.'[1] At 102 she loved to dance the Argentinian tango, told jokes and still felt sexy.

Sensitised and awakened by Bel, I find the media is also on my wavelength. In New York, Eva Zeisel marked the occasion of her 105th birthday with publication of *A Soviet Prison Memoir*. Portrait photographer Editta Sherman at age ninety-nine had a Thanksgiving Day parade viewing party for more than forty members of her family, including great-great grandchildren at her Central Park South apartment. Tayo Shibata in Japan published her first collection of poetry at ninety-nine. It sold over 1.5 million copies.

The ABC/Flickchicks documentary, *The 100+ Club*, features Australian women chasing their dreams in the second century of their lives. For 103-year-old Olive Webber, her nineties were the happiest years of her life. And Ruth Frith, 102, flies off to Perth to compete in the Masters' Athletics Championships. Although I wasn't consciously looking for role models about how to live, I lapped up all their stories. What most impressed me was that they took up new challenges late in life. Ruth only began competing in athletics at seventy-four and Olive started singing lessons at eighty-nine. Change is not just for the young, you can do something new at any age.

Not only are very old women being productive—working, exhibiting, publishing, performing and competing—but they are having a great time. They all agree you have to be healthy and this, like everything else they do, takes effort—sometimes called attitude—and it is worth it.

A few months after I saw Bel, I had a fat file labelled 'Fabulous Femmes over 90', and I realised I was on a quest. While medieval knights might set off to kill dragons, sparked by their adoration of lovely damsels with long tresses and pointy hats, a funny and feisty old woman now sent me galloping off to slay my fears of ageing as an inevitable decline into dithery-ness, dysfunction and death. Thank you, Bel.

During 2012 and 2013 I interviewed twenty-eight women, aged between eighty-five and 100. Each interview lasted two hours or longer, with follow-up emails and chats on the phone with the women and their children as this book progressed. Because I wanted the insights they offered to be relevant to all of us, I chose women from varying backgrounds, in different economic circumstances, educated and not so educated, single, widowed and married, and with a wide range of life stories.

Who else but the women who've gone before us, who pioneered living to ninety and beyond, can teach us how to make the most of the last third of our life? They have generously shared with me their lives and their lessons, making me want to live those coming years as fully and joyfully as they have. I hope that reading about them will do the same for you.

Warning! This is not a book about how to live longer. If that's what you're looking for you will be disappointed. But it is fuelled by the fact that we are living longer. The women I talked to are the lucky ones, having outlived by ten years or more the average life expectancy for their cohort. Average life expectancy at birth for women born in the 1920s was sixty-three. Those who made it to sixty-five, could expect to live to seventy-eight.[2] Things have changed.

If you're sixty and a Japanese woman you can now expect to live the longest, to eighty-seven on average. For Australian women it's eighty-five; women in the United Kingdom, eighty-three; and those in the United States, eighty-one. The figures are in the same range for all developed countries but nowhere as good in poorer strife-ridden countries.[3]

In the last few years, men have started to catch-up on the longevity league tables. The gap in life expectancy between men and women at sixty ranges from seven years in Japan to just four years for those in Australia and the United States.[4] This contraction has been attributed to various factors, including the decline in heavy industry and more women smoking.[5]

To the surprise of the forecasters, who predicted in the 1980s that life expectancy would plateau, it continues to grow.[6] The rise in the number of people aged sixty-five and older has just as much to do with population growth—the boomer generation has now entered the statistics—as it has to do with increased longevity.

In 1901 only 4 per cent of Australians were sixty-five or older. By 2012 this had grown to 14 per cent of the population, and by 2040 it is predicted to be 20 per cent.[7]

The women I interviewed all told me they had never given a thought to how long they would live. I was astonished. I have been thinking about this ever since my mother Rysha died. I worried that her genes were also mine. My mother, had she lived, would be ninety-two. But she died before she turned sixty. I think of those three decades as the could-have-been, might-have-been, should-have-been years. Since talking to these women I feel this loss differently, understanding better all that she could have experienced in those thirty years. I now have a much better idea of what she missed. And this will make it worse for me if a car runs me down, or I get cancer like she did, knowing what could be there for me.

Dying at sixty didn't seem so terrible when I was thirty. The accepted wisdom then was that my brain reached its full development by puberty, and my brain cells had been dying off ever since. I knew that as I aged the machine that was my brain was wearing out and after fifty this slow and inexorable deterioration would accelerate. Definitely downhill all the way, right? That's what we understood then, a third of my life ago.

Since then there has been a revolution in our understanding of the brain. Out with the hard-wired theory and in with the soft-wired. Scientists have discovered that the brain is malleable. It is not a static organ and we constantly grow new neurons. Brain plasticity is a developmental model where the anatomical composition of the brain responds to learning, thought and action. This new knowledge about how our brain responds to the stimulus of our experience and environment has radically changed our view of ageing.

Neuroscientist Dr Michael Merzenich, Emeritus Professor at the University of California in San Francisco, is a pioneer in neuroplasticity, a field in which he has a three-decade-long track record. He argues that targeted activities and programs, what he calls 'brain fitness programs', can 'help prevent, arrest or even reverse the effects of cognitive decline'. Learning new and challenging things, he says, creates positive changes in our brain and will 'help people ensure their brain spans match their life spans'. Among the challenges Professor Merzenich recommends for your brain are learning a new musical instrument, a new language, a new dance, doing difficult jigsaw puzzles (of over five-hundred pieces) and playing table tennis.[8]

Although unlikely to be familiar with Merzenich's theories, the women I interviewed are following his program naturally. Many of them learn languages and play the piano, read the latest books, swim and exercise. They develop new projects, travel as much and as far as they possibly can to new places, and do their very best to stay engaged with life and with people. I'm impressed with the sustained effort they put into creating full and interesting lives, whether completing a PhD, or sending a card to every grandchild and great grandchild on their birthday, or working out the logistics of their next trip or celebration. They are not sitting around waiting for life—or death—to happen to them.

'Don't think that you're ever too old to learn new things,' was Bel Kaufman's advice. I've learned so many new things through the writing of this book that at times I thought my brain would burst. The women showed me that there is so much more to learn if I'm lucky enough to have those extra years to live.

In this latter third of our lives, we have the time to put what we've learned, and are continuing to learn, and our skills and experience, to work for the things that we care about. The opportunity for activism is here—remember, you're never too old to change the world. Older women are involved in political organisations, and in organising and lobbying for causes such as saving the dingo, protecting human rights and those of animals, and caring for the environment.

As well as being part of multi-generational and mixed-gender groups, older women also set up their own activist organisations. One of my favourites is Great Old Broads for Wilderness, a nation-wide US group founded in 1989 'by a feisty group of lady hikers', who use the deference to their age and experience to get publicity to protect public lands. In Australia, Grandmothers Against the Detention of Refugee Children was formed because older women felt they had speak up for the more than nine hundred imprisoned children and work for their release. The potential for us to flex our political muscles never goes away.

After you've read this book I'm hoping that you'll want to ask yourself the question I'm now trying to answer: What am I going to do next?

Contributors

THERE WOULD BE no book without the generosity of the twenty-eight women who invited me into their homes, answered my questions so thoughtfully and talked to me about their long and rich lives.

Why twenty-eight, you might ask? It wasn't because I wanted to stop. I was having a great time doing the interviews and there are many more women out there, with different and fascinating stories to tell, but as my editor firmly pointed out, there would never be a book if I kept on doing interviews.

Thank you all for your warmth and generosity, for being willing to talk to me, and most of all for your honesty with someone who came as a stranger and left your homes feeling more like a friend.

I hope that you feel good about the book you inspired and guided. I know that readers will enjoy meeting and getting to know you as much as I have.

 **Dr Jean Allison** was born in Melbourne Australia on 4 October 1927. After Dandenong High School, she studied medicine at the University of Melbourne. For twenty-five years she practised anaesthetics at the London Mission Hospital in Hong Kong, retiring and returning to Melbourne in 1993. Jean is a keen bushwalker and active in professional associations and her local Uniting Church, and in advocating on environmental and refugee issues.

Dr Margaret Barnett became a world authority on genetic changes in leukaemia. She was born on 4 October 1927 in Benalla, Victoria, and was educated at public high schools and the University of Melbourne Medical School. Margaret established and headed the Research Lab for cancer cytogenetics at St Vincent's Hospital. After retirement Margaret worked at the Cancer Council and as a guide at the Melbourne Zoo. Her husband died in 2006. She has two children and five grandchildren. Margaret lives with her cat Jacques and tries to travel as much as she can.

Two hundred and forty-nine people attended **Dodo Berk's** 100th birthday party. Born on 18 September 1914 in the Bronx, Dodo grew up in Brooklyn, New York. She worked at RH Macy & Co (now Macy's) department store until her marriage. Dodo has been a widow for twenty-six years. She has a son and a daughter, four grandsons and a great granddaughter. She is the oldest and longest-residing resident in her apartment block, the former Lido Beach Hotel.

Lady Florence Bjelke-Petersen is best known as the wife and widow of Joh Bjelke-Petersen, the longest-serving, and probably most polarising, premier of Queensland, and for her famous pumpkin scone recipe. She was born in Brisbane in August 1920 and lives in the house she moved into when she married, on the family farm near Kingaroy. From 1981 to 1993 Lady Flo served as a senator in the federal parliament. She has four children, fourteen grandchildren and a growing brood of great grandchildren.

 Born in July 1916, **Mary Broughton** attended a private girls' school and completed an arts degree at the University of Melbourne. She married in 1939 and was widowed at forty-five. She has two children, five grandchildren and four great grandchildren. Voluntary work has been a large part of her life especially with the YWCA, Red Cross, Uniting Church and Shoreham Historical Society. A very keen gardener, Mary is involved with the Lyceum Club and the Mont Albert Reading Circle. She now lives in a home for the aged.

 **Stephanie Charlesworth** was born in Kew, Melbourne, in May 1925. She was the first social worker employed by the department of immigration. After marriage and motherhood—she has seven children and eleven grandchildren—she completed a Master of Social Work and then a law degree. Stephanie is a pioneer in the field of family mediation. Into her busy schedule she fits research and writing of her family history, gym, meditation and the Catholic couples' program she and her husband brought to Australia.

 **Margaret Fulton** is Australia's first celebrity chef. Through her cookbooks, and as food editor of *Woman's Day* and later *New Idea,* she has had an enormous influence on what Australians cook and eat. Born in Nairn, Scotland, in October 1924, Margaret came to Australia when she was three years old. She married twice and has a daughter, two granddaughters and two great grandchildren. Margaret continues to be involved with food and cookery with the reissue of her cookbooks, and in the family food business established by her daughter and granddaughters.

Beth Gott is a botanist best known for her pioneering work on the indigenous plants of south-eastern Australia. Born in Moonee Ponds in Melbourne in July 1922, she attended state schools and gained her PhD from the University of London. Beth's husband died in 1990. She had three children and has five grandchildren, and has always worked, although not always for pay. Beth is responsible for the Indigenous Garden at Monash University, continues to expand and update her extensive databases, attend conferences, give talks and write on the subject in which she is the expert.

Sister Mary Gregory joined the Good Samaritan Order at the age of twenty-one. She was born in February 1923 in Grafton, New South Wales, and worked as a social worker and educator. In 1985 she attended Fordham University in New York City, where she completed a Master of Religious and Children's Education. Sister Mary lives in the assisted living section of a large housing complex and is involved in an advisory role with organisations that promote social justice in the local area and beyond.

Lady April Hamer was born in Melbourne Australia in 1921. She completed an arts degree at the University of Melbourne and married Rupert (Dick) Hamer, the former premier of Victoria, in March 1944. They had five children. Lady Hamer has eight grandchildren and a great grandson. Her duties as a politician's wife were especially demanding from 1972 to 1981. Her husband died just after their sixtieth wedding anniversary in 2004. After moving into an old-age home,

Lady Hamer continued to attend her current affairs class, study Italian, and read widely. She died in January 2015.

Barbara Hamer worked as a social worker until she married David Hamer, who went on to be a federal politician in both the house of representatives and the senate. Born in January 1926 in Melbourne, Australia, Barbara has three children and eight grandchildren. As well as fulfilling her duties as a politician's wife, Barbara was active in voluntary work, particularly at the board and advisory level, including the Australian Arts Council and the Council of the University of Melbourne. She has been a widow since 2002. Barbara plays the piano every day, is running her family business and farm, and is involved in the Hamer Family Foundation.

Born in St Kilda, Melbourne, in March 1922, **June Helmer** studied pharmacy at the University of Melbourne. June had three children and has five grandchildren. Returning to study in her fifties, June completed a Master of Fine Arts, taught in the Fine Arts Department and wrote *George Bell: The Art of Influence* (1985). She worked tirelessly for the Jewish Museum of Australia, and then catalogued with Dr Cunningham Dax his collection of art by people with mental health issues.

Florence Howlett has lived in Coburg for ninety years. She was born in Nottingham, England, in September 1918, arriving in Australia when she was three. Her husband died just before their seventy-fourth wedding anniversary. Flo has five children, fifteen grandchildren, twenty-six great grandchildren, and a great-great grandchild. She lives in an old-age home where she takes part in their full range of activities. She is a keen knitter and reader.

Dr Elisabeth Kirkby is Australia's oldest university graduate and the oldest person in Australia to be awarded a PhD. Her thesis compared the Great Depression with the global financial crisis, both of which she experienced. Born in January 1921 in Bolton, England, she came to Australia in 1965. Elisabeth was an Australian Democrat member of the NSW Parliament, ran a sheep and wheat farm, and played a lead role in the primetime television show, *Number 96*. She has three children, four grandchildren and a great granddaughter.

Born the eldest of nine children in Port Melbourne in 1916, **May Lowe** worked as a seamstress until she married. For many years she volunteered with Meals on Wheels and raised money with an anti-cancer group in her local area. She has four children and five grandchildren. May has been a widow for thirty years. She is a keen football fan and a fervent Swans' supporter, enjoys a flutter and still likes to sew.

Bertha Lowitt was born in Brooklyn, New York, in November 1917. The first half of Bertha's life was devoted to left-wing political activism, as a public speaker and Communist Party organiser. She worked as a stenographer, and during the war as a 'Rosie the Riveter'. Bertha has a daughter and a grandson. In her fifties she went to college and became a teacher, and has since worked in paid and later unpaid positions in education. Bertha's husband died in 2002.

Joan Lowrie still lives in St Kilda, Melbourne, the suburb where she was born in March 1919. She worked from the day she left school at thirteen until she was eligible for the age pension, for most of that time at the Myer department store in Melbourne. She has been a widow for twenty-four years and when I last spoke to her was planning her annual Melbourne Cup Day party.

Joyce McGrath has had two careers: first, at the State Library of Victoria where she worked until she was sixty-five, and later as a portrait painter. Joyce was born at Red Cliffs in the Victorian Mallee in October 1925. She contracted tuberculosis from her father and spent much of her childhood in a sanatorium. Despite increasingly limited mobility Joyce remains involved with the Victorian Artists Society and maintains her networks, contacts and interests via her computer.

Lorraine (Maxie) Meldrum lives a few streets away from where she was born in May 1922. She is a widow and has two daughters, five grandchildren and five great grandchildren. Maxie was involved in voluntary work in her local area. For most of her life she read a book a day. Until her health started to deteriorate she enjoyed painting and sculpture, golf and croquet. She writes short stories and attends a U3A creative writing class.

Domnika Pasinis was born in 1913 in the village of Niki in Northern Greece and died in Melbourne in February 2014 at the age of 101. When her husband emigrated to Australia, she remained in Niki from 1939 to 1949 throughout World War II and the Civil War that followed. After joining her husband in Australia, Domnika worked in the family business, fish and chip shops. Her husband died in 1990. Domnika had three children, and has five grandchildren and four great grandchildren. At her death she'd been living in an old-age home for twelve years.

Born to immigrant Greek parents in June 1927 in Parkville, Melbourne, **Kali (Kalliope) Paxinos** left school at sixteen to do a dressmaking course. Her marriage in 1947 was arranged. She has five children, eight grandchildren and five great grandchildren. In her fifties she worked as a teacher's aide with immigrant students at Swinburne Technical School. Searching for a way to cope with her youngest son's schizophrenia led Kali to the Richmond Fellowship and a new career in mental health. Her husband died in 2004.

Frances Reynolds was born in January 1923 in St Marys, New South Wales. She graduated with a science degree from the University of Sydney in 1944, and worked as a dietician until she married. Frances has two children and two grandchildren. She and her husband live in the home they bought when they moved to Melbourne in 1970. Both still drive and travel to their beach house and interstate. Frances plays bridge, attends lectures, is a keen reader and volunteers at her local op shop.

Dame Margaret Scott is best known as one of the founders and first head of the Australian Ballet School, a position she held until 1990. Born in Johannesburg, South Africa, in April 1922, Dame Margaret is married with two children and two grandchildren. She lives with her husband in the home where they raised their sons. Dame Margaret has been the recipient of many honours and awards for her contribution to ballet and remains deeply engaged with dance and dancers.

Dorothy Shultz is a pseudonym as she wishes to be anonymous. She was born in 1928 and lives with her husband not far from Melbourne. She has been working part time until very recently and at eighty-five is shifting into voluntary work, with the conviction that what's important is to keep 'contributing'.

Suzanne Simon was born in July 1923 in Launceston, Tasmania. After she married in 1949, she never worked. Suzanne had four children and has six grandchildren. Into her eighties she travelled widely and enjoyed swimming, tennis and skiing. Suzanne's husband died in 2011. She lives in her own home and loves to read.

In 1938, **Rose Stone**, then aged sixteen, travelled alone to Australia without a word of English. She was born in Biala Podlaska on the Polish–Russian border in March 1922. Rose has two children, two grandchildren and three great grandchildren. After her divorce she used her sewing skills to support herself. Her days are packed with bridge, two book clubs, going to movies, theatre and concerts. The best moment of Rose's life was 'crossing from the old self to the new self in the women's movement'.

 **Betty Walton** has lived in ten different countries. She was born in Edinburgh, Scotland, in May 1927. Betty received a Masters of Arts in German and French literature from the University of Edinburgh and has taught drama, literature and languages throughout her life. She is married with three children and six grandchildren. Although she had to give up her tennis at eighty, Betty continues to teach drama at the U3A and is part of an Italian language group at the Lyceum Club.

 Being interned with other Japanese Americans in December 1942 was the turning point of **Masuko (Koho) Yamamoto's** life. At the barracks in the desert of Topaz, Utah, she learned Sumi-E, a Japanese style of brush painting she has been practising and teaching ever since. Koho was born in April 1922 in Aliviso, California. Although she closed her painting school in 2010, she continues to teach and paint in the Greenwich Village, New York, apartment she has lived in since the early 1970s.

1

A Working Life

O F ALL ASPECTS of making the most of the last third of our lives, work is the one my friends and I are grappling with most immediately. We're in our fifties, sixties and early seventies and it's work watershed time for us.

Only a handful of women I know in Australia are still working full-time. Over the past five years most have retired, been pushed from, or left full-time employment. The workplace culture wants us out the door, firmly saying 'time for you to go'. Friends and spouses no longer working beckon with offers of exotic travel and enticing leisure pursuits. The adorable grandchildren clamour to hang out with us and daughters and sons need help with school pickups and childminding.

What should we do?

The experience of the group of women I interviewed can help us decide. How long should we keep working? Should we go part-time? Are these the years when we should focus more on looking after ourselves and those we care about?

The strongest message from the women who've been at this crucial point in their working lives is to 'stay', and so I say to my contemporaries, 'Don't retire. Keep working.' Those women who left work under duress or caved in to societal and family pressures are telling us to hang in there and not give in to the 'go' sayers, or those holding out carrots of allurement. You still have much to offer and you'll regret giving up your job.

Doctor Margaret Barnett was an international authority on haematology, the study of blood disorders, who set up the cytogenetics lab at St Vincent's Hospital in Melbourne. Over the thirty years Margaret worked there, she occasionally thought about what she'd do in retirement. 'But I had never taken it seriously because I thought I was going to keep on working for the rest of my life,' she said.

The chop came bluntly. 'I was the head of a large department I had built up and I got a letter saying, "Thank you, Margaret, for all your time at St Vincent's, we wish you well in the future," and that was it, I had to go.' Government regulations mandated that she retire when she turned sixty-five. Being retired against her will she says, 'I hated it. I could have worked a lot longer, at least ten years more, until I was seventy-five.'

No wonder Margaret was in shock, having to give up her lab and her work, her 'wonderful life' and 'being king of the castle'. She'd been 'a member of an international group' working on genetic changes in leukaemia and suddenly she couldn't even get a research grant, 'because I was too old, well I was sixty-five'. It was a harsh readjustment. 'I just thought I wasn't useful anymore. It was a horrible feeling.'

Losing the work that 'inspired' her severely dented her sense of self-worth. More than twenty years after her forced retirement, Margaret still feels the loss of meaning and purpose that work gave her. And what of the loss of her contribution to curing leukaemia?

It's not only the victims of compulsory retirement regulations who say, 'I could have done another ten years'. Lady Florence Bjelke-Petersen became a Country Party senator for Queensland at sixty-one and retired at seventy-three. She thoroughly enjoyed her years in federal parliament and reckons her greatest achievement in life—apart from bringing up her family as good Christians—is 'the twelve and a quarter years of serving our people of Queensland to the best of my ability'. Her advice, at ninety-three, is the same as Margaret Barnett's: if you're feeling the pressure to retire, stay doing what you love and are good at for another ten years.

Even if you're committed to working into your sixties, seventies and later, it's not going to be easy to resist the expectation that older people must move on. Elisabeth Kirkby has experienced this twice. In 1980 'the men' were not pleased when Elisabeth was awarded the Number 1, and only winnable slot, on the Australian Democrat Party ticket for the forthcoming senate election. She 'stood down' and no Democrat got in. She got more votes at Number 2 and would have got in on preferences had she stayed in the Number 1 spot, so the outcome was worse for her and the party. From 1981 to 1998 Elisabeth was a Democrat Party member of the NSW Legislative Council. She did not leave this job by choice. At seventy-seven she retired 'because the party believed that a younger person should have the opportunity'. She says that there's no way she could have stayed with the pressure she was under. When I met Lis she was ninety-one and would still make an excellent member of parliament. I'd vote for her tomorrow.

If work is important to you, and you're enjoying it and doing a good job, remember the I-should-have-stayed-another-ten-years rule from those who have gone before. Don't be someone who looks back in regret at having stopped working way too soon.

Legislative and policy changes have now made it feasible for us to work longer. A few years ago, it would have been considered laughable to investigate the prospects of work, especially paid work, for women over sixty-five. In Australia and the United Kingdom most jobs had a mandatory retirement age of sixty-five. Women were eligible for the old age pension at sixty, five years earlier than men. The United States never had this differential benchmark.

Those days are gone and all countries are gradually making the pension age the same for women and men, and also raising the age at which anyone is eligible. In Europe, the United States and Australia it is being incrementally and slowly raised to sixty-seven, and in the United Kingdom to sixty-eight. And compulsory retirement has gone out the window. In 1986 the United States outlawed mandatory retirement, with an exemption for workers in colleges and universities that expired in 1993.

States in Australia began banning age discrimination in employment in the early 1990s. It has been unlawful across the country since 2004, with the same process happening in New Zealand by 1999 and Canada by 2009. The hundred-year trend towards earlier and earlier retirement is over and, according to the experts, not coming back. Forget about getting the gold watch and the golden handshake and rejoice that you're not being pushed out the door. We're among the lucky ones—we can keep working.

Because we have that possibility more and more of us are working longer. The end of compulsory retirement and the raising of the pension age have fuelled a dramatic rise in older women's employment. In Australia over the past decade the number of women working in their early sixties has trebled and participation rates for women in their late sixties have more than doubled from 8 to 18 per cent.[1] The trend is predicted to continue with the biggest increase in women's labour force participation coming from the 65- to 74-year-age group. That's us! In the United States this increase will be around 90 per cent, which adds up to 2,303,000 older women working. Partly this is caused by the baby boomers, born from 1946 to 1964, getting older, but it is also because more women of our age want and need to work.[2]

Different work patterns

Probably the biggest difference when comparing the working lives of women who are now in their eighties and nineties with those of their daughters and nieces is that so many of the older women left paid work as soon as they married. I don't know anyone of my age who stopped working when they married, whereas more than half of the women I interviewed did so after their wedding.

Dodo Berk's first and only job was at RH Macys & Co (now Macy's) department store in New York City. She married in 1936, in the middle of the Great Depression, and even though her first child was not born for another six years Dodo never worked again. The same holds true for university-educated women like Mary Broughton and April Hamer, who married immediately after finishing their arts degree, and for many women with professions like June Helmer, a pharmacist, Frances Reynolds, a dietician, and Barbara Hamer, a social worker. And it wasn't just financially secure women who did this. Flo Howlett, Kali Paxinos and May Lowe really needed the extra money but they too stopped work on their wedding day. As Frances Reynolds says, 'You didn't work when you married. I am talking about 1950.' Rich and poor, educated or not, on marriage your job became looking after your husband and your home.

The assumptions about women and work of the earlier generation might seem laughable to us today. Not work after you're married? Why not? Frances Reynolds describes how her husband was away for work for long periods of time. She was needed at home as 'the backstop', to keep everything together. Flo Howlett proudly tells me, 'I was a home mother who looked after my children', as does May Lowe who says, 'I never worked in my married life'. Flo had five children and May four. It's also clear that their husbands wanted them at home.

A good mother stayed home and cared for her children, a good wife was the rock on which the husband depended so he could go into the world and be a provider. Your husband expected it and so did everyone else. Rose Stone explains how things were in the 1950s:

I didn't just have two children. I had three children. I
had to feed him, look after him, do his washing. He'd
come home from work and sit—I served. I just accepted
it. I thought that was my role in life. I didn't have a car.
I had to do all the shopping, all the cooking—I didn't
have a washing machine. Not that things weren't easier
than Poland where I was born. I still had a lot of things
to do. I had to take the kids to school, go and pick them
up. I had to be ready with the food when he came home.
I remember when I was dragging my daughter to gym
and one night we came home a bit late so the food wasn't
quite ready. He kicked up a fuss. I had to cook in the day
to have it ready for him.

Today most married women work and many more older
women want to work. In January 2014, in a Gallup Poll of nearly
two thousand baby boomers, men and women, one in ten said
that given the choice they never wanted 'to clock out for good'.[3]

Older women who did work after they were married and
continued in paid employment into their sixties, seventies and
eighties have lessons for us in these different times.

Work is good for you

On the day I meet her, 'the woman who taught Australians how to
cook' is tasting pullet eggs and pronouncing judgement on yeast
cakes. More than four million Margaret Fulton cookbooks have
been sold and they continue to sell. You may see her with her
great grandson Harry in television commercials for Woolworths
supermarkets, or watch her on YouTube making scones with her
granddaughter Louise in an advertisement promoting St George
ovens. Whether as a guest on *MasterChef* or being interviewed by
Andrew Denton on *Enough Rope*, this little grey-haired old lady
sure packs a punch.

Never afraid to speak her mind, she slammed reality-cooking programs on television, saying, 'I don't want to watch people very pleased with what they're doing but doing everything wrong.' As well as being a National Living Treasure and having a musical written about her, Margaret was named one of the 100 most-influential Australians in 2006 by both *The Sydney Morning Herald* and *The Bulletin*. Sure she enjoys the fame and the awards, but there's also the sheer pleasure she takes in her work. She loves being able to:

> chop away, slice, stir. I find it enormously soothing to get into the kitchen. When things seem really black—on the other side of the world, or on the other side of the fence— knowing that my family are going to come and share this with me and things are going to be good again ... it's just wonderful, when you get into the kitchen and do something and then you produce a lovely scone, a lovely pikelet, a lovely roast dinner—it's a wonderful backup we've got in our lives.[4]

When I asked her whether she planned to keep working, Margaret said 'I don't call it work any more. It's just living.'

Women who keep working, like Margaret Fulton, tend to enjoy what they are doing and so it's not surprising that working longer is good for them. The consensus is mounting: retirement can damage your health, and the longer you're retired the greater the health disadvantages. Using research strategies that allow for the fact that people may retire because of illness, one study after another is finding a positive link between work and health in old age. Retired people are 40 per cent more likely to suffer from clinical depression and 60 per cent more likely to have a diagnosed physical ailment than those who are still working.[5]

Studies specifically set up to question the hypothesis that working longer is good for you have come down heavily on the yes side. One such US study, of 6511 people, confirmed the causal link between work and wellbeing. Even an 'undesirable job' is better for your health than no job at all, although not as good as one that is less stressful and demanding, with the advice being that part-time work is a good option for those in 'undesirable jobs'.[6]

Many people intuitively know this. Retirement? No way. 'Never,' says Koho Yamamoto. 'I am going to paint on and on until I die.' Her works on paper completely cover the walls of the narrow passage and tiny rooms of her Greenwich Village, New York, apartment. The five flights of stairs she goes up and down at least twice a day are no problem for this ninety-one year old.

In one of those ironies of fate, where something wonderful comes out of an injustice, Koho found her vocation after the Japanese attack on Pearl Harbor in December 1942, when Japanese Americans lost their homes and their properties. These American citizens were suddenly told they were an enemy of the United States and put in internment camps. In the barracks in Topaz, Utah, Koho became the prize pupil of famous artist and teacher Chiura Obata, a master of Sumi-E, a special technique of Japanese ink painting. In a bleak place of sandstorms and sagebrush Koho went to art school and she has been painting ever since.

Now working from home, Koho supplements her social security pension with the money she earns teaching and from the sale of her paintings. There is growing interest in her work since she turned ninety. In 2012 she had two one-woman shows, and in 2013 she had back-to-back exhibitions in two New York City galleries.

Koho's health has never been better in what she says are the best years of her life, doing what she's done for more than seventy years. 'Every day, I try to paint,' she says, a glowing example of the benefits of working longer.

Elisabeth (Lis) Kirkby is another woman who attests to work being good for you. It was the new job that pulled her out of the trauma and depression of losing her marriage. At sixty, when most people are thinking of retirement, Lis was elected as the first Australian Democrat member of the Legislative Council of New South Wales. After the end of her marriage she focused on trying to get elected. 'By the time I was elected in 1981,' she says, 'having to go to Parliament House every day, having to deal with all kinds of things that I had never had to deal with before, I mean a huge learning curve. That is what dragged me out of sitting around being miserable.'

Lis has always come out of the low points in her life—her mother's death, being left by her husband, being dumped by her party, confronted by drought—by trying something different and challenging. Work and learning new skills engages and nourishes her.

Work also helped Kali Paxinos through a very difficult phase of her life. Just after she retired from Swinburne Technical School her youngest son became mentally ill. 'Things were really bad and I had to find ways to cope,' she says. Within a year she found help at the Schizophrenia Fellowship and began volunteering for them. Soon Kali was employed to work with families coping with mental illness, particularly migrant families. Although her only qualifications were her 'living experience and answering phones on the helpline', Kali became an expert in a whole new field. Her unique ability to work with families from culturally diverse communities became widely recognised and utilised. After seventeen years she set up in business as a carer consultant. Now eighty-six, Kali is still in demand as a speaker for Mental Health Conferences throughout Australia and New Zealand.

Longevity

Data provided by actuaries and other researchers suggests that working longer and retiring later, increases longevity. Retiring at seventy instead of sixty adds twelve months to a woman's life expectancy. In arriving at these figures the actuaries took into account that people forced to retire early because of sickness are likely to die sooner, and that some people who retire at sixty-five will die before they get to seventy. Evidence is accumulating that the health benefits of working longer lead to longer life expectancy and that perhaps the discipline of work helps us remain active and live longer.[7]

The 'work longer–live better', or the 'work longer–live longer' theory, though, doesn't apply to the women I interviewed. Dodo Berk hasn't had paid employment for a minute since 1936. Mary Broughton never was in the paid workforce, and neither Flo Howlett nor May Lowe worked after they married. Yet all are over ninety-five, have never had a serious illness and are as well or better than many of the women who worked into their eighties and beyond. Among the I'm-never-going-to-retire contingent are Margaret Fulton, who had a quadruple bypass in 2005, and Koho Yamamoto, who three years ago had chemotherapy for colon cancer. The still hard-at-work-botanist Beth Gott has had a mini-stroke, a pacemaker for her irregular heartbeat and a stent in her leg because of a blockage in her artery.

The researchers' focus is on people who work to a certain age and then stop—the classic division of paid work and retirement—whereas most of the women in my sample of interviewees spent very few years out of their long lives in paid employment. The data on longevity compares retiring at sixty with retiring at seventy; it's not about working into your eighties and nineties. Another reason for why I don't think the findings apply to the women I spoke to is that the cohort being studied by the researchers are people of my age, boomers in our fifties, sixties and seventies for whom paid work has been an integral part of our adult lives. Post second-wave feminism and the equal opportunity reforms of the 1970s, paid work is a big factor in our identity and sense of self-worth, which was not the case for most of the women in my older group.

Consciously or not, the researchers are also fuelling a political agenda: if we work longer we'll be less of a pension burden on governments and the younger generations. Based on such research findings, governments throughout the world are developing incentives for employers and workers to extend working life. 'There should be no normal retirement age in the future,' is one of the new catch-cries.

The real reasons we want to keep working

Beth Gott loves her work:

> I just like being a botanist. People bring me things and ask, 'What's that?' And so I say, 'I will find out for you.' I enjoy being consulted on my area of expertise; somehow it makes you feel that you are still valuable. I enjoy giving a talk and having people come up to me afterwards and say, 'I really liked that.'

Although at ninety-one she's not doing as much teaching, research and writing as before, Beth is still *the* go-to expert on plants used by the Indigenous people of south-east Australia. Her busy working life includes being responsible for the Indigenous Garden at Monash University, writing, presenting papers at conferences and giving talks to landcare groups and field naturalists. Most of her time is spent expanding her extensive Aboriginal ethnobotanical databases on the indigenous plants of Tasmania, Victoria, New South Wales and parts of South Australia. Right now Beth is investigating how and why Australian Aborigines used fire to maximise the growth of their staple foods. Being a botanist gives her enormous satisfaction.

The message comes across loud and strong from nearly all the women I spoke to: they want and need to contribute to the world beyond themselves and their families, to feel and be useful, to add value and be valued. Rose Stone says, 'I believe in getting involved with helping people. You've got skills. Pass your skills on.'

Margaret Barnett was very much engaged with the world until her late seventies, 'But now I am not and that is what is killing me now. I guess "killing me"—that's a good word.' At eighty-seven, she says, 'I don't feel useful. Every now and again I think what am I doing on this earth? I am not doing a thing. I live here comfortably, I go to luncheons, I go to talks, I belong to clubs, and that's it. You know, it's pretty dull.'

It's interesting to compare Margaret's last ten years with Jean Allison's. Jean is the same age and also a doctor, and she is thriving on a life packed with engagements. As well as being involved at various levels of the Uniting Church, she's on several AMA committees and recently became active with GetUp on their refugee and environmental campaigns. Giving a talk about retirement to the Society of Anaesthetists, Jean said, 'Well we've all heard this morning how important it is to have exercise and running on the treadmill like a hamster … lifting weights, it's got knobs on it. What you must do is to cultivate an interest that gives you exercise.' To prove her point Jean showed a photo of the Melbourne University and Alumni Bushwalkers on a boardwalk at Wilsons Promontory, surrounded by tea-tree. She said, 'This is the kind of walking I do now.' At eighty-seven, Jean leads a long walk once a month for the Alumni Bushwalkers.

Someone who is absolutely convinced that feeling useless would finish her off is Bertha Lowitt. She worked full-time from when she finished high school until she was seventy-seven. When I interviewed her in her home in Brooklyn, New York City, she was ninety-six, very deaf, walking with difficulty, and champing at the bit to get back to work for at least one day a week at The Museum of Jewish Heritage. Her life is diminished, she says, 'If I can't go to the museum and do tours, which I loved so much, I still repeat in my head some of the ways in which I used to ask the questions.' Her voluntary work at the museum provided Bertha with even more satisfaction than she'd had from her paid jobs as a stenographer and a teacher.

The Jewish Museum of Australia provided another woman I spoke with, June Helmer, with a similar sense of worth. She says about her fifteen years working with the museum, 'I was lucky to use my middle to old age in such a useful way.' This desire to be useful holds true for most of the women who've done little or no paid work. They continued using their skills well into their seventies and eighties, working voluntarily. For Mary Broughton, contributing to the community is very important. 'I am a lifetime member of umpteen things,' she says of her years working for the YWCA, the Red Cross, the Friends of the Botanical Gardens and other causes she believes in. Even at ninety-seven she can't retire from doing the cataloguing at the Shoreham Historical Society— they value her knowledge and expertise. This is echoed in what Barbara Hamer says about being on the Council of the University of Melbourne until she was seventy-six: 'It was an active role and you felt needed. I was happy.'

The need to do more than entertain yourself in your old age is something that Stephanie Charlesworth has strong views about: 'I think that women who had interesting careers, particularly sixty, sixty-five year olds, ought to be thinking about "oh, what now?" not just that I will be able to do all those travels now.' Stephanie believes that in our old age we, 'need to think about doing something continuing and meaningful, and that it doesn't neces-sarily have to be paid work, but needs to be something where you get satisfaction out of knowing you are very effective'. For Stephanie—and all those women who believe in being useful— old age should be about more than filling in time. You still need to be goal-oriented, and to add value to your society by using your skills. She says, even travelling is more fun if you have a purpose rather than just sightseeing.

Among my own friends the need to feel useful is there for most of us. Whether it's paid or unpaid, our sense of self-esteem, wellbeing and life satisfaction is tied up with being engaged, feeling that we are contributing to the wider society. We're in paid work, although few of us now work full time, we're on boards and committees, we're teaching at U3A, we're out there in the world trying to make a difference just as we have all our adult lives. We agree with Dorothy Shultz, who is eighty-five and the youngest woman I interviewed, she has just now made the shift into unpaid commitments and says, 'I see contribution as the important thing.'

Working to earn money

Among the twenty-nine women I spoke to only one needs to work to earn money. Although she lives very modestly in a tiny rent-controlled apartment, Koho Yamamoto must supplement the meagre payments she gets from social security with teaching and selling her paintings. The added benefit of her teaching is the connection it allows with younger people.

Most people I know want to fund lifestyles that are far more expensive than Koho's. Flo Howlett, Joan Lowrie, Beth Gott and Kali Paxinos live comfortably on the age pension. Flo is shocked by how much her grandchildren spend at cafes—a waste of money she believes. We boomers are not a thrifty lot. We want to eat in restaurants, take yoga classes, travel to exotic places and go to rock concerts or operas, depending on our tastes. You can't do that on the age pension. More than 1.3 million Australian baby boomers believe they will need to work beyond the age of seventy-five because they haven't saved enough for retirement.[8]

It's likely that in the future more of us will need to work to pay for our lifestyle, so it's comforting that even work we don't enjoy is probably good for us. Whatever our motive for working— whether it's health, a sense of self-worth, the need to contribute, or for the money to fund the things we want to keep doing—we need to know how to do this, how to stay employed.

The women who work into their eighties show grit and resourcefulness out of the ordinary. Margaret Fulton, always believed 'that of course I could do it', and was never one to give up. For decades Koho Yamamoto worked at menial jobs that she hated to pay for art classes and pursue her vocation. Beth Gott needed to be resourceful to work as a botanist, even overcoming the ban on pushchairs in Melbourne trams at peak hour in the 1950s. Because she had to drop her youngest daughter at the babysitters and get to work on time, Beth bought a big bag to hide her stroller and carried the baby on board. 'Confronted by an inspector I said, "That's a bag, not a pusher."'[9]

How Lis Kirkby got her first job tells us a lot about her ability to leap into opportunity later in life:

> It was like many things in my life—absolute serendipity. I was making the fire one day with newspaper and wood. Holding the newspaper I saw this wanted ad for an assistant stage manager and an address. When my father came home, I said, 'I think I am going to write to them,' and he said, 'Okay, well write to them.' So I wrote a letter and he changed one or two things in it and sent it off. They replied, and I went to see them and they accepted me.

What she calls serendipity, I call spunk. War was imminent, Lis was eighteen and had just spent a miserable time running the household while her mother was dying of cancer. She grabbed the chance, and took her first step towards fulfilling her dream of becoming an actress.

If you do want to stay in paid work you'll need some of these same qualities plus a strong faith that you've got something valuable to offer no matter what age you are.

It doesn't have to be paid work

For most women, being engaged and useful is more important than whether they make money. Once our children are older and our mortgages hopefully paid off, we are likely to have more time to devote to interesting unpaid work. That's when Rose Stone was able to commit herself to 'the highlight' of her life: the women's movement.

After her divorce Rose made a living using her sewing skills and managed to work her way into better jobs teaching sewing at TAFE and the Centre for Adult Education. With better pay she could work fewer hours. Although she enjoyed her work and needed the money, what gave real meaning to her life was volunteer work, helping to set up and run the Women's Liberation Halfway House, the first shelter for battered women in Melbourne. Rose says that she's never been the same since 'crossing over' to viewing the world with feminist eyes. 'My life was terrific,' Rose says, 'I found out what was in me.'

Rose is not alone in finding voluntary work more satisfying than her paid work. After all you can choose your volunteering job, and people choose something they care about, that they want to do. Plus you can usually choose your hours of work, and if you don't like the work you can leave. And the research supports these views, with 25 per cent more of those who volunteer being satisfied with their job than paid workers.[10] An added attraction is there are far more voluntary jobs out there than paid ones.

In discussing paid versus voluntary work Stephanie Charlesworth pointed out that society places more value on paid than voluntary work, which raises the question of whether we feel more worthwhile when we're paid. She cites the loss of status that many men experience on retiring, from having had the routine of a responsible job to suddenly confronting days that need to be filled. Stephanie's concern is that as women's jobs and lives become more like men's, this loss of status and purpose will affect us too.

It is true that women like Barbara Hamer and Mary Broughton and the others who were never paid, or were only briefly in the paid workforce, had no sharp break in their lives when they hit sixty-five. They continued with their voluntary commitments and pursued the interests they'd been developing over the years. But most of the women I spoke to with full-on careers were also involved in voluntary work. Margaret Fulton has long been campaigning for the preservation of dingoes and more recently with Greenpeace on the continued banning of GMO crops in Australia. Jean Allison was on the advisory board of International Social Service, and on the committees of various church and professional groups. While working full time, Joyce McGrath was on the council of the Victorian Artists Society and Committees of the Lyceum Club.

Looking at the arc of women's lives over the past thirty years the paid/voluntary work distinction is blurred and perhaps irrelevant. Where, for example, does Sister Mary Gregory fit on this continuum? She's not been paid since she was twenty-one, when she joined the Good Samaritan Order, but boy has she worked. True, being a nun is itself a secure job, with food, clothing and shelter taken care of, and a small allowance. Or there's Barbara Hamer, whose experience of paid work after marriage was a part-time job for two years in her fifties. As well as the demanding unpaid jobs she's been doing in the past thirty years, Barbara has also run the farm she owns near Canberra and her family business interests, which are definitely money making. And although never having had a paid job, Mary Broughton has been supporting herself by managing her money effectively since she became a widow at forty-five.

What is clear is that in the last third of your life, whether you are paid or not becomes less relevant to your satisfaction or sense of status, unless of course you need the money to live (but more on that later). What matters is whether you enjoy the work you are doing and it's seen as useful by you and others. Betty Walton's comment hits the spot when she says, 'I never retired. The only difference is that I'm not paid and that doesn't matter.'

Just as there are big differences in the nature of the paid work that women did—compare Joan Lowrie being a cashier at Myer with Dame Margaret Scott running The Australian Ballet School—so there are in voluntary work. And I'm not talking about satisfaction because that doesn't necessarily relate to whether you are doing sewing alterations or painting a portrait. Both can be equally rewarding and satisfying. The difference I think is crucial is in the degree of responsibility you take on in voluntary work. Perhaps this is what Stephanie Charlesworth means when she says, 'I have been on the board of PLAN Australia for fourteen years and I have been on other adoption boards and tribunals but I have never been a volunteer in an op shop, I have never wanted to go to community morning teas.' Working in op shops and raising funds is both valuable and satisfying. But Stephanie needs to exercise the skills and expertise she developed at a certain level of responsibility. Luckily there are all manner of valuable voluntary jobs to match individual skills and interests.

In 2005 my friend Marion Webster and I, with the help of a group of six other women, started Fitted for Work, an agency to help unemployed women get jobs by providing them with free interview clothes, presentation advice and coaching. Marion and I had shared experiences in working in paid positions in not-for-profit organisations. She had philanthropic expertise and connections and I had experience working as a volunteer at Bottomless Closet in New York City, the agency on which we modelled our new enterprise. The responsibilities we took on were huge. Looking back we admit that, had we known what starting a new service from scratch entailed, we would never have embarked on it. It wasn't so much about workload but in running any small business you can't leave the issues and worries behind you when you lock the door and leave at night.

For fifteen years I've been a volunteer at Bottomless Closet in New York City. Each week I work with clients to find outfits for them to wear to interviews and to their new jobs, edit and tweak their resumes until they are perfect and practise answering interview questions. As well as unpacking and sorting boxes and bags of donated clothes, I do anything else I'm asked to do. It's very satisfying and enjoyable. I connect to people—clients, staff and volunteers—I'd never have met otherwise. Once I leave for the day I never think about it. If I have a doctor's appointment or something else comes up, as long as I let the volunteer coordinator know well in advance, it's fine for me not to turn up. And I can go on holidays and trips whenever I like.

I'm useful in both roles, and I need to do each properly and well. But it wouldn't have been fine for me to say sorry I've got a dentist appointment if a Fitted for Work grant proposal was due or if I had to meet with government officials or potential donors. The difference is in the level and nature of the responsibility I had taken on, not about whether I was paid for what I did. And there may come a time when I no longer want the responsibility but I'd still like to contribute in some way. You need to choose how and where you use your skills and can make a difference and this will change over time—interests and abilities don't stay static.

Don't wait to be asked

When asked what voluntary or paid work she's done in the twenty years since she retired from the senate, Lady Florence Bjelke-Petersen says, 'Nothing in particular, no, nothing. You know when I retired from the senate I suppose I thought that was a sign I could retire completely.' And here's the enigma. Lady Flo is a woman 'who has always been game to try things'.

Her first invitation to make a speech came on her honeymoon in New Zealand. 'My heart sank,' she says, but she rose to the challenge. And she's still ready to give things a go. When I phoned and asked to come and interview her she said 'yes' right away, 'Why not?' But she doesn't seem to be a woman who initiates those challenges or one who creates new pathways or sets new goals for herself. She was in the same job as a secretary for fourteen years and, in those formative years from eighteen to thirty-two, she didn't travel overseas or upgrade her qualifications or branch out from the Queensland Main Roads Department. And why did she stand for the senate? Lady Flo says that she never would have thought of it, 'but Joh had the bright idea' that she'd be good for the people of Queensland. Lady Flo again rose to the challenge.

Sadly in the last twenty years there hasn't been much asked of her to do out there in the wider world. Where are the companies and not-for profits asking her to be their patron and sit on their boards? Don't get me wrong, she's a very happy and contented women. But she'd be a wonderful mentor of younger women, a terrific radio show host, and much more. I can't help wondering what she would have done if only she'd been asked.

Kali Paxinos could have had a similar story. She left school at sixteen, and did a dressmaking and then a typing course. At nineteen Kali had an arranged Greek marriage, and went on to have five children. In her fifties a forward-looking headmaster plucked her from sandwich making in the school canteen to work with the migrant children teachers were unable to cope with. By the time she retired, Kali was an expert in understanding and integrating migrant children. Perhaps she, like Lady Flo, would have stayed retired if her youngest son hadn't become mentally ill. At the Schizophrenia Fellowship Kali was able to transform the traumatic family experience of her son's illness into helping others deal with the same issue, and she trained workers to do a better job with families like hers.

Something powerful resonates in Lady Flo not putting herself forward. My friends and I were bright girls, who jumped the hoops that school and university put under our noses. Then one day we were grown up with husbands and children and mortgages. From here on we had to choose our own courses and goals and we were flummoxed. Another friend describes our lives up to marriage and children as a series of boxes we ticked—finish school: tick; get a degree: tick; find a husband: tick; have a child: tick. Then the real challenge came when we had to plot what came next.

We are now at a spot where once again we have to set our own courses. Employers are not out there waving salary packages and 'leadership programs' under our noses. Those younger than we are want us to shuffle away to retirement villages or better still even further, to Queensland or Florida. We've got to decide what we want to do and how we want to do it and it's no use waiting around to be asked.

Planning, flexibility and adapting

The women who successfully worked into their ninth decade, as well as having faith in what they had to offer and loving their work, were flexible and forward looking. When Beth Gott moved to Connecticut because her husband got a job in New York, she found voluntary work with an anthropologist specialising in the Connecticut American Indians. On returning to Australia she began going on digs at Victorian archaeological Aboriginal sites to identify the plant material, and so began her ethnobotanical studies of plant use and management by the first people of south-eastern Australia. 'I followed my nose,' she says, describing how she pursued her interests and her instincts, like a hound or a detective sniffing out where the clues led her.

In trying to identify the plant remains from the archaeological digs she realised that there must be a great deal of information in nineteenth-century books and articles, in reminiscences and diaries, that had never been collated. 'So that was when I started to get it together and what ended up in the databases that I've got now. I was following my nose because that's what I liked doing.' Beth has never had a full-time or permanent university appointment. Over the years she received grants from the Institute of Aboriginal Studies in Canberra, and has taught courses in botany departments at Monash and Melbourne universities. Her books came out in the early 1990s when Beth was in her seventies. This is a woman who came into her 'brilliant' if poorly paid career late in life. Yes, she has always been a botanist but the real blossoming has come after the years of childrearing were over. And there is more to come. Beth says, 'Botanists never retire'.

Lis Kirkby also moved with her husband's job, 'Because in those days that's what you did.' They first moved to Singapore and Malaya in 1951, and again to Sydney in 1965. Here she restarted her acting career, later shifting into politics. At seventy-seven, when she was pushed out for being too old, she'd already prepared for her new life as a wool and sheep farmer.

Of course some find leaving an established career liberating. About being compulsorily retired, Stephanie Charlesworth says, 'I remember towards the end of my university year it was just like the feeling I had toward the end of my last year at school. Freedom.' Stephanie had completed a law degree at sixty, while teaching in social work at Melbourne University, and through her new studies and articles she had the networks to move into a new field. For Stephanie, having to retire from the university at sixty-five was an opportunity for her 'to pick and choose what I wanted to do', and she chose family law and mediation. She had planned her move well and worked for another twenty years. Clearly it is important to have a five-year plan, while staying open enough to shift goals if need be.

By the time she made the career move, Stephanie had good networks in her new field. Who you know always counts and this is even more so when you're looking to get a new job in your sixties. Being married to Joh gave Lady Flo the profile that helped her election as a senator. Bertha Lowitt was similarly fortunate after she retired from secondary school teaching. Her husband was the CEO of Fedcap, an employment, not-for-profit service for people with disabilities, and she was able to move into a job with him. Nepotism and established networks are a big help in being able to work longer.

Are some jobs not made for the old?

Among the working women I spoke to, all have jobs where their hours are flexible and under their own control. The painters like Koho and Joyce choose their own hours. Writers and researchers like Lis, Beth and Stephanie also have flexible hours and can write from anywhere. If you don't need the money you might consider going back to study—you can do this at your own pace and in your time and it might just lead you to a new field.

Being a star in your area helps expand your options so try and get to the top of a heap, however small and specialised it may be. Margaret Fulton retired from the constant deadlines and stress of magazine work when she had a quadruple bypass operation in 2004. Now the grande dame of Australian cooking can easily pick and choose what she does and when she does it. Kali Paxinos and Beth Gott are recognised for their unique knowledge and expertise so can choose the projects they work on.

One of the best ways to make sure you can stay working for as long as you like is to be self-employed. Margaret Fulton is the head of a thriving family enterprise with much of the detailed work being done by her daughter and granddaughters. Lis Kirkby ran her own farm. In 1987, when Betty Walton was sixty, she and her husband bought an English language school in Bergamot in Northern Italy. Back in Australia, Betty founded The Middle Court Players in 1991 and ran the company for nine years.

Buying the school at sixty and becoming a small business owner, and setting up the theatre that she ran until she was seventy-three, are ways Betty created a working life for herself beyond the conventional age of retirement. Domnika Pasinis is another who worked beyond the age at which she was eligible for the pension, in the family fish and chip business.

In looking for a job in your sixties, seventies, and eighties it is smart to retrain for a field where there are labour shortages. That's what Stephanie Charlesworth did when she studied mediation. But be realistic. Sadly some of the currently listed Australian skill-shortage areas mightn't be suitable. If you've got geology or engineering qualifications and can live in outback conditions, you could go for the mining jobs—there seem to be lots. As always chefs, pastry cooks, bakers and hairdressers are in short supply but these jobs require physical stamina as you're on your feet all day. We also need physios, sonographers, audiologists, nurses, optometrists and midwives but the retraining for all these jobs is academically demanding and expensive and some, especially physiotherapy and midwifery, are incredibly demanding on the body.[11]

There are nonagenarian women doing all kinds of demanding jobs. Elinor Otto is ninety-three and working full-time wielding a heavy riveter at the Boeing Aircraft Plant in Long Beach California, and 92-year-old Sara Dappen works full shifts at MacDonald's in Story City, Iowa. There are many more like them so if your dream is mining or midwifery, go for it.

You'd think that because of its intense physicality, being a dancer is not an option even in middle age. Dame Margaret Scott put her dancing career on hold after a back injury and the birth of two boys. She was adaptable enough to move to teaching, beginning with classes in a church hall, and then becoming the founding director of the Australian Ballet School in 1963. She stayed in that job until she was sixty-eight. And yet in 2000, when she was seventy-eight and about to dance in Murphy's *Nutcracker*,

Dame Maggie said about performing, 'I'm still totally addicted.'[12] There's always the exception to prove the rule and another such exception is Gillian Lynne, British dancer and choreographer of *Cats* and *Phantom* who was still working a full diary at eighty-seven.

There are probably jobs no one should do in old age. Doctor Jean Allison is adamant that seventy is the 'absolute maximum' to retire from anaesthetics. 'One loses one's skills. I could see what was happening to people that stayed on working too long,' she says. 'You have got to stay so alert. You've got to have eyes in the back of your head all the time and you have to concentrate on every breath and every heartbeat.' The facts support Jean's opinion. The average retirement age for anaesthetists in the United States is sixty-four, and fifty-three in Britain. Although she's dead set against practising, Jean is in favour of staying involved. She is on the Retired Doctors' Committee of the AMA and part of the Retired Anaesthetists' Group. She has attended the World Congress for Anaesthetics more times than anyone else because Jean's interest in the field is still strong and she has experience and knowledge to share.

Husbands and children

Jean is a single woman without children and can suit herself whether she moves back to Melbourne or attends the World Congress for Anaesthetics. As a nun Sister Mary Gregory has no set retirement age, nor was her working life fractured by the demands of a husband and children. She didn't need to consult her family about taking on a new challenge in her seventies when, instead of retiring, she moved to the Claymore Housing Estate in the Campbelltown area of south-west Sydney to develop an Animation Project. 'I had no idea where Claymore was. I didn't know anything about it. At that stage it was the most disadvantaged area of Sydney and it really had a bad reputation, which was a shame because the people weren't like that at all.' Anyone who has worked in community development knows the energy and strength it takes to support people working for change. And here was Sister Mary doing a job that burns out young workers in their twenties and thirties.

Koho Yamamoto regrets the twelve subservient years of her long-ago marriage and has been determinedly independent ever since. Joyce McGrath's parents died young, she never partnered, and has no siblings. Although this life has drawbacks, with no one but herself to care for, Joyce had the time and energy to develop her second career of portrait painting at the same time as she was working as a full-time librarian. Many of the women I surveyed who are working later in life are single. This is not surprising when we remember the prevailing ethos that women should stop work on marriage. Until 1966 a single woman working in the Australian Commonwealth Public Service had to resign her job on the eve of her marriage.

Not one woman I know, who's around my age, has never married. My generation felt just as much pressure—if not more—to marry as our elders did. We were the tail end of this period, on the cusp of equal pay, having been born in and benefitting from the affluent years after the World War II. Second-wave feminism was a faint smoke signal way over on the horizon. At university and not as part of any course, I read Simone de Beauvoir's *Second Sex* and Betty Friedan's *Feminine Mystique* and pitied Friedan's frustrated American housewives, never for a minute imaging that they had anything to do with me.

Our mothers read out newspaper notices of engagements and marriages, hinting that if we didn't do something about it soon we'd be on the shelf. And in my final year at university there were the 'Dip Ed Diamonds', young women of twenty-one, completing teaching qualifications they cared far less about than their sparkling engagement rings and wedding plans. My friends and I also married young, in our early twenties, the difference to our mothers' generation being that we planned to work and travel and do other things before we had children. After all we had the pill, had read Mary McCarthy's *The Group*, and some of us had had to have abortions.

Among the older women I interviewed only Bertha Lowitt put off having a child, because she needed to work full time and continue with her political work. She was the exception because in her day you were supposed to have children right away. Kali Paxinos explains that, 'We had to. This was the law of the land at the time—marriage had to show that you produced.' Her Greek-born parents did not go so far as to check the bed linen after her wedding night but that certainly still happened among people she knew. And once children arrived, as April Hamer so clearly puts it, 'They take up your life almost completely.' She had five children, the first barely nine months after she married and the last when she was thirty-nine.

My friends and I had our children after working a few years. It was the 1970s and the height of second-wave feminism. Most of us rushed back to work, at least part time, as soon as we could after having children. Some took time off for mothering. I only know one woman in my sphere whose life can be described as 'homemaker' or 'wife and mother', everyone else worked. Having a supportive husband, who at the very least accepted our need to work and at best shared the housework and childrearing, was very important.

The same holds true if we want to keep on working into our old age. It still helps to have a supportive husband, one like Bertha Lowitt's. When she got home from work she would 'open the door and *The New York Times* crossword puzzle was open with a sharpened pencil on the table'. Her husband did all the shopping and cooking. 'All I had to do was warm it up; the table was set. When I stopped teaching, and I started to do the shopping nobody knew who I was. They wanted to know what happened to that young handsome guy.' Sadly there are not many husbands like Bertha's around. Having only one child and a supportive husband enabled Bertha to work full time and continue her night time and weekend political work.

One reason Kali Paxinos continued working and Lady Flo didn't is that Kali overcame the initial resistance of her husband and kids. She says, 'The family was a bit disturbed when I told them I was going to get a job,' but they needed the money and soon her husband and the children became very supportive. Whereas once Sir Joh was no longer in politics he wanted his wife back home with him.

Without supportive husbands there is no way Stephanie Charlesworth and Dorothy Schultz could have returned to study after having children. Stephanie has seven children and went back to study when her twins were two. She believes this career break was positive and that she came back fresh, after having had fifteen years at home with her children:

> I just got so much pleasure out of my work and I think it was partly because I came to it late. Looking at young career women today they're back at work within six weeks of giving birth and they didn't have those days and weeks travelling with the children and all the companion-ship and all that I had.

Stephanie and Dorothy's working lives follow a pattern very common among working women of my generation. They stop work when they have children, study and improve their qualifica-tions and are ready to rocket back into work in their late forties and early fifties. Unfortunately too often that is exactly the time that age discrimination kicks in; just as we're ready to work full bore and full time, no one wants to employ us.

What's stopping us?

Eighteen per cent of Australian women working into their late sixties is still not a big chunk of this age cohort—evidence that ageism is still powerfully at work in our own psyches and in the attitudes of employers and society.[13] The new invisible barrier of 'too old to work' is as strong and subtle as the forces that kept Rose Stone from the English classes she wanted and needed. In the 1950s, if you were a woman and worked you were stealing the jobs of male breadwinners. Today if we want to stay working we're accused of adding to youth unemployment. Yes, we are seeing some changes, as it's now okay to work to sixty-five, instead of leaving at sixty, perhaps even to seventy, but after that? Forget about it. In the United States about one-in-twenty women over seventy-five are working, and in Australia it's a mere 2 per cent.[14]

There is absolutely no doubt that 'older workers' experience discrimination in getting and keeping jobs. The term 'older workers' can apply to anyone over forty-five, but more generally it's over fifty. If the research into age discrimination and employment was done on those seventy-five and over, or even eighty and ninety and over, the level of discrimination would go sky high.

Not one person I know when they were over sixty has got a job applying for it cold—that is, without knowing anyone in the employing organisation or company. Even when I was nearing fifty I knew enough to leave my date of birth off any job application. Resume writing advice books always offer the same tips for older workers: include only fifteen years' work experience for a managerial job, ten years for a technical job, and five years for a high-tech job; leave your other work experience off your resume or list it without dates in an 'Other Experience' category; use a functional resume rather than a chronological one. The assumption underlying this advice is that employers don't want to employ workers over forty.

Evidence of discrimination is not merely anecdotal. The most impressive data on prejudice against hiring older adults—and older women in particular—comes from studies using mock resumes. One researcher created 4000 mock female resumes and sent them to different companies in Boston, Massachusetts and St Petersburg, Florida. The applicants' ages ranged from thirty-five to sixty-two. Turns out that younger women were 40 per cent more likely to be hired than those fifty or older.[15] In another study of both men and women, 202 resumes were sent to 452 companies in Western Australia. The researchers found that older females were the ones most likely to be rejected.[16] These experiments have been repeated many times in different locations and with different industries, always with the same result: older women are the least likely to get an interview for jobs in which they are just as well qualified as all the other applicants.

It's depressing to find that 67 per cent of older Australians believe they've been turned down for a position because of their age.[17] But it's not surprising because most of us carry some of the stereotypes and prejudices that underlie this discrimination.

Surveys of employers have found that unfounded stereotypes are widespread. We've all heard the rationales: older workers are more expensive, set in their ways, lack up-to-date skills, are technologically illiterate, and won't be around long enough to justify the cost of hiring and training. On top of this employers also believe that older employees won't cope with working for someone who is younger or less experienced. Employers in the United States usually provide health insurance so the belief that older workers are 'sick and frail' means they fear hiring them as this means heftier premiums and benefit costs.[18] Not only is there evidence that older workers are more productive than young workers but there is absolutely no basis to the belief that employing them will increase youth unemployment or block youth careers. In fact economists believe that employing more older workers will enhance opportunities for youth by boosting economic demand.[19]

Sadly, as well as not getting hired, older workers also get fired more often. Because proving age discrimination is so difficult to establish only the most blatant cases get to the courts and tribunals. Take Debra Moreno, an office coordinator at Hawaii Healthcare Professionals, whose manager said she was a thorough and efficient worker. The fifty-four year old was laid off in 2008 after the company's owner reportedly said that Debra Moreno 'sounded old on the phone' and looked 'like a bag of bones', the irony being that Hawaii Healthcare Professionals provided home healthcare for seniors.[20]

Age discrimination cases make up by far the smallest proportion of complaints brought to the tribunals and commissions that deal with discrimination in Australia, the United States and Great Britain. Only 8 per cent of complaints that come to the Australian Human Rights Commission relate to age discrimination as compared to 37 per cent under the disability legislation.[21] The low figure has no relationship to what really happens. In the United States, one in five workers between forty-five and seventy-four say they have been turned down for a job because of age. And one in ten say they were passed up for a promotion, laid off or denied access to career development because of their age.[22]

Susan Ryan, the Australian Human Rights Commissioner, points to the fact that older workers have internalised the stereotypes and have had their self-confidence undermined by the broadly held views of their incompetence and grumpiness. She says that older workers are more concerned that 'kicking up a fuss' will be used against them, and their age cohort comes from a culture that implies they are likely to be more stoical. This stoicism is true of some of the women I interviewed, including Lady Flo and Lis Kirkby, who said, 'Well, that's just the way it is.' Others like Margaret Fulton and Bertha Lowitt overcame discrimination and are perfectly capable of 'kicking up a fuss'.

A few recent landmark cases give us heart. We've all noticed how few older women are working in television. At fifty-one, Miriam O'Reilly had worked for the BBC for twenty-five years and was doing a great job presenting on BBC1's *Countryfile* program when her employment was terminated. 'People said to me "that's showbiz",' she writes, and told her to keep her head down. Instead she took the BBC to court and in 2011 won her case. As a result the then director general of the BBC, Mark Thompson, publicly admitted there were 'too few' older women presenting on BBC TV and pledged to be more representative.

In Canada in December 2012, a decision of the Alberta Human Rights Commission actually gave Joan Cowling, seventy-two, her job back. She was told her position was being redefined for someone with fewer qualifications. She applied for the job anyway and was unsuccessful. The commission found that her employer, by using language like 'growth' and 'developmental' position and 'seeking a person who could stay in the position five or ten years', were specifically excluding her at age sixty-seven. She was re-employed and, amazingly, neither side seems to harbour bad feelings about the matter.

Not all employers conform to their stereotype when it comes to employing older people. The median age at the Vita Needle Factory in Massachusetts is seventy-four, with Rosa Finnegan, who's just turned 100, being the oldest. Older workers are valued by the company for their loyalty and commitment—many have worked there for ten to fifteen years—as well as their attention to detail and the quality of their work. Because the company's senior citizen workers are eligible for Medicare and work part time, the employer saves on medical insurance.[23]

As well as employer prejudice and discrimination and the negative attitudes we've internalised, there are age limits and restrictions to workers' compensation, income protection insurance, superannuation and professional licensing, which act as structural barriers to workforce participation for older workers. Changes to encourage those on the age pension to stay in part-time work cut out when you reach seventy-five. After that you can no longer earn up to $6500 a year without jeopardising your pension. So Rose Stone barters her sewing skills in exchange for home repairs and Kali Paxinos and Beth Gott claim only expenses for the talks they give and the advice they provide. If they weren't financially penalised for working, they'd be able to be paid for the work they do.[24]

Voluntary work, especially at a grass-roots level, also becomes more difficult to get and keep as you get older and this is without taking into account any 'infirmities' someone might have. Liability and insurance issues act as barriers to older volunteers working. Mary Broughton describes how new legislation made the job of the Catering Committee of the Friends of the Botanical Gardens increasing difficult. Mandatory refrigeration was required, depending on 'how long it took to get from the place where it was made to its destination', and committee members did not have fridges in their cars.

'If you want to know the worst part of old age it's that you're a blessed nuisance. Nobody wants you. You want to do things but nobody wants you to,' says Frances Reynolds, who needs to feel useful and tries to be as active as possible. A change in local council regulations led to her leaving her voluntary work for the Meals on Wheels service. Frances also used to borrow books for those who couldn't get to the library—the housebound and people in nursing homes or in care—but now the librarians do this task. When Frances turned ninety, 'overnight they have got to have another person' in the op shop where she's working. Frances believes that this has something to do with insurance. On the day I spoke to her, she had just found out that once you are over eighty-six you can no longer donate your organs. 'I thought that's the icing on the cake! You think, all right, I can leave my organs, but they don't want them.'

Frances drives and can do anything that younger volunteers can do and the truth is that younger volunteers don't want to do the work she's prepared to do. It's bad enough that she and others are made to feel useless, but volunteering adds $14.6 million to the Australian economy every year and older Australians contribute by far the most volunteer hours.[25] The Advisory Panel on the Economic Potential of Senior Australians made two recommendations in this complicated area. The first focused on improving the federal and state legislation for protecting older volunteers and the second on getting insurance companies and seniors together to improve the availability and affordability for older volunteers.[26] To date, none of the panel's recommendations have been acted on.[27]

Where do we go from here?

We older people need to come out, to assert ourselves to ensure that we can work for as long as we want to and are fit and productive. Lady Flo would have stayed in the senate another ten years and Lis Kirkby could have resisted the move-over-for-a-younger-person push she got from her Democrat Party colleagues if decisions were made on the capacity to do the job instead of years clocked up. It shouldn't be about how old you are, but about who can do the best job. We need to learn to look past the wrinkles and sunspots, and even the walker, and see what's on offer. Older people should be doing it for ourselves. And it starts just as it did for Rose, when she crossed the line into women's liberation. It is not the fault of the two million Australians over fifty-five who want to work that they can't get jobs, it's age discrimination.

On the Australian Human Rights and Equal Opportunity Commission website they smash some of the myths about recruiting people over the age of fifty-five. Turns out that mature workers don't cost more. In fact, they're significantly less likely to resign, they call in sick less often, and they experience fewer work injuries. All of that stuff saves money, especially on recruitment and training. But 'the times they are a-changin'', just as they did for my cohort in the 1960s. US Equal Employment and Opportunity Commission age discrimination complaints, though still tiny in number, were up 40 per cent by the end of 2012 on the 2006 numbers. As the oldest baby boomers ride their wave into an extended working life they are hitting the barrier of age discrimination. They bring with them the experience of activism, organisation skills and experience in leading the fight to end discrimination for gender, race and sexual preference. And we're going to have the numbers. Hey, Bob Dylan, you're seventy-two! How about a song that helps us over this barricade?

Right now those of us over sixty-five make up about 15 per cent of the Australian population. That's a sizeable chunk of the voters and we're growing to a predicted 23 per cent by 2041. As I write that date I look again at that year. In 2041 I'll be ninety-five and for the first time in my life I can imagine myself—if I have the capacity—still working then. Scary, and exciting!

HOT TIPS For a working life

➤ Repeat this refrain: 'I can work another ten years.' Write it into your computer calendar so the reminder pops up every birthday after you turn sixty.
➤ Don't let outdated concepts of retirement deter you from working as long as you want and need to.
➤ Don't let unfounded prejudices about older workers go unanswered—you have as much if not more to offer.
➤ Be inspired by women who've worked into old age despite the barriers they had to overcome.

➤ Remember you must set your own course for your future work and it may take you a while to find what this is.

➤ Find a supportive group of women like yourself who want to keep working—stay away from the naysayers.

➤ You will need a supportive partner, someone with their own late life interests that don't depend on you.

➤ You will need supportive children who understand that you can't be a full-time babysitter for the grandchildren.

➤ Choose a job or profession in which you can continue to improve as you age

➤ If you are in a job that depends on the physical capabilities or boundless energy of youth start planning your shift into a new field well before your use-by date.

➤ Don't be single-minded in your work focus. Create a second string, and have another interest or project waiting in the wings in case you get pushed out.

➤ If you've made a name for yourself in your field you're more likely to be in demand.

➤ Never think you're too old to start a new career. New work and learning new skills will be exciting and you can do it.

➤ Be flexible—be open to change, nothing stays the same. You will probably have to remake your working life more than once.

➤ Be ready to grab new opportunities—say yes and give it a try.

➤ Keep up with your field, especially new technology.

➤ Check out areas where there are job shortages and be prepared to retrain at fifty or sixty, as you've still got several decades to give to your new field.

➤ Being your own boss is your best chance of staying in paid employment that allows for flexibility. Think about starting your own business.

➤ Ask yourself do you need the money or the status that paid work gives you? You can get more job satisfaction and status from voluntary work.

➤ Try voluntary work as there are so many urgent issues out there and we have the time and skills to contribute.

➤ All the same rules above apply whether your work is paid or unpaid.

➤ Contributing—doing something meaningful that is recognised as being useful by others—will make you happier.

➤ If you don't enjoy your work, retire or find another job.

➤ Remember that work is probably good for your health. Stay engaged even if you cut down your hours of work.

➤ If you believe that you need to make room for younger people in your field, then plan your move into a mentoring and advisory role.

➤ Don't wait to be asked, as you'll be waiting for the rest of your life. Lean in harder than you ever have and put yourself forward for what you want to do.

➤ Think about how much responsibility you want to take on in your work. A CEO may want to work in a soup kitchen for a few years.

➤ Use your friends and contacts. Networking and nepotism are more important than ever. You will not get a job by sending your resume to the Human Resources Department.

2

Love and Loss

RECENTLY THREE OF my friends' husbands have died. They are in shock, reeling from the impact of their loss. Anthea is fifty-eight and met her husband as a teenager, at a youth camp. 'I thought I was resilient,' she says, 'but I'm staring at the thirty years ahead without him, with no one to come home to, who talks you down from your angers and frustrations.' Having been a woman chock-full of energy and enthusiasm, Anthea now describes herself as having lost her mojo. Renee and her Henry were together for sixty years. She's a writer who's written not a word since he died and hardly leaves the house. 'I'm not lonely, just sad because I miss him so terribly.' Susan's the opposite, 'I have to get out of the house or I'll go mad.'

All three are careful not to show how lousy they feel. They know misery and grief are not attractive, and nowadays likely to be stigmatised as depression. 'Why don't you get some anti-depressants?' or 'Take a trip' are common responses to visible grief. While no longer wearing traditional widow's weeds, a grieving widow is a visible reminder of our own mortality. Everyone is trying to keep their spirits up, and who wants to be around a downer?

By the time I meet my widow interviewees their husbands have been dead for at least two years. None are in the initial stages of shock or grief, although there are powerful memories of this period. Suzanne Simon will always miss her husband. She lost 10 kilograms after Alec died. 'I was terribly sick,' she says. 'I am sure it was grief, and my GP says it was grief too. I didn't want food, I didn't want anything.'

Eleven years after her husband Julian's death, Bertha Lowitt still shouts, 'Why did you leave me?' at his photograph.

Beth Gott describes her marriage as 'a meeting of true minds without impairment'. Her metaphor for their togetherness is the merging of their libraries. They laughed at the same jokes and worked for political causes together. After Ken died in 1990, Beth was still working, so it was more the weekends that were hard for her. 'I used to feel so lonely,' she says. 'I didn't have anyone to talk to. My husband and I were really word people, you know.' Nearly twenty-five years later she says, 'I know it's very sad but it happens, you have to face it.'

If you are married it is highly likely that you will have to face this loss. Eighty per cent of all widowed Australians are women. The reasons for this disparity are that women live longer, we marry men who are older and we are far less likely to remarry.[1] The figures are the same in the United States, where it's estimated that a quarter of married women will be widows by sixty-five, and that half the remaining women will lose their husband by the time they turn seventy-five.[2]

How you cope with the loss of your partner is going to be a major factor in making the most of the last third of your life. You need to expect to face your partner's death and be prepared for it—as much as you can. After talking to the widows for this book I'd agree with Stephanie Charlesworth that, 'You never lose the sense of loss but you learn to live with that sadness.'

As well as the emotional loss there are practical losses too. One woman describes widowhood as finding she now needed forty-eight hours each day to do the things she did and her husband used to do. You are going to have to learn to do all the things your spouse once did.

Lady April Hamer had never contemplated life alone, never thought about getting old, until her husband of sixty years died. 'It wasn't something I'd envisaged beforehand.' Never to have imagined, or in any way planned for, being alone made the transition to widowhood that much harder for her. As she says, 'You need to rearrange your life entirely.'

The remarkable 99-year-old Dodo Berk has no time for grieving widows. She was married to 'the handsomest man at New York University night school for fifty-two years'. Dodo never mourned, she only mourns 'if I didn't have it or I didn't do it'. When I press her about her husband, she says, 'Why mourn? I had everything.' Yet even Dodo had to remake her life, beginning with looking in the mirror and saying to herself, 'Dodo, you're going to be fine.'

Widowhood as liberation

Not everyone is lucky in love and marriage and not every death of a husband is a loss. For some women it brings freedom from fear and misery. Dodo Berk describes her aunt at the end of her uncle's funeral saying triumphantly, 'It's my turn now.' We all know women, set free from a difficult and demanding spouse, who blossom in the last third of their life. With recent surveys showing widows having higher levels of wellbeing than either married or single women, it's clear that being on your own has things going for it.[3]

Joan Lowrie was ninety-three years old when I spoke to her. By then the man she married when she was twenty-seven had been dead for more than two decades. Only when she was sure we were completely alone did Joan furtively lean over and whisper, 'I don't tell anybody. My husband was a chronic alcoholic. I had to nurse him. He was in and out of hospital. Pretty rugged.

The only thing he gave me was the war widow's pension. I had a horrible life, a horrible life.' She never once mentions his name as if to let that slip out would unleash a black cloud of bad memories. There are no photos of him: 'I don't want to remember him to be perfectly honest.'

Joan is a tall, well-built and forthright woman yet I sense how frightened she was of the man she married. She says, 'My life was hell,' and when I ask why she didn't throw him out or leave him she tells me he would have found her wherever she ran to because, 'Some of these alchies [alcoholics] are at your door all the time . . . And where was I going to go with an elderly woman [her mother]? I couldn't do it. They say people leave them but it's very hard.' Joan didn't believe she had any options. Yes, she was concerned about where she could go with her aged mother, but deep down she was afraid that he would never leave her alone, no matter where she went. His death in 1990 lifted the load of care and constant worry. For Joan, widowhood brought liberation and some of the best years of her life.

Maxie Meldrum buzzes with energy as her hands circle and swoop to underline the points she makes. When she talks about her husband Frank, she is at her calmest. Frank died in a nursing home, four months before his hundredth birthday. They'd had a wonderful, loving marriage, but Maxie says. 'When I lost him I was pleased, he went so easily. I didn't grieve at all.' Frank developed dementia in his early nineties, when he was still playing golf three days a week with his friends, and it took its toll: 'He became paranoid. When I left him alone I would come home and think what's he done now.'

Maxie says, 'I looked after Frank for about two years and I lost ten kilograms over that time. I had large breasts which I didn't like then, but now I have little paper bags hanging down.' After about five years, Frank went into a nursing home, where he was happy. When he died, 'The kids said, "Oh, what a pity." I said, "No, it was a wonderful death because he just went."'

With Alzheimer's and dementia, you've already lost the person you loved. Rose Stone says, describing the decline of the lovely man she took up with in her fifties, 'By the time he died in 2010, he was no longer Fred.' Fred got vascular dementia, and three years and many strokes later, he went into a nursing home. Rose says, 'The loss of Fred was a slow loss, the Fred I knew slowly disappeared. It was nice that he died. For six months he didn't want to eat and just sat there reading the newspaper upside down.'

Becoming a widow was not traumatic for either Maxie or Rose. They had been remaking their lives, as single women again, for many years before their partners' deaths.

We'll meet again

Lady Flo Bjelke-Petersen's husband Sir Joh died in March 2005. For much of their married life, everyone in Australia knew who they were. Sir Joh was a colourful, more than life-sized, controversial politician—people either loved or hated him, depending on their political persuasion. Asked in 1994 how she felt about the possibility of losing her husband, Lady Flo said, 'We have the hope that we'll meet again one day beyond this life. That's the Christian's hope. But we have to accept that God's plan—he knows what's going to happen in the future, we don't. That's all I can say to you about that.'[4]

When I spoke to her eight years after his death, in the home she'd shared with Joh, and where they'd raised their four children, she still says in her slow thoughtful way, 'I don't know what God plans so you have to accept what you get.' She describes how toward the end of his life, 'It was quite a different kettle of fish from when he'd been alive and telling you what to do and all the rest of it. Oh, yes, he wasn't well the last twelve months or so, he was in bed most of the time.' As she talks I sense him slipping away to what Lady Flo believes is a better place. She has confidence in God's plan, and that in another life beyond this one she'll be reunited with her loved ones.

Someone who also gets comfort from the belief that there is another life after death, in a beautiful place, is 91-year-old Koho Yamamato. In Greenwich Village, New York City, she is living the happiest years of her life with the underlying conviction that people are not gone when they die: 'You know many people say when they die, it's so beautiful there, it's so so happy, and I would like to believe that. I think maybe we turn into another person, or maybe we continue living as another living thing or we might be staying there in happy heaven.' When Koho says, 'I am not very religious', she is talking about observance rather than her beliefs: a mix of Buddhist beliefs in reincarnation, as either new people or other beings, with western ideas of a 'beautiful heaven' where we all hang out together, just as long as we've not done too many bad deeds in this world.

Wouldn't we all like to believe that? I know I would, if I could. But I can't suddenly become a completely different person and chuck my deeply held scepticism. It's not that I can't change or won't change but there are limits. At the core of my being I value 'rationality'. My humanism cannot integrate what for me is a completely unsubstantiated belief in reunification in an afterlife, or reincarnation. If I was another person, I would now set off on a pilgrimage from church to temple to ashram.

None of the widows became suddenly religious after the deaths of their husbands. Although only five of them have the comfort of believing in a life beyond this one, more than half the people in the world believe in 'the sweet hereafter'.[5] We think of Australia as a secular country and yet a surprising 53 per cent of us believe in life after death. The British and Swedes are a bit more optimistic about the world to come than Australians but still way under the 80 per cent of believers in the afterlife in the United States.[6]

So how do others cope with the loss of our nearest and dearest, the nearly 50 per cent of us who don't believe we will be reunited with our loved ones in the next world?

Does time heal?

The received wisdom is that a widow usually recovers from grief within a year. Among my friends the extreme symptoms tail off within twelve months; they cry less and less. There is a craziness about them in that first year—falling into swimming pools, missing appointments, forgetting keys, losing weight or gaining it, depending on their proclivities, and many other signs of stress. They buy way too much food and cook their husband's favourite dishes.

The year timeframe makes sense to me. In some religions, the year following the death is considered an extended period of mourning, and older grievers can choose to wear black clothing. On the anniversary of a death Roman Catholics offer a memorial mass. The Jewish Kaddish prayer is recited daily for eleven months and after that annually on the anniversary.

More than 50 per cent of bereaved people recover from the severe symptoms of grief within six months, while others can take from eighteen months to three years to recover. Widowers tend to suffer more from the death of their spouse than widows because they are less able to reach out to friends and others for support.[7] Researchers conclude that, 'Loss is forever, but thankfully acute grief is not.'[8]

This timeframe generally holds true for the widows I spoke with. They are all past the acute grief stage, and getting on with their 'rearranged' and rebuilt lives. Mary Broughton, Dodo Berk and the others who've been widowed for decades have full and fulfilling lives. But for some there's still the loneliness, the feeling that this new life is second best, a patch-up job, compared with what they had with their husbands.

Suzanne Simon was widowed at eighty-seven. She had a very happy marriage: 'It was the best thing that ever happened to me when I met Alec, I really adored him. He died two and a half years ago and I have never really recovered, I don't think I ever will.' Four years before his death Alec Simon was already unwell enough to stop them going on their usual overseas trip. Suzanne misses him terribly. But is Suzanne's belief that she'll never recover related to how recently her husband died?

Flo Howlett's husband Johnny died at around the same time as Alec Simon but there the similarity stops. The Howletts had been married just a couple of months short of seventy-four years when he died in November 2011. Two years before that they'd sold their home and moved into adjacent rooms in an aged-care home. At ninety-five, Flo's advice for how to cope with the losses of people you love and care for is to 'take it as it comes'. 'When Johnny died,' she says, 'I didn't carry on or anything like that, I didn't break down and sob and sob and sob. I haven't been able to cry for years and when he died I still couldn't cry. Can you believe that?'

Flo sees herself as tough and able to handle anything that life throws her way: 'I had so many bad times growing up and getting up to this age that I am a bit hardened.' When I asked what hardened her she replies, 'Just struggling while keeping everything together. Just struggling.' And then she repeats: 'I have had a very tough life.' Perhaps how Suzanne and Flo coped with the deaths of their husbands has more to do with their completely different life circumstances and experiences.

Flo, the youngest of ten children, was brought up by a single mother and went to work in the local wool-spinning mill just five days after turning fourteen. There was no money to keep her at school. According to Flo, her mother had an even harder life,

'A terribly hard life. She used to go out to work cleaning people's houses, you know for five shillings for about four hours.' The Howletts never owned a car, have not been on any overseas holidays, and always lived in working-class Coburg, in the northern suburbs of Melbourne.

Suzanne was the youngest of two. She attended a private secondary school, loved riding horses, and was helped to independence by a small inheritance from her mother. When talking to me she never mentions the Depression. Suzanne and Alec, and their children, travelled overseas regularly, and the four children attended expensive private schools. She lives in a light-filled, architect-designed house in the leafy and wealthy suburb of Hawthorn in Melbourne.

Like Suzanne, Flo didn't work after she was married but unlike Alec Simon, Flo's husband was not such a good provider. 'Well it was hard, I had three kids in three years and then Johnny backed horses and drank beer and that took money, and I was struggling all the time, you know. I suppose that may have been what hardened me inside. And of course he did shift work and I had the kids on my own such a lot,' she tells me.

Both have had their share of personal tragedy. In describing how she coped with the death of a baby at twelve months Flo says, 'I don't know what helped me, just myself, I guess. I just kept going—and I'm just tough.' Suzanne has also been through terrible times: the loss of her mother when she was a child of ten, and her youngest daughter dying of cancer at age thirty while, at the same time, her other daughter was suffering from a serious mental illness.

The different ways that Flo and Suzanne describe the loss of their husbands are perhaps expressions of their individual adaptive styles; how they integrate their experiences into their individual personality, formed by nine decades of life. When Flo says, 'to take it as it comes', she expresses her stoicism in the face of the hard knocks that she expects from life, which includes losing your husband. Suzanne is more able to express her feelings. She doesn't see herself as tough or hardened, and wouldn't want to be. She believes that her mental health has been adversely affected by the losses in her life. 'It can't be otherwise,' she says, 'You can't get over losing a beautiful daughter or a wonderful husband and then the original loss of a mother was the start of it all really because it wasn't properly dealt with.'

There are practical differences, too, that frame how both women experienced the death of their spouse. The Howletts had already moved into care, into rooms next door to each other, which made it easier for Flo to transition to widowhood. Her routines, the new friends she made and activities she got involved in were all in place by the time Johnny got sick and moved to the higher care floor upstairs.

Yes, time definitely does heal. But there are women, long widowed, for whom the sense of loss remains potent, and who still deeply mourn the life they had with their husbands.

Coping with sudden death

Does the way you cope afterwards have anything to do with how your husband dies, especially if he dies unexpectedly? There is no shortage of literature and advice on coping with the sudden death of a loved one. The consensus is that the shock and unexpectedness makes grieving and adapting to the loss longer and more difficult. It leaves you more vulnerable and less able to cope.[9]

On 24 March 2004, the death of Sir Rupert 'Dick' Hamer, a former premier of Victoria, was reported in *The Age*:

> Lady Hamer celebrated 60 years of marriage with Sir Rupert earlier this month, and said her family were helping her come to terms with his sudden death at their Kew home on Tuesday at the age of 87.

'He was in perfectly good health,' Lady Hamer said. 'He was having a rest and I found him when I came home. I suppose it doesn't really hit you for a while.'

April Hamer had no chance to prepare herself or to gradually adjust to this dramatic change in her life. She had never thought about getting old: 'No, never, until Dick died. Because from good luck we were both very healthy.' Sixty years a wife and the next moment a widow—what a shock! Lady Hamer was not able to say goodbye to the love of her life. The irony, of course, is that we'd all like deaths like Dick Hamer's—peaceful and painless and in our sleep. April Hamer agrees: 'Absolutely, he was a lucky man, good one day and gone the next.'

Asked to reflect on old age she says, 'You have to keep doing things as much as you can and not let things get on top of you.' And her emphatic response to a reporter who asked her about the secret of a long life was, 'Perseverance!'[10] In the ten years since her husband died April has made a life with her children, study, church and charity work yet, during our time together, she talks more about Dick than herself. And the best times of her life, she says, were when her husband was alive.

Doctor Margaret Barnett's husband also died suddenly, after forty-eight years of marriage. One Saturday morning they were at their farm in Bonny Doon, in the foothills of the Victorian Alps. She was talking on the phone to her son, Peter, who was on his way to America:

> I had a long talk, hung up and went out to tell John how Peter was getting on. And he was lying there, dead in the yard. It was horrible. I was by myself and I had to ring the police, had to ring the ambulance, had to ring up and tell the girl on the phone that I knew he was dead, it was

a horrible business. He blew an aneurism in his heart and
he just went like that.

Margaret explains to me that she went through a very bad patch
after John died, and went to see a psychologist. 'Unfortunately I
didn't think it helped all that much. It took a lot of getting used to,'
she says of the shock of finding herself suddenly alone. Margaret
dealt efficiently with the practical aspects of life after John died. She
left the retirement flat he'd chosen and moved to another closer to
where she had connections. She sold half the farm at Bonny Doon
almost immediately. Although she is now used to being without
John, there are many things she still misses of their life together.

Understandably you can feel less secure, and lose confidence
in the future when someone is snatched away from you without
warning. Unexpected death is harder to come to terms with than
if there is time to prepare for the loss.

Coping with the sick and dying

Often there are years of looking after a sick husband, dealing with
his illness and its effect on him and the family. Suzanne Simon's
husband's last years were not good. Looking back, she says:

> I really feel that I should have insisted on having a carer
> because it was too much for me. If I'd got a really nice
> attractive carer with whom he could talk about Vienna,
> and opera, and all those sort of things while I was slaving
> at the sink, it would have been better for him and better
> for me. But he said, 'Oh, no, I don't want a carer, no I
> don't want anyone.'

Suzanne's story is a warning to us to look at alternatives to
the self-sacrifice model, to look after ourselves. My father also

didn't want to go to hospital or have a carer, and by the time he died, three years after his stomach cancer was first diagnosed, my mother, like Suzanne, was physically as well as emotionally exhausted, in a state where she was less able to deal with grief and loneliness. The message is, we need to stay strong and well to deal with the intensity of the emotional needs of a dying husband, and his fears of hospital, pain and death. So ask for, and get, help with the day-to-day nursing, feeding and cleaning up.

Even when your husband is in a nursing home there are different ways of living for the prospective widow. Rose Stone, for example, chose not to visit her partner every day. 'If I'd gone every day I wouldn't have made Fred better, I'd only have made myself worse,' she says. 'I wasn't lost because I hadn't given my life up to looking after him. There was a blow, but I wasn't a lost soul.'

When there is time to prepare, it means letting go, and knowing there's going to be a life for you after death. This is something you've got to ready yourself for.

Remarriage

None of the widows I spoke with had remarried or re-partnered, not even Mary Broughton. She was widowed more than fifty years ago at the young age of forty-five but says, 'All the nice men I knew were safely married. I knew no bachelors. It never entered my head, there was never anybody. I never thought of marrying again.' To have had a good marriage for twenty-two years, to lose a fine husband in your mid-forties, and not to look at another man or even have thoughts about remarriage—it's hard to fathom.

Rose Stone was newly divorced at about the same age that Mary was widowed. Like Mary, her children were grown and at university, but Rose felt quite differently about being single. 'The reason that people look for something, anything, is because the loneliness is amazing. You're so used to being with a family.' After the divorce Rose found herself alone, and terrified and describes what many widows experience: 'In the 1960s if you went out with a woman it was a poor outing. And you never went out on your own to have a meal. If you went out with a woman it was because you couldn't get a man. I was really looking for another husband.'

I am surprised by my other interviewees' lack of interest in finding a new partner because the widows who I knew of that generation—my mother, my mother-in-law, my mother's friends—all took up with new men. But none of the widows in my mother's circle remarried and few let their new partner move in. My mother's friend Cyla's new man did move in with her, and a day later she asked him to move out again. 'I wasn't going to go back to washing someone else's socks and ironing their pants. I'd had enough of that.' Their living apart arrangement worked. After he moved out, they were together for another twenty years.

Only 3 per cent of widows in Australia remarry.[11] Other data suggests that this figure seriously underestimates the interest of widows in forming new romantic relationships.[12]

Margaret Barnett and Barbara Hamer were both widowed in their late seventies. Margaret says, 'Having someone to go out with makes a big difference. I never had to be by myself very much. You know John had always been around mostly. I could cope when I went overseas to conferences by myself.' With her husband, Margaret had been on many adventurous travels and they'd gone to seventy-eight countries—usually just the two of them with a car and a driver. 'But,' she says, 'it's ground to a halt a bit since John died. I don't enjoy it nearly as much as when he was there, we were a good couple.'

The 'big difference' Margaret talks of is the sense of security she feels. A woman can be more vulnerable on her own, especially in a foreign country, and perhaps the man will even carry the bags! But as we age, men get weaker and become vulnerable too.

Like Margaret, I don't like travelling on my own except for work. I need someone to share the experience with. And I'm the same about restaurants, plays, movies, art exhibitions. I don't even enjoy cooking for myself. But perhaps more than the preceding generation, I enjoy doing all these things with my female friends.

Barbara Hamer is not one of those widows who never considered re-partnering. She wouldn't have minded finding someone else, 'But the ground is pretty thin at that age. I didn't really want to take on another old man to look after and to be honest I don't think many of them are up to much.' As we've seen, it's hard enough looking after your lifelong partner through sickness and dying. Of course you think about this before taking on a new old man. Who wants the potential responsibility of changing the nappies and mopping up the sick of someone we've known for only a few years?

I can imagine being a widow but I can't see myself with a new partner, and I'm determined never to remarry. Perhaps I'd feel differently if, like Mary Broughton, my mother or my friend Andrea, I'd been widowed in my fifties or younger. As Barbara Hamer found, older widows have fewer options, and the men who are available tend to prefer younger partners. The younger you are when you are widowed, the more likely you are to re-partner.

Widows are far less interested in new romantic relationships than widowers. Eighteen months after the death of a spouse, 15 per cent of widows and 37 per cent of widowers sixty-five and older are interested in dating.[13] Many widows are loathe to give up their newfound freedom and independence. They grow to love just pleasing themselves and feel liberated in not having to look after someone else. No wonder many consciously choose to remain unpartnered.[14] I see myself as one of these widows, not because I believe there can only ever be one man in your life but because of not wanting to put in the effort needed to find and nurture a new relationship. The man, any man, will already be a fully formed person and likely to have siblings and children and more baggage, just like me. I look around at my friends who've done it and I see that it's very hard work.

Among my friends who have re-partnered very few have remarried or moved in with a man. Those who do remarry often do so for economic reasons. It's a way of getting better health benefits, and sharing the cost of accommodation and living expenses. Most women don't feel that they need to re-partner for companionship. Because widows have many friends and wide social networks, only 20 per cent have started a new relationship—compared to 60 per cent of widowers—within two years of the death of their spouse.[15]

Of course, I could feel completely differently when it happens to me. But I'm willing to bet serious money that I'll never remarry. And I won't co-habit either even though the number of people in their eighties and nineties living with partners without getting married is growing very quickly.[16]

Rose Stone credits the length and strength of her thirty-year relationship with Fred Lester to the fact that they never lived together. Both had lived alone for a long time and were involved in different things: Fred with athletics and Rose with the women's movement. But most important of all, Rose knew herself. 'I knew that it wouldn't work for me if he moved in. My conditioning was built in so deep that I would have started doing everything for him and then I would have resented him.' In the future widows who do want companionship and intimacy are more likely to be in 'living apart together' (LAT) relationships, like the one Rose and Fred had. By keeping separate households you can maintain an independent life and sustain an intimate ongoing relationship.

To make the right choices about whether to re-partner or not, you need to be conscious of what you are like and your needs. You might be a Mary or a Bertha and never want to look at another man. Or you could join one of the ever-increasing numbers of singles clubs and internet sites and agencies specifically set up for older people to meet a new love. Fortunately you've got choices. And there is much less societal pressure nowadays to be one of a couple, as well as expanding opportunities for single older women to do things by themselves and in groups.

Enmeshed, entwined and separate lives

To better survive and thrive do you need to create a separate life for yourself well before your husband dies? Barbara Hamer thinks so. She says:

> My husband and I were very independent, we didn't depend totally on each other. He was in the navy, so he wasn't there half the time, and then he went to parliament and wasn't home half the time either. So I had to battle on, on my own and be responsible for a lot of aspects of life which some women when they marry somebody they just leave it all to the husband to do. And then they are lost because they don't know how to deal with all that.

In contrast her sister-in-law, Lady April Hamer, tells me, 'My life's a bit different, because I didn't have a career. I did things with Dick.' As well as dealing with her husband's sudden death, April Hamer had much more of her life to recreate when Dick was gone. Suzanne Simon also never had a career. Her husband Alec was a huge influence on her life and he didn't want her to go to work after they married, he didn't want her to go to university when the children left home, and he didn't want anyone except Suzanne to care for him when he got sick. Suzanne says, 'I was looking for love and he had plenty of love to give.' They were a close and enmeshed couple—even more so after supporting each other through the death of their youngest daughter.

Rose Stone, who never lived with another man after her divorce, is a true believer in not making a man your whole life.

She advocates a life of activism, community engagement and staying busy as the answer to making a life after loss. Bertha Lowitt has a similar catch-cry: stay active. She and Rose also have in common their Yiddish-speaking backgrounds and engagement in left politics. But more than politics and anything else, the core of Bertha's life was her husband, Julian. 'I fell for him, hook, line and sinker,' she says. Usually when I ask women about the best moment of their lives, there is hesitation. Bertha doesn't miss a beat: 'The best moment was when I first knew that Julian was in love with me, when I finally realised that he's mine.'

As Julian did all the shopping and cooking until Bertha retired, all she had to do when she came home from work was kick off her shoes, and turn on the oven when she was ready to eat. Julian even bought her clothes: 'I wouldn't buy a thing without him.' For the ten years before they retired, Bertha and Julian worked for the same organisation, Fedcap, providing training and jobs for people with disabilities. 'We spent a life together with such warmth and love,' Bertha says:

> It was a relationship that was a friendship, a deep, deep love, a mutual respect for each other, would that all young people would have that kind of life together. So when he died, it was taking my life away, almost. I told my daughter, I don't think I can live without him. And it's eleven years so I guess you live.

I ask her whether she believes she'll meet Julian somewhere else. She laughs and says, 'No, I wish I could. I always say at night, "If I could just take a look at you, for just ten minutes." And then I say, "What? Am I kidding myself? He is dead, there is nothing left of him." He was cremated so it's ashes to ashes.' She says that, 'The week after he was gone was impossible.' But she soon made herself do things, and began working three or even four days a week at the Museum of Jewish Heritage as a tour guide and in the education department. 'It was hard for me to be at home,' she says, 'even now I hate to be home.'

It's in the dark hours, eleven years on, that Bertha's sadness takes over, and she admits to herself that she's lonely. Telling me about these feelings she begins singing, '"Are you lonesome tonight? Do you miss me tonight?" I sing myself to sleep at night, I don't sleep too well. So I sing these crazy songs from those days: "Long ago and far away I dreamed a dream that you were standing here before me".'

Some of the grieving widows are like dense-feather eiderdowns. After their husbands die, some of those feathers are flattened or lost and the eiderdown sinks a little, its ebullience diminished. Yes, the loneliness is worse the crazier you've been about him, or the more enmeshed your lives were. Imagine, your husband choosing and buying your clothes. Bertha would not have given up even one second of her life with 'the most wonderful human being' to have eased the loneliness and sadness of the past eleven years without him. Is it the depth of the attachment and the fusion of their two lives that blind women to the knowledge that they need to prepare for a life after the death of a spouse? These smart women know the statistics and can look around them: you've got an eighteen to one chance of being a widow once you get to ninety.[17] To my surprise not one of them—not Bertha, Suzanne Simon, April Hamer, Margaret Barnett or any of them—seem to have given it a thought.

I often think about what I will do if, and what I will do when, my husband dies, and what he will do if I die first. And I talk about it to my husband, my children and my friends. Once when I was talking about what I'd like for my funeral and memorial service, a woman accused me of being morbid. I'm not morbid. It's happening to people around me. The taboo about talking or even thinking about death feeds into a pretence that it's not going to happen to you or those you love. But it will, and it will help to make some advance emotional preparation.

Does it have to be like this after a happy, entwined marriage? If you met 86-year-old Kali Paxinos you might be fooled by her appearance into assuming she's a typical *yiayia*, a Greek grand-mother, set in the ways of the old world. You would be wrong. The eldest of three daughters of Greek immigrants, Kali was nine-teen when she married. Her 'challenging and happy marriage' of fifty-seven years to Stan Paxinos was an arranged one. Kali and Stan had five children and never became wealthy, although they did eventually own their own home. Just as they were about to take it easy, with a little more financial security and their children having left home and settled, their youngest son, Peri, developed schizophrenia. They were terrible times for the Paxinos' family.

Kali and Stan were a loving and mutually supportive couple. At seventy, Stan began having heart problems and before he died he told Kali that he was ready to go. Now ten years later there are times that she misses the intimacy with Stan, and their long life together, but Kali is not lonely. She was never dependent on Stan, emotionally or socially. She describes enjoying her evenings at home listening to the radio, knitting, and doing mending for her children. 'I've always got something to do,' she says.

Looking at Kali's life at eighty-six, I can see that she is still very much needed. Her youngest son's schizophrenia is better controlled now. He lives with her and they eat most of their meals together. With five children, eight grandchildren and five great grandchil-dren, there's usually someone popping over or a celebration to attend. Kali loves to cook and there are always homemade biscuits and cakes in case any of the family drops in. And she's also still in demand for her professional expertise, preparing and giving talks at Mental Health conferences. Above and on top of all of these fac-tors, explaining how she's got on with life at more or less full blast, is Kali's flexibility.

Some of us who taught together in the humanities department at Swinburne Technical School in those heady educational days of the 1970s still meet for lunch at least once a year. The year Kali turned eighty we gathered in the back room of a restaurant. Suddenly Kali climbed up on a chair so that we could all see—as she says herself, she's grown in confidence over the years but not in height—that she was wearing trousers for the first time in her life. Even though her husband had encouraged her to wear pants and jeans, she'd stuck to her father's ideas. He said that women who wore trousers were whores. 'Why I didn't do it earlier I don't know,' she says. 'I think I just heard that voice of my father. I suppose you can be dominated by little things.'

Kali has the ability to change, and accept change in small ways, like starting to wear trousers at eighty, and in more significant ones, like adapting to a son's mental illness and in not being lonely after the end of her lovingly entwined marriage. But demographic changes suggest this all might be less of a consideration in the future. In Australia the median age for widowhood is going up. In 1985–1987 it was at age sixty-nine, and by 2000–2002 it had risen to seventy-five. This goes along with data that life expectancy for men is catching up with women, so perhaps there will be fewer widows in the future and our period of widowhood will be shorter.[18]

Becoming an adult orphan

If we're lucky, we live at the centre of a rich emotional and social network. Take me as an example. I'm connected with my husband, children, grandchildren, my brother and his family, my cousin and her family, my in-laws, friends—old and new—colleagues and neighbours. How will this network change as we live into our seventies, eighties and nineties? Is there anything we can or should do to sustain and enrich the web of relationships that nourishes us?

One of the things that will happen in the last third of our life, whether earlier or later in this period, is that we will become orphans. We can expect to outlive our parents. An unusual number of the group of women I interviewed had mothers who had died very young—half before they were sixty-five. The women who'd lost their mothers in childhood wanted to talk about this loss and how unhappy their childhoods had been thereafter. Koho Yamamoto contrasts the poverty and misery of her early mother-less life, when no one wanted her, with the past twenty years, the happiest years of her life.

There's a palpable sense of missing out on a mother's love and care in Maxie Meldrum's and Suzanne Simon's stories, of fathers who should have thought more about their schooling and their futures. Sister Mary Gregory was eleven, about the same age as Maxie and Suzanne, when her mother died and she went to live with her grandmother. By the time Rose Stone was twenty her mother, father, younger siblings and most of her family had been murdered by the Nazis. This tragedy made her both vulnerable—so much so that she rushed into marriage—and highly independent. Beth Gott's mother died of typhoid at forty, and Elisabeth Kirkby had just finished school when her mother died of cancer at forty-two.

Whether or not an early death of your mother prepares you to deal with other losses later in life, losing your mother at a young age is not the norm. The most likely age for losing a parent is when you are over fifty. Right now two-thirds of us are entering the last trimester of our lives as adult orphans.[19] Because it is so universal and seen as a normal process, there is little research on the experience of adults losing a parent. Adult children are supposed to have established independent lives and be able to move on and focus on the living. Our culture is not interested in the old and the response to the death of an elderly parent is often, 'Oh, your mum died at eighty. Yeah, she had a good life, get on with it.'

One of the few studies done in this field found that the death of a parent has adverse effects on adult children for three and seven years. Adult orphans start drinking more, don't look after themselves, are anxious and depressed but, the good news is, they get better around the seven-year mark.[20] Some adult daughters actually feel that more is gained than lost when your mother dies. They are able to explore new careers, divorce their husbands and have sex with other women once they are free of the weight of their mother's expectations.[21]

Elisabeth Kirkby was able to pursue a life in the theatre after her mother's death. In 1938 she was in her final year at school. Her mother wanted Elisabeth to train as a nurse and arranged for her to be taken into Nottingham Royal Infirmary as soon as she matriculated. 'I didn't seem to think I had personally any control over it. I just did as I was told,' Elizabeth explains. Her mother knew there was no money to send her to university, and was 'really horrified at the thought of my becoming an actress, which is what I wanted.' By the end of that year her mother had died of cancer at the very young age of forty-two. Very soon after that Elisabeth got a job with the Oldham Repertory Company, following her dream of becoming an actress.

'The death of your parents can be the best thing that ever happens to you,' is the provocative sentence that opens Jeanne Safer's book, *Death Benefits: How losing a parent can change an adult child's life—for the better*. Safer became an orphan at fifty-seven on the death of her 92-year-old mother. She writes about the release from caregiving and the burden of complex decision-making, and the freeing up of time and emotional energy. This was also partly true for me on becoming an orphan at thirty-seven. Being an adult orphan is definitely a new stage of your life and can be an opportunity for reassessment and change. If my mother had lived, I doubt that I would have decided to move to New York in my fifties. Safer's book is part of a shift from seeing the death of a parent for an adult child as 'a normal process' to seeing it as a profound life-changing experience. Those of us who have experienced it, know this to be true.

With life expectancy now in the eighties and still rising, and with the huge increase in the ninety-plus age group, more of us will have parents living into the last third of their lives at the same time as we are also moving into the last third of our own lives. Many of the children of the women I interviewed are my age, some even older. With her children pushing seventy, the irrepressible Dodo Berk quips that both her children are benefitting from seniors' discounts.

Not many of us are going to become super centenarians but their existence highlights how complex the hierarchy of care and loss can become. At ninety-five, Kitty Sullivan sold her car and moved into a retirement community, opposite where her mother lived. Her mother, Sarah Knass, was in a nursing home and, at 118, the oldest living woman in the world. She died a year later in 1999. Sarah's grandson was seventy-three. Her great granddaughter Kathy Jacoby, at forty-nine, had a daughter of twenty-seven and a three-year-old grandson. Kathy said that she didn't know which one of her relatives to visit first. How could she find time to help her daughter with her toddler when there were three generations of older relatives to keep an eye on?

Certainly more and more of us are going to have our mothers around in our sixties and seventies. When Diana Athill turned seventy, her 92-year-old mother, 'was deaf, blind in one eye and depending on a contact lens for sight in the other, so arthritic in her hips that she could hardly walk, and in her right arm that it was almost useless. She also had angina (still mild and infrequent) and vertigo (horribly trying and not infrequent).'[22] Her mother needed her and Diana felt that the parent, who looked after you as a child, should expect the same at the end of her life. But Diana couldn't, and didn't want to, give up her job in London. After a year of long weekends in Norfolk, commuting to work in London, with complicated home-help arrangements and other assistance for her mother, Diana was miserable and exhausted, with high blood pressure and a big weight gain. By deciding to keep every third weekend free for herself, she worked out a compromise that kept her sane and healthy and also worked for her mother. On her ninety-sixth birthday Diana's mother felt faint while supervising the planting of a new eucalyptus tree in her garden. Two days later she died and her last words were, 'It was absolutely divine.' About as good as it gets for life and death.

I lost my mother so young and I am envious of Diana Athill, and of the children of the women I interviewed. But as my brother once pithily put it when talking about our friends coping with their parents' Alzheimer's and other old-age and end-of-life problems, 'By dying early our parents saved us from all this.'

In coping with the death of a loved parent, Margaret Fulton is a wonderful role model. She was only twenty-five when her mother died of uterine cancer at fifty-eight. Margaret credits her focus on food and family as coming directly from her experience as the youngest of six children, being nurtured by the meals her mother cooked. Her mother's legacy of the evening meal, where the family gathered to eat and talk about everything good and bad, is what Margaret went on to recreate. On losing her mother so young, she said in an interview in 1995:

> It was hard but, don't forget, I had been brought up by a woman who wanted to make me independent. So I didn't feel the loss, because I felt that what mother had given me was inside me and nobody could take that away. So whether she was alive, or whether she was whatever, she gave me the resources to do anything I wanted to.[23]

It's not that Margaret has no regrets. She told me, 'I always was sorry that my mother didn't live to see me and the success— I am calling it success. She would have been very pleased. It is sad but I do think the very fact that you know people have faith in you whether they are alive or dead is very important.' Margaret has not lost her mother because she feels that her mother is an integral part of her, an influence on how she thinks and feels.

Betty Walton expresses exactly this same feeling when she says, 'My mother is so often with me.' I feel the same—my mother is also often with me, as is my father. Like Stephanie Charlesworth, another woman who misses her parents, 'I want to ask them things and tell them things.' Our memories of those we've loved and who have loved us are a part of our very being. Thirty years after my parents' deaths, Margaret Fulton could be echoing my thoughts when she tells me, 'I remember my mother and my father with very strong feelings of what wonderful people they were and how lucky I was.'

The hardest loss

We must prepare ourselves for the deaths of our parents, that's as it should be, but we are never ready for the death of a child. Beth Gott's son, her middle child, died of multiple sclerosis when he was thirty. 'He had a non-remitting form, which just got worse and worse and worse,' she says, 'a horrible way to die.' It's our worst nightmare; that one of our children might die before us. We worry and wait and get through the dangerous years when the lure of drugs and the chances of dying in a car accident are high. Phew, the kid's turning thirty, and we breath more easily. Beth's son and Suzanne Simon's youngest daughter, Jenny, were not so lucky.

Jenny was diagnosed with breast cancer at thirty, while at the same time Suzanne's other daughter was suffering from a serious mental illness. Suzanne was seventy-two when Jenny died. The intervening four years were, 'Terrible, terrible years. Jenny died in 1995, and I really wanted to die too. It's all very well to say you want to die, how do you die? You jump off a cliff or something and that's a terrible thing for the children, for your family to have to cope with.' She recognised that would have been a selfish thing to do when her husband and the other children needed her.

Losing a child is something that a parent never gets over. Sadly, it turns out that 19 per cent of parents have experienced the death of a child.[24] My friend Sally, whose son died in a car accident, tells me that when bad things happen, 'I find that nothing phases me. I got through his death so I know I can get through anything.'

If we live long, long lives the chances of outliving our children will probably increase. But there is no way to prepare for such a catastrophe. Don't even contemplate it because it is not likely to happen. If by some terrible chance it does, take comfort from the women who have survived this. Perhaps it has made them stronger and more resilient in dealing with other losses, but no one needs to be made strong in this way.

Siblings

Our relationship with our siblings is likely to be the longest in our lives and it becomes particularly important in the last third of our lives. There is a tendency to drift away from them in early and middle adulthood, while we are concentrating on our young families and our jobs, building adult lives. Often the need to care for ailing parents becomes a powerful catalyst for siblings to work together, and events like the birth of grandchildren, illness, divorce and retirement lead to renewed contact and bonding. For people aged fifty to eighty the sibling relationship is as important as that with parents and children.[25]

Four of the women I spoke to have no siblings: Margaret Barnett, Joyce McGrath, Dorothy Schultz and Betty Walton. This puts them in a very small minority, as having brothers and sisters is still the norm, with about 80 per cent of adult Americans having at least one living sibling.[26] After our parents die, siblings are the ones with whom we can share precious memories and experiences. Your brother is the only one who remembers the time you fell out of the tree and broke your nose. For him too, the smell of burning onions will trigger fond memories of your mother's kitchen. And who else can you reminisce with about the nutty neighbour who crept around cutting his lawn with nail scissors?

Sister to sister is the strongest sibling relationship, with more frequent contact between them than either sister to brother or brother to brother.[27] Interestingly it's sisters who also have the most conflict, but by the time we're in our sixties, we're usually over the jealousy, anger and resentment that may have been there in childhood. There is a dramatic increase in contact between siblings in later life and the great majority choose to stay in touch with each other until death.[28]

In looking at my group of women interviewees, the likelihood of siblings being around in your old age depends on where you come in your family, and whether you've got brothers or sisters. If you're not yet ninety and like Jean Allison, the eldest of sisters, your chances are good. Both Jean's sisters are alive and well and she's especially close to her younger sister. May Lowe is ninety-seven and the eldest of nine children, the youngest born when she was seventeen years old. Of those nine, two of her sisters are still alive, one at ninety-one and the other eighty-five. At the other end of the spectrum is 95-year-old Flo Howlett, the youngest and last surviving of ten children.

Frances Reynolds, ninety, is the only one with older living siblings. From the original six children, she has an older brother of ninety-five in Queensland, and an older sister of ninety-two in Sydney. She and her husband were planning a road trip to visit them both.

About a third of my group have a living sibling. All of those who do are in touch with their sisters and brothers and, depending on how nearby the remaining siblings live and how mobile the women themselves are, see them regularly. Lady Flo Bjelke-Petersen's younger sister Margaret, at nearly ninety, was driving up to Kingaroy from Brisbane—225 kilometres away—to stay for a while around the time of her big sister's ninety-third birthday. Meanwhile May Lowe's sister Phyllis says she's probably getting too old at eighty-five to make the long flight from Perth to Melbourne.

Your connection with brothers and sisters, if you are lucky enough to have them, grows in strength and significance as you get older. One way of nurturing sibling and other family relationships is to become the archivist and documentarian of family history and memories. Barbara Hamer, the oldest of four, describes herself as the 'kin keeper' in her family. She has self-published *Nuts and Bolts*, a story of the family business, and is now working on a memoir. When I met her, Stephanie Charlesworth was rushing to meet a deadline: the hundredth anniversary of the marriage of her parents. She achieved her aim and created two albums of family history and photographs in time for the celebration. Stephanie is the oldest alive of her family and is now working on a more complete version of her parents' family history.

Friends

When my friend Sandra's husband was dying he said, 'You will be okay; you've got your friends.' And she is okay, although it did take some hard years for her to get through losing him. For me, my friends—nearly all women from school, university, work and life—are a crucial part of my life. Not a day goes by that I'm not in touch with some of them. We see films, eat meals, drink coffees, go to lectures, potter through galleries or walk together. And always we talk and talk and talk. Not all of us are girlfriend people. Kali Paxinos, for example says she's never been one, and she has a full life of family and colleagues. But most women are like me and our friends are very dear to us. While most men's only confidant is their wife, we have our girlfriends to share the good and bad times with.

Only one of my close friends has died: Pfui pfui. I spit over my left shoulder, an old superstition I don't really believe in but do automatically to deter the angel of death from swooping down to punish me for my good fortune. I miss her but I didn't feel the same rage and pain at having her taken away as I did about the dying and death of my mother. Perhaps because I never thought of her as mine in the way I think of my parents, husband or children, and the fact that there were other closer mourners.

Joyce McGrath agrees that coping with the loss of those who are close is much harder. She's a single woman of eighty-seven, with no siblings and no children and says that people she knows are 'dying all the time, but I haven't got people that close to me [and, it's not] like your immediate family members, you know. That's all happened to me in the past. When I was young. My father was only thirty-three. My mother was sixty-five.'

Even if psychologically we can handle it, a life without friends would be emptier, lonelier, diminished. When Mary Broughton starts counting she's shocked that of twenty-seven cousins there are only four left and that 'I'm the oldest by miles'. At ninety-seven she no longer attends school reunions as she has no school friends left. For Bertha Lowitt the losses strike deeper. Bertha's friends were an integral and big part of her life—a group of like-minded politically active women and men who were harassed by the FBI, some of whom she'd known from childhood. They looked after each other's children, lived close by and spent week-ends together at the holiday houses they'd built in the same street in Connecticut. Sometimes, when she's watching her favourite show on TV, *Jeopardy*, she goes to call up a friend to share a story, then stops herself and remembers that, 'All my friends, except two, have died.' Her sisters are dead too. To dispel any idea that she might be feeling sorry for herself, she then lifts her head, looks straight at me and says, 'Holy mackerel, I am ninety-six. At ninety-six I am glad I can sit here and talk to you.' The fact that she has made new and younger friends in her work at the Museum of Jewish Heritage does not make up for the friends who knew her when she was young, who shared her ideals and fought the same battles.

I wasn't surprised by the huge crowd at Dodo Berk's hundredth birthday party. Her mobile phone rings and rings. While we're talking about networks, Dodo cultivates hers assiduously. She is not one to sit back and wait for life to come to her. In the evenings she does not watch television, she gets on that phone and rings people. She nurtures and develops her friends, so Dodo always has somebody to be doing something with.

Although most of us are unlikely to be able to emulate Dodo, you needn't worry about an old age without friends. The received wisdom used to be that elderly women became increasingly friendless because of death, retirement and widowhood. Turns out that the over sixty-fives have more friends than the middle-aged and as many as the under twenty-fives.[29] Older women have more time to put into friendships, and become closer to their existing friends. Most take up new activities in retirement, like hiking and painting, and make new friends with similar interests.

Retirement for Jean Allison meant coming back to Melbourne after decades in Hong Kong. Since she's been back she has created a web of activities through her church, her walking, her professional interests and her political activity. In all of these pursuits she's met new people and made new friends. Other women broaden their networks through their involvement in the activities provided at senior centres and retirement homes.[30] That's what happened to Flo Howlett after she moved into an old-age home.

Sister Mary Gregory, too, is making new friends and developing new interests since she moved into assisted care.

Coping strategies for all our losses

Sister Mary at ninety, is finding that most of the people she knows who are dying are now younger than she is. It's not so much a belief in the afterlife that has helped her to deal with the losses of her parents, a younger brother and many friends as The Rule of Saint Benedict, a book of instructions the Good Samaritan Sisters follow. For Sister Mary, what especially applies is the notion that 'we should keep death daily before our eyes'. Like her, we will all cope better when we accept death as a part of life. It is going to be an increasing part of our life as we age. The women facing or living their tenth decade are comfortable with death, accepting that partners, siblings and friends—and they too—have a finite time left.

For others like Mary Broughton and Suzanne Simon, it will be your children and the need to support them that will keep you going, through the losses of other loved ones. Lady Flo says that she found great comfort in having three of her children living around her. 'When your husband has died it's certainly a difficult situation. Anyway, I am very blessed. I had John here beside me. I wasn't too bad, and the girls [her daughters] were here. Helen lives over there and Ruth lives the other side, so I am pretty well set up.'

I can't help but wonder, though, if there's something missing in this discussion of children. The children and grandchildren aren't with you in bed when you are trying to sleep. They have their own lives, usually very busy ones, and their own grief to deal with. Although it won't make up for the loneliness, having children and others who need you does keep you connected to the world and ensures you make some effort. And that is advice that comes across overwhelmingly, whether overtly or by the example of how they live their lives: stay engaged.

Keep working at staying connected and involved with your family, your friends and the world. Bertha Lowitt's advice for coping with loss is:

> The only thing I can tell people is to remain active. I don't care what you do, you belong to things, you're part of organisations, you go to the theatre, whatever, remain active. Devote yourself to certain things because when you're alone you think mostly about who you lost, and I can't begin to plead with people, remain active. I mean to me it's the answer I mean otherwise you just hole up and die.

As well as getting involved in activities in her new home Sister Mary Gregory remains a lifelong member of local community groups and is still actively involved in program planning with an Aboriginal Reconciliation group, and an associate member of the Mygunyah Camden Aboriginal Residence Group. She's still deeply connected to the Good Samaritans, the order she has been a member of since 1944, and someone from the order usually drops in every day to see her for a chat and catch-up.

All the women I talked to are still active, and some became more involved in their communities after the death of a loved one. May Lowe began volunteering with her local anti-cancer group after her husband died of the disease and Bertha increased her number of days at the Museum of Jewish Heritage. Among my friends, the adult orphans and young widows in their fifties, sixties and seventies, it is their work as much as their family that keeps them going through the initial period of mourning. After that they grow and flourish through new friends, interests and activities.

Stephanie Charlesworth tells me that about 90 per cent of her friends and relations are dead. She says, 'You never lose the sense of loss, you don't "get over it", but you learn to live with that sadness.' No one meeting the vibrant Stephanie would call her a sad person. Like Margaret Fulton and Kali Paxinos and others, the dead and loved ones are a part of her: lost and yet not lost.

There has been a shift from the view that 'healthy' grieving for a dead loved one—whether husband, parent, child, sibling or friend—is a process of gradual detachment. Research and observation now point to the bereaved maintaining an ongoing and evolving relationship with their dead. We're starting to understand that we never really detach from them, instead we continue our conversations with them. If the relationship wasn't that great in real life, we remake it to suit our ongoing needs and ditch the parts we don't like.

Research shows orphaned adult children having just as strong a bond with their parents, and rating that bond more positively than the ones who had parents still alive.[31] Once they are dead we can idealise our parents, keep what was best in the relationship and throw away the rest. Now we're the children of good, wonderful parents. Presumably this also applies to husbands, children, siblings and friends. Did Bertha's beloved Julian snore? She never mentioned it. If you push me, I'll admit that my mother and I spent years driving each other nuts. But that's not what has stayed with me. I remember a loved and loving mother and our good times together. It's what we remember that matters and how we create and organise our memories.

Often we recreate the memory and the relationship by talking to others—to our children about the father who's no longer around, with a brother or cousin about dead family members. One of the ways that Dorothy Shultz copes with loss is by 'going down memory lane'. When she's walking, or just before she goes to sleep, she conjures up a person she misses and meanders through her memories of their lives. It's a wonderfully conscious way of making sure that the dead are still with us.

Some people need to do more and continue their relationships with the dead by memorialising them as Barbara Hamer did in writing a history of her family's business. Stephanie Charlesworth says, when talking about writing about her parents, whose families she can trace back over a thousand years, 'I suppose that's part of my motivation and, I must say, my emotions.' What she is interested in is the influences on her of her parents and the culture they lived in because 'when I die they will be gone'. Stephanie feels compelled to document her parent's lives and pass this on to her own seven children and eleven grandchildren.

As well as writing books and making movies, others fund scholarships and prizes to honour the person and their interest. For a mother who was a nurse in Singapore you can create a World War II essay prize in her university's history department, and for my dead friend a scholarship for rural students like her. So perhaps it's time we all labelled those photographs, so we don't forget who the people are, and copy our home movies to digital media, or take-up genealogical research. I'm motivated by my interviewees to get going on some of these ways forward, these projects, just as soon as I finish this book.

HOT TIPS For love and loss

➤ Know and accept that you are likely to be a widow and an adult orphan, and you will lose friends and family.
➤ You need to picture a life without parents and partner before it happens.
➤ Be prepared to rebuild your life completely after the death of your husband.
➤ Look after your health while you're caring for a sick and dying husband, parent or someone you love. You need to stay well and ask for help and use professional care if you need to.

➤ Make widowhood and the loss of your parents less stressful by having a grip on the finances beforehand.

➤ Remember that loss is forever but acute grief is not. You will feel terrible initially but if you're not mending after three years, seek professional help.

➤ It's fine to mourn, to miss those no longer with us and to be sad, upset and distressed, especially on the milestones and anniversaries of the relationship.

➤ Rituals are an important way of helping you through the early stages of grief—funerals and death rites, answering condolence letters, obituaries and memorial services or your specific religious and ethnic customs.

➤ Make no dramatic changes or important decisions for the first year—don't change your job, sell your house or re-partner. You are not going to be in a rational state of mind.

➤ Make sure that you have a life of your own beforehand, so develop some interests that are not dependent on a partner for their enjoyment.

➤ Keep busy and engaged as soon as you can after the loss as it fills up your days and gives meaning to your life.

➤ Better still, give something back. Do something that helps others, as you'll have more time than you had when you were half of a couple.

➤ Talk about the person you've lost to family and friends who knew her or him. It's good for everyone to share memories and feelings.

➤ Now and then take 'a walk down memory lane', like before you go to sleep or at some other time. Pull up and enjoy the memories of someone you loved and lost.

➤ Become the 'kin keeper' in your family. It's a great way to reconnect with siblings, cousins and the younger generation. Collect together all those precious memories in the form of photos, oral histories, documents and more.

➤ To help with the loneliness and especially the empty house syndrome, share your house with someone else, for example by taking in a student or a refugee.

➤ After the first twelve months, celebrate anniversaries of the dead one's birth and death.

➤ Memorialise those you've lost with something to remember them by—create a scholarship, plant a tree, put together a photo album. It'll make you feel good.

➤ Get comfortable with death—it will help you to accept the inevitability of loss.

3

Being Well

T HE MORNING WAS perfect. A light breeze played with the leaves on the track. It was mild with the promise of sun for our first day of hiking the Goldfields Track. I was doing what I loved, with my husband and friends: walking, talking and exploring new territory. We had three leisurely days to hike from Castlemaine to Bendigo in central Victoria. Sweet, slightly dusty eucalypt scent tickled my nose. What could be better?

Forty minutes later, waving my arms around illustrating a story I was excitedly telling, I lost my footing and fell hard on the wrist I'd put out to try and save myself. My broken wrist was set quickly and efficiently at the regional Bendigo Hospital. Our friends walked on without us, and I went home and collapsed into a mental slump of self-pity. For weeks I couldn't pull my pants up without help, couldn't cook, couldn't drive, couldn't write or do anything for myself except read and watch DVDs. It wasn't about pain. That only lasted a few days and was fixable with drugs. I cried often and mulled over the whys and wherefores of how I fell and why I fell and why me, and why my right wrist.

My routine in those early weeks was a whirlwind of medical visits for X-rays, to the orthopaedic surgeon for a new cast, and to the technician for special slings and other bits and pieces that were all apparently essential to my recovery. On top of this I had weekly physiotherapy and hydrotherapy sessions. My injury took up my life in waiting for taxis, sitting in trams and more sitting and waiting in medical receptions. No wonder I was depressed. I wondered if this was what it was going to be like in the years to come, as bits of me started to go and I could no longer do things for myself. I was foreshadowing being old, disabled and miserable—a life that revolved round organising visits to see busy health professionals where you wait an hour, then see them for five minutes and they tell you about their football team, or their son's success in the rowing team, but often have little time to answer your questions.

Writing this, I'm reliving and reviving my fear and anger. The wrist mended and I went back to hiking, under strict instructions not to walk and talk at the same time. But I'd had a terrifying glimpse into my future. It took meeting a group of 85 plus-year-old women to shift my fears and challenge my stereotypical picture of old age as being about decline and disability, an inevitable and speedy slide on the downhill chute to the grave.

You can be very old and really well

Old people are supposed to feel the cold more, aren't they? My interviewees proved to be a hardy lot in the Melbourne winter. I kept my woollen coat on, and buttoned up. 'Are you cold?' they'd asked as they watched me pull my coat closer still. 'Oh no,' I lied, 'I'm fine.' Frances Reynolds and Lady April Hamer apologised that their heating wasn't working, not that it bothered them. Others obviously didn't feel cold enough to have heating. I shivered at Dame Margaret Scott's and at Rose Stone's place I finally caved in, asking her to please put the heater on. As my afternoon with Stephanie Charlesworth got chillier and chillier she did pop on a light cardigan but I hadn't even taken off my coat. Only Joan Lowrie mentioned that she didn't get out of bed one morning because it was so cold. Perhaps it's a generational thing. After all they lived many more years in a time before houses had central heating, and maybe that toughened them up. I'm of the softer, later generation. Tough old birds. That's what I'd like to be—a tough old bird.

Because I didn't interview anyone who was bedridden or in a hospital or nursing home, my sample is slanted towards the well. Even so, I'm impressed by how well they are. And among this group of healthy women, Dodo Berk is a phenomenon. She's almost reached her century and takes 'one little pill', a beta blocker, a day. Her health is so good that she didn't bother with an annual check-up last year. Her hearing is perfect, she has all her own teeth, and she doesn't wear glasses, although she did have her cataracts done. Laughing wickedly Dodo says, 'Doctors tell me I'm a freak of nature because of my remarkable health.'

Her social calendar is packed. She'd been out late to 'a bash' for the Alvin Ailey Dance Theatre, and my interview had to be squeezed in before her lunch meeting. 'If you go to a party, go to a party, kid,' Dodo tells me with an imperious wave of the hand. I interpret this as 'go for it', 'get into it' or stay home. Dodo is 'never frustrated', 'never disappointed', because there's always a Broadway show to see or a trip to go on. When she wants to go somewhere, Dodo catches buses all over New York City. Scientists tell us that our energy declines from the age of twenty so imagine what Dodo could have gotten up to eighty years ago.

Mary Broughton, May Lowe and Florence Howlett are over ninety-five and although not as remarkable as Dodo, they are really well. Mary has never had any serious health problems and takes nothing but the occasional Panadol. Physically fit, and used to fending for herself, she's happy to get a tram on her own to the city—pretty impressive for someone who's ninety-seven. Flo Howlett is no great pill taker either, getting by with only a daily aspirin and a vitamin D tablet. 'Really and truly, I was very lucky health wise. I've had few upsets. Once I had sciatica, which was agony, but luckily I have been pretty healthy,' she says about the good health she's enjoyed for ninety-five years. 'I like good health and I like good children, and at the moment I have got both,' says May Lowe. Her medication is minimal for a ninety-seven year old: one pill for blood pressure and a vitamin D tablet. 'I have a packet of Aspros I might have to throw out because they have been in there so long.' May's doctor tells her to expect that letter from the Queen in 2016 and I picture the Queen surrounded by huge heaps of letters she has to sign for the ever-increasing number of centenarians. May's memory is perfect and although her sight and hearing aren't what they used to be, they are good enough.

My sample of well women is similar to data from the Australian Longitudinal Study of Women's Health (ALSWH), which conducts regular surveys of more than forty thousand women. Among the oldest cohort, 70 per cent said they were as healthy as anybody they knew and only 5 per cent said they were in poor health.[1]

So what distinguishes the really well?
Dodo epitomises being well—physically, psychologically and socially. She can mostly do what she wants to do, she feels great and everyone loves her and wants to be around her. 'I'm not depressed, ever,' says Dodo. It's impossible to separate Dodo's excellent physical health from her positive personality. Dodo believes in nurturing and protecting her positivity. In guru mode, looking me dead in the eye, Dodo decrees, 'Don't hang around with negative people—drop them like a hot potato,' and 'Kid, don't look for criticism, it kills you.'

In contrast, when I spoke to centenarian Domnika Pasinis she was tired of living. Physically she was in pretty good shape and could live to 110, her carers predicted. But 'what for?' Domnika says, when she is so tired all the time and one day just follows another. Sadly she died aged 102, a year after our interview.

Meanwhile, in New York City, Dodo is always happy and occupied even when she's alone. She plays solitaire, word games, bridge and canasta with herself. If she's not out, she's busy making lists and talking with all the people she knows on her mobile phone. More than a glass half-full person, Dodo's glass is overflowing.

Though not as bubbly people-magnets as Dodo, what characterises the other really well women is their positive mental outlook. Lady Florence Bjelke-Petersen, describing her chronic back pain to a reporter, said, 'This back thing hasn't been a joy, but I know there are others much worse off, so I never complain. I'm grateful to have made it to ninety and to have enjoyed such a varied life, all the while surrounded by a wonderful and loving family.'[2] She's a glass half-full person all right. Being well depends on looking on the bright side and, fortunately, this is more achievable as we age.

Happiness and old age

I'd kill to have Dodo's sunny don't-sweat-the-small-stuff disposition. Being me—not so far renowned for bringing laughter and lightness—I'm going to have to try for an extreme personality makeover. Although there's probably little chance of my ever achieving Dodo's level of positivity, I don't discount moving closer in that direction. I'm going to get happier: the research that tells me so is incontrovertible.

Commenting on his study of one thousand people over eighty-five, Professor Tom Kirkwood, who heads the Project 85+ Study at Newcastle University in the United Kingdom, says, 'It's a myth that they are bowls of misery, unhappy with their lot, and always going on about ailments. Four out of five of them actually think they are doing pretty well.'[3] This study confirms yet again that the older we get the happier we will be. Whether you're in Sweden or Zimbabwe, rich or poor, the U-bend of happiness holds true. By eighty-five you'll be happier than you were at eighteen. In your forties and fifties you'll be at your most unhappy and from that point you climb up and up the other side of the U-bend, getting happier as you get older. And if that's not enough good news, women are also happier than men.[4]

Without the countless happiness studies of the past forty years conducted in every corner of the world, we wouldn't believe it. How can it be that in this youth-obsessed society, we will be happier as we wrinkle, lose our mental acuity and many of our physical capacities? Being measured in these studies are both life satisfaction—looking back over your life and assessing it—and your current emotional state—were you happy yesterday and why? One of the pioneers in trying to work out why we get happier as we age is Professor Laura Carstensen, Director of the Stanford University Longevity Centre. She's identified what she calls socio-emotional selectivity: the tendency of the old to remember the pleasant in favour of the unpleasant. She's also found that stress, worry and anger decrease with age.[5] At the core of this increasing positivity is our recognition that we won't live forever. As our time horizons get shorter our goals change and we get better at living in the present.

The U-bend of happiness holds true across generations. It doesn't depend on a set of life experiences like living through the Great Depression or World War II. We can all look forward to becoming happier and more positive as we get older.

Does having money matter?

Among the group I spoke with are women living in the wealthiest suburbs, who have never known a moment of want or concern about money. Some are in excellent health and others, like Maxie Meldrum, Suzanne Simon, April Hamer and June Helmer, are not. Also in the group are women who grew up in poverty and struggled to make ends meet, often not having enough to last the week until their husband's next pay. Their past financial status has absolutely no correlation to their current health—mental or physical. Kali Paxinos, Flo Howlett, Joan Lowrie and Beth Gott are all living on the age pension and are no less well than the women with big assets and incomes. The poorest of the women, Koho Yamamoto, would like to be better off, especially so she could afford a larger apartment and more art supplies. Yet she's never felt better in her life. Of course, if you're without enough to eat, or a roof over your head, or access to a doctor, that would be a different matter. As long as you've got the basics you can be old and healthy.

Is it family supports and connections?

You may think that being mentally and physically well in old age is related to having partners and children and grandchildren and other family. Yet among the really well are women without partners or children. Again Koho is the standout. She's never wanted children, and has thrived since she dumped her husband from a long ago marriage that lasted twelve years. Although Koho had a very happy one-off visit from her nephew in California a few years ago, she has felt no need to develop this relationship further. Among the healthiest of the women is Jean Allison, a great walker and talker, full of beans and fully engaged at eighty-seven. Even though she is close to her sister, Jean never married or had children. Family does not correlate with health or ill health, with the proviso that none of the women I interviewed live isolated or lonely lives. All are still connected to other people, whether family, friends, colleagues or students, and the world around them.

Which brings us to a tricky question: what is good health? Even when she was eighty-eight and having chemotherapy for colon cancer, Koho Yamamoto said, 'This is the happiest time of my life.' By the time I spoke with her, three years later, she told me that she was completely cured. Having had her cataracts 'done', she only needs to use 'an eye glass' or magnifying glass to read.

Her fitness regime involves going up and down the five flights of stairs from her apartment at least once a day. When I ask about aches and pains or arthritis she says, 'Not at all, thirty years ago I had all these aches and pains, it comes from within, now I have no problem. I feel great.' According to Koho it's all about keeping her mind strong: 'Your spirit controls you, no aches or pains or anything. I haven't caught a cold for at least ten years, not one cold.'

She's a phenomenon, as remarkable as Dodo. You wouldn't believe she was ninety-one as she springs up to show me the iPad her student bought her, or dashes into the passage for a copy of a handmade book of her illustrations. She has so much energy, too much to sit still. Koho can achieve anything she sets her mind on. There's a feeling of strength, of the power of will, radiating from this slight woman.

Koho, like Dodo, Kali Paxinos, Lis Kirkby and some of the others, can be described as being in perfect health. They have nothing wrong with them. Others, including Mary Broughton, May Lowe and Flo Howlett in the 95-plus age range, and many more in their late eighties and early nineties are living very full lives, unhampered by the number of years they've clocked up. They may have objectively assessed health deficits—deteriorating eyesight, hearing loss, arthritis, osteoporosis, heart problems—but these are not stopping them from doing what they want to do and care about.

Being able to do what you want

Seeing well is important to us. Mary Broughton's eyesight is not great because of macular degeneration, but that is not stopping her from reading widely and often, or doing anything else she wants to. Six months after I interviewed her, Flo Howlett was also diagnosed with macular degeneration. Her daughter Glennys wrote, 'Here's hoping it's going to be okay as she gets enormous pleasure from reading, knitting and TV and would hate to end up partly blind.'

With macular degeneration you lose vision in the centre of your eye. About 30 per cent of people over seventy-five have signs of this condition and can have difficulty reading or recognising faces, although usually you have enough peripheral vision for other activities. Although Mary Broughton and Flo Howlett have it, so far it has not affected the quality of their lives. They can watch television and read and knit and walk and garden, just as they've always done.

Someone who is really feeling the negative effects of macular degeneration is Maxie Meldrum. At ninety-one, she's had it for longer and more severely than either Mary or Flo. She said, 'Well, if you can't see and if you have only got very limited vision, only peripheral vision, I have gone on, but it hasn't been much fun.' Maxie can read 'a bit better' on her iPad, where she can increase the font size and brighten it. Because of her poor eyesight she has trouble knowing 'whether things are dirty or not, it's awful' and can be 'very embarrassing'. Not being able to see is terrible for Maxie, who describes her life as having gone downhill since she was eighty, when looking after her husband Frank 'and the macular started the dreary trail'.

At ninety-six, Bertha Lowitt's hearing loss and mobility are stopping her from doing what she wants to do most: contribute to society and get around independently. She's on that treadmill of twice-weekly trips to the physical therapist and a least one doctor to visit each week. She can't get there under her own steam so needs to wait for the unreliable New York City Access A-Ride service that provides cheap transport for the disabled. She has had a host of health problems, starting with colon cancer ten years ago. Bertha also has a pacemaker, but it's the arthritis in her spine and back that gives her 'crazy' pain at night. When I ask whether she takes medication, she points: 'If you look under the table you will see five bottles there.'

Her deafness and the fact that she can no longer climb stairs or take public transport have definitely affected her quality of life. She used to go to a gym and liked to swim but can't get there any more. Looking forward to a friend's seventieth birthday, she checked out the location and decided not to go because of a flight of stairs she wouldn't be able to climb. Worst of all, she can't get to work at her beloved museum.

Talking to Bertha and the others has helped me to see health in a new way. Ill health is not about having a confirmed diagnosis or specific symptoms or even physical limitations. It's not Bertha's heart condition or her arthritis, it's that she can't go to her friend's birthday or to the museum. Ill health is not about what's wrong with us in some objective way, it's about what we can and can't do that we want to do.[6] I'll never be able to participate in le Tour de France but that's fine with me, as I don't want to. But I want to be able to use my computer and I need good wrists for that.

With any health condition, there's the objective aspect—what's actually wrong with you and how it limits you—and the subjective—how you feel about what's happening to you and how you deal with it emotionally and practically. That mental heap I fell into after I broke my wrist does not speak well of my emotional capacities for dealing with what was, in the bigger scheme of things, a minor fixable physical mishap.

When I asked Sister Mary Gregory about her health she responded, 'On the whole it's good.' She has been at 'death's door' with an aneurism, had a hysterectomy and then was 'very ill for a long time' after a bowel operation. She takes blood pressure tablets and admits, 'I have got quite a few things wrong with me.' Sister Mary says:

> I have glaucoma but I can read, and yes I have moderate
> loss of hearing and wear hearing aids but I can do quite

well without them too. I have arthritis and one leg is a bit shorter than the other but I get along. They asked me to take the walker with wheels when I go out over ground that's not too even, but I get around without that most of the time. I go down to the shops and to have my hair cut and things like that.

Sister Mary is happy with her health and what she can do despite a whole litany of health problems. She can walk and take public transport so she can attend meetings and conferences. She shops and can look after her own needs. She loves to read and to listen to classical music. She's engaged with her friends, her siblings and nieces and nephews and other relatives and with people and issues.

Comparing Sister Mary with Joan Lowrie highlights questions about how we judge good health. Joan, at ninety-four, has nothing wrong with her except a sore back that she describes as 'not a sharp pain, sort of an ache'. She uses a cane and a walker but never leaves her home. Despite nagging from the physiotherapist who visits her weekly she won't walk, not even up her street. She is the only one of the women I spoke to who is housebound, and that's by choice. Even Domnika Pasinis, when I spoke to her at age 101, was going on outings with her children and grandchildren. Joan admits to being bored but is not unhappy and looks forward to sitting in her yard in the sun when the weather warms up. So who is healthier: Sister Mary or Joan? Objectively there is little wrong with Joan. The mystery is why Joan has chosen to limit her life in this way. Bertha Lowitt would be outraged.

In October 2013 Joan Lowrie did leave her house for an operation under general anaesthetic to remove a skin cancer from her leg. Fortunately she is well again, back home, and planning a Melbourne Cup party in her backyard.

Where do you set the limbo bar?

According to any objective assessment Joyce McGrath is unwell, although she would never describe herself this way. Over the past two years her hip and knee have deteriorated dramatically and her mobility is severely restricted. She takes painkillers every six hours. Joyce cannot shower herself and depends on a paid carer to shower her after her weekly hydrotherapy session. She can't drive or shop or do her own washing or vacuuming. She employs people to do all these things for her. There's an electric wheelchair sitting in the middle of her living room but it's of no use to her until she gets electronically opening doors installed. Then she'll be able to get to her painting studio and perhaps even go up the street on her own. Right now she gets around on two sticks but is finding that her hands are getting very sensitive with all the work they have to do to support her. With all these restrictions and the pain, Joyce is a very positive person. 'Never felt depressed in my life,' she says, and puts this down to her experiences as a child.

At eighty-seven, Joyce's problems stem from the tuberculosis she caught as a child from her returned serviceman, soldier-settler father. All her life she has had a stiff right hip and one leg shorter than the other. In those days, before streptomycin and penicillin, the only treatment for TB in the bone was sunshine and fresh air, and so Joyce was placed in a sanatorium when she was four and stayed there for five years:

> I was taken there from the Children's Hospital in the city in an ambulance. When I got down there I was put in a cot and didn't see my parents or relatives or anybody for a month. When I first got put in the cot, I stood up in the cot and I screamed, and I screamed because I didn't know whether mother knew where I was. Nobody said anything to you, people didn't in those days talk to children

about anything. I didn't know where my parents were. I just screamed and nobody came, if they did come I didn't know what to say and so I just knew that there was no use keeping on, nobody was going to take any notice of me. I think resignation comes into it. I resigned myself to the impossibility of changing the situation I think very early on. So I think that stayed with me all my life. If there is nothing you can do about it, then there's no use worrying, but if you can do anything, do it.

Dealing with disability and pain is nothing new for Joyce. 'I'm used to it,' she says, and focuses on working out how to keep painting and staying involved for as long as she can. Happy that she can see well and hear well, and has a good brain, she works at staying in touch with people and what's happening in the world via television and her computer. Visiting Joyce you see how restricted she is, how hard it is for her move around and look after herself and her surroundings.

In contrast, when you meet Suzanne Simon you find a fit-looking ninety year old, who seems to be in the prime of life, walking well, smartly dressed, and with everything about her and her home perfectly tended and in its right place. It's a shock to hear how much her back and bowel problems have affected her quality of life. Since the colonoscopy she had in 2011, Suzanne says, 'I am really housebound in the morning. I have to go to the toilet all the time, otherwise I would have accidents.' Even if this means missing her friend's ninetieth birthday celebration, Suzanne will not leave her house before the afternoon. Her doctors say that her condition can be fixed with another operation, but Suzanne won't have it. After having been in hospital three times in 2011, where 'the reins were out of my hands completely', she says that she won't go back. 'Supposing that operation wasn't successful,

I would have a colostomy bag, and I told the doctors that I would never live with the bag. I wouldn't, I couldn't, I wouldn't want to.'

Suzanne knows that other people live happily for years with a bag, but for Suzanne it would be a devastating blow to her self-image. It's not that Suzanne doesn't love life and her family but she's set the bar for what she'll put up with at a much lower rung than Joyce McGrath and she has a right to decide how she wants to live. Because of her lifelong disability and childhood experiences, Joyce McGrath doesn't expect to be as well or have as much control of her physical state as Suzanne does.

The last hurdle

One of the reasons that Joyce McGrath and Suzanne Simon respond so differently to poor health and disability is that Joyce is a practising Catholic. For her and the other women who are believers, it is the Supreme Being who is ultimately in control of both life and death. Among my interviewees, it's this religious belief that separates the women who will take death as it comes and those who want to decide how and when it is time for them to go. Call it assisted suicide or dying, or the more blunt voluntary euthanasia, this is an issue that affects the quality of our last decades.

To include all perspectives, I wanted to speak with women who were miserable and not enjoying the last third of their lives; women who wished they were no longer alive. The one woman I found in this situation did not want to be interviewed. While we all want the Sir Rupert Hamer death—peaceful and in our sleep—many of the women I spoke to are ready for death. They tell me that they've had wonderful lives and were prepared for it. As they said, it's the dying not being dead that worries them.

Maxie Meldrum and Suzanne Simon, who loved their seventies and eighties, said they could only love their nineties if they were able to control the timing and manner of their deaths. They are organising the means for their final exit. My interviews were held not long after Beverley Broadbent went public with her plans to end her life at eighty-three. Her health and mental powers were failing, she said, and she 'would rather go a year early' than risk not being able to die when she chose to.[7]

Over the last two decades the legal 'right to die' or 'death with dignity' has become available in the Netherlands, Belgium, Switzerland, and in the United States in the states of Oregon, Washington, Montana and Vermont. A bill on the subject is before the House of Lords and a case about it is being argued in the Supreme Court of Canada. Popular support for the right to die for terminally ill people is widespread and increasing: 80 per cent of those surveyed in Australia,[8] 70 per cent in the United States,[9] 70 to 75 per cent across Europe and the United Kingdom,[10] and an enormous 85 to 90 per cent in Canada.[11] In Australia, in federal and state elections, you can vote for the Voluntary Euthanasia Party.

For those of us who do want the choice and feel strongly about it, it's the perfect moment not just to get the pills for our own peace of mind, but to put our efforts into forcing politicians, who sometimes pander to a vocal minority, to enact the will of the overwhelming majority. We need to flex the political muscle of our numbers.

What we should and shouldn't worry about

We're all too aware that at any time something could happen and in a flash we would stop being well and become incapacitated. Problems with her foot have made Barbara Hamer 'very unstable'. She worries about falling and says, 'Of course I am furious about it. I mean I used to nip up and down to Canberra. I could manage my luggage, but it has got so that I have real trouble pulling the damn thing along, even when the taxis drop me at the airport.' But as Barbara says, she can handle this. It's the fear of something worse that really worries her. 'Any day now I could fall over and I might be taken to hospital and they might find all these other things like your blood pressure or your bowels or something else doesn't work and you are at the mercy of the doctors and things like that. You are helpless.'

Even though it can happen at any age, as we get older we are more likely to fall and more likely to break something if we do fall. As our body parts regenerate far more slowly, it'll take longer to recover, even if they don't find anything worse than a broken rib once you're in the hospital emergency ward. Joan Lowrie, who never leaves her house, is less likely to fall than the more adventurous going places and doing things. Yet, sitting at home, Joan got a skin cancer and had to be hospitalised. We all know the big fear of being in hospital—the risk of getting a really nasty infection. It is a big scary world out there and as we get older we need to decide whether we are risk takers. How far do we want to restrict our lives for fear? Me? I'm going to pass on treks to Everest and Mont Blanc, and I'm very careful on ladders but I know you can injure yourself badly by bending down to pick up a paper clip or stretching to reach a shelf in the fridge. The risk we take is for each of us to choose.

When I first interviewed Rose Stone in mid 2012, she said she no longer went out in the evenings, and was 'doing half, a quarter, of what' she used to do. 'Age creeps up on you,' she said. For a tired woman of ninety, Rose was in great shape. The flight of stairs to her flat doesn't worry her and she often took the tram to go for a walk along St Kilda Beach. She shopped, cooked and washed for herself. Her calendar included two book groups, bridge once a week, meetings with friends, theatre, movies at ACMI, Shakespeare readings and more. Just imagine what she packed in before if this is a quarter of it. To top it off she encouraged me to join her in her regular exercise program and proved how much stronger than me she was.

Fast forward a year and Rose is no longer so well. She has a ruptured disc in her back that presses on her sciatic nerve. It's okay when she sleeps or sits or even going up and down stairs but hurts like hell if she walks. 'I'm taking taxis everywhere,' she tells me. 'With the weekly physio at $100 a pop, and acupuncture at $100, it's lucky I can afford it.' Rose is not accepting this limitation and pain as permanent, and she is putting her time and energy into getting better. Whether you're ninety or fifty, you can fall over and bang your knees or do your back in with an awkward move, and you're in pain and incapacitated. Don't panic, as you are likely to get better, just as Rose eventually did. Before you rush off to surgery follow Rose's advice: try all the other alternatives first.

One of our greatest fears is losing our minds. Mary Broughton is particularly worried about forgetting names. 'That's the thing that happens now—it's a miracle I remember my own name. Just a name will go and then it will come back.' When I tell her that this happens to me, and I'm thirty years younger, Mary remains unconvinced and shrugs it off with, 'That's what everyone tells me.' Anomia, or not being able to remember names, starts when we're thirty and, as we age, we find it harder to remember telephone numbers, the prime ministers of Australia and where we parked the car. Being slow at, or not being able to remember names and facts, can no longer be attributed to age-related cognitive decline. Recent research argues that those blank moments—'senior moments'—are not because older brains are slower, but because we know more. Like a hard drive that is full of programs and software and data, our minds have so much more in them that it takes us longer to find the particular word or fact we're searching for.[12] Next time you blank on a word, remember that it's not forgetfulness but that you know so much.

April Hamer and June Helmer were not in great shape when I spoke to them. Both were showing symptoms of conditions that will get worse. June Helmer has Parkinson's and April Hamer is having memory problems. These conditions are diseases, not part of the normal ageing process. The excellent physical and mental health of most of the women I interviewed shows that we shouldn't panic every time we read an article or hear about someone who gets dementia or Parkinson's. Statistics shows that you are far less likely to get these diseases than be injured on the road.[13]

Parkinson's affects only about 1 per cent of people over sixty and this increases to 4 per cent for people over eighty. Alzheimer's is not widespread, despite the beat-ups of press coverage like, 'The toll of Alzheimer's disease is reaching epidemic proportions. Someone is diagnosed with Alzheimer's in the United States every 69 seconds—a somber reminder that we must do more if we are to find an effective treatment for this devastating, debilitating condition.'[14] Sounds terrifying doesn't it? But misleading. We are not heading for Alzheimer's or Parkinson's armageddon. Be suspicious of figures about how widespread diseases are that are put out by the various organisations seeking research funds from the government and the public.

If you added all the alarming articles together—heart, all the different female and other cancers, Alzheimer's, Parkinson's, and so on—it seems amazing that any of us are still alive. Take this statistic: 'Alzheimer's will affect up to 45 per cent of Americans over 85.'[15] Is the 'up to', 44 per cent or 4 per cent, or a number in between? In an independent random study of people in their nineties, 5 per cent were found to have dementia with another 14 per cent suffering some memory loss or confusion.[16] This is a lot less than the figures—one in ten Americans over sixty-five and 'nearly' 50 per cent of people over eighty-five—bandied about by the associations. When it comes to our brain functions, things are getting better according to Danish researchers. On mental ability tests of 95-year-old Danes, the current group performed better than those tested ten years ago.[17]

Among my American friends quite a few are rushing off to have tests to see if they are likely candidates for, or have signs of, the diseases. When I ask why they say it's better to know so they can plan ahead. I think they're mad. Why have this knowledge blighting your life when you can't do anything about it? Professor David Snowdon, the researcher of the famous Nun Study of Aging and Alzheimer's Disease, agrees with me. Since 1986 he has annually tested 678 nuns from seven provinces in the United States, as well as having done autopsies of their brains when they have died. To his surprise the autopsies showed that some nuns had the telltale twisted protein in their brain cells but no signs of memory loss. Snowden says it does no good to find out if you're susceptible until there's a cure or, at the least, palliative treatment available.[18]

How terrible would it be to live with foreknowledge of something that may never result in any symptoms? These diseases are terrible but right now there is nothing we can do about them. Late in 2013 it was reported that scientists may have found a way to use lasers to identify and destroy the clumps of protein believed to cause Alzheimer's and Parkinson's.[19] If and when treatments are fully developed, I'll think about getting tested. But here Joyce McGrath's advice resonates: 'Don't worry about what you can't do anything about.'

Marvels of modern medicine

Many of the women I spoke to would not be alive and well today if not for recent advances in medical treatment. Koho Yamamoto and Bertha Lowitt would have died of colon cancer, and if Bertha had survived that cancer, her heart condition would have got her before she became too deaf to work at the museum. Frances Reynolds is a very active ninety year old who has survived two bouts of breast cancer thanks to radiotherapy and chemotherapy treatments and has now been well again for sixteen years. She would also have died from heart failure if she hadn't had her defective aortic valve diagnosed seven years ago and had a pinch valve put in. Now she's on what she calls her 'longevity pills', one 'for reflux and a blood thinner for the aortic valve'.

Half the population is on blood thinners and that includes many of the women I spoke to. Beth Gott has been taking one since she had a mini-stroke. She also has a pacemaker for her irregular heart beat and a stent in her leg because of a blockage in an artery. Margaret Fulton, who quips, 'I am kept alive by a very good GP,' has been taking blood thinners since her quadruple bypass in 2005. Although she has had her aortic valve replaced Margaret Barnett is not taking blood thinners because they would cause bleeding in her head, where she has a shunt that relieves her normal pressure hydrocephalus. If not for new surgical techniques, Betty Walton and Sister Mary would be dead from aneurisms.

New techniques and treatments have saved the lives of about a third of the women I spoke to, and not only saved their lives but enabled them to live a better quality of life. Cataract surgery is now so standard that unless I asked directly, most of them didn't even remember to mention they'd had it. All but five of the women have had their cataracts removed. No wonder my American eye doctor is already recommending it to me with the carrot that I'll see better than I have since I was ten years old. So that's something to look forward to: better eyesight.

'Without hearing aids I am practically totally deaf. Sometimes I wish I didn't have hearing aids, when I get in the middle of George Street in the traffic.' In reality, Elisabeth Kirkby knows she needs to hear well to live the full life of study, theatre, parties and travel that she enjoys. Hearing aids don't come cheap, with prices of between $7000 and $12,000 being quoted by their wearers. Suzanne Simon showed me hers:

Look at them, tiny little things. They cost $4500 each, that's $9000 in your ears. One night, brushing my hair, I flipped it off and where would it go other than in the glass of water. I pulled it out and thought, 'My God, have I lost $4500?' But I dried it—apparently they are waterproof.

About half the women use hearing aids and for all but two they work so well that you would never know they had any hearing loss. Bertha Lowitt's deafness is not treatable enough for her to be a museum guide anymore but she has no trouble hearing in most of the day-to-day activities she's involved in. Since her son-in-law installed her alert device that flashes a red light when her phone rings, she doesn't miss any phone calls either. Margaret Barnett has been deaf for twenty years and would be 'deaf as a post' if she took her hearing aids out. Hers is an inherited condition and does limit her life. 'In a group I am hopeless, and I get a bit upset,' she says, 'because I can't follow what people are saying.' Some voluntary work options are closed to her: 'I wanted to read to schoolchildren but you see I can't because I can't hear what they are saying to me afterwards.' Margaret has given up the theatre but still hears well enough to enjoy the ballet and take a cruise from Rabaul to New Zealand. Just recently she's been enjoying television again, having discovered, 'A thing called the streamer, with which I can hear exactly what they're saying on the television. Before I could hear the noise and I would turn it up, but turning it up would just muffle it. But now this has absolutely made a difference to me.' In the future hearing aids and assist devices are likely to get even better.

The women have had hip and knee replacements, arthroscopies, laminotomies and laminectomies that keep them mobile and active. The walking frame only came into use in the early 1950s but now you can get around even when your legs and balance go. Lady Flo uses one when she does her shopping and has her hair done in Kingaroy, and the walker enables May Lowe to do her washing and cooking and to get about independently in her home.

Best of all, as Frances Reynolds so pithily put it, 'After menopause you are so relieved at not having your blessed period.' Hallelujah! That's a gift of good days every month when we might have felt lousy. Maxie Meldrum had it bad: 'Blood used to flow like mad, it was embarrassing. Blood everywhere, in great lumps like bits of kidneys coming out, disgusting, absolutely disgusting. They are the worst pains I have had. Period pain knocked me out. Even on my wedding day I was terribly nervous in case I poured blood everywhere.' Maxie says that the best years of her life were from her fifties, after her hysterectomy, 'because I didn't have this cloud of blood hanging over my head. I was really good.'

I don't want to paint too Pollyanna-ish a picture of medical advances, as there is still plenty of bad stuff out there. It's definitely not all rosy when it comes to deciding on tests or treatments but things have changed. Beth Gott's mother wouldn't die of typhoid at forty-eight today, and antibiotics would have zapped the infection that killed Suzanne Simon's mother.

Dilemmas of modern treatment

'Stay away from doctors but visit your dentist regularly,' is Dodo's advice. But the truth is that all of us, including Dodo, go to the doctor. If you're not seeing or hearing well, if you break a limb or find a lump in your breast, or that nagging pain in your stomach persists, you'd be mad not to. Most of the time the doctor will be able to help with drugs or other recommended treatments. The women I spoke with had GPs, eye doctors, hearing specialists, urologists, cardiologists, gynaecologists and more. What Dodo actually meant was: don't let your life revolve around seeing doctors. And be careful of becoming addicted to the routine of tests, especially X-rays, MRIs and other imaging techniques. With these you will see your sadly deteriorated disc or loss of bone density or the arthritis in your hand and think, help, I'm falling to pieces. What you've got to focus on is not the deterioration but dealing with the symptoms and pain, and overcoming any limitations these might create for you. The trick is how to choose what will improve our lives and options for being well.

Dodo's experience is of doctors and the health system in the United States, where everything is more gung-ho and testing orientated. The American can-do and let's-fix-it mentality—something that I admire about them—can also lead to unfortunate outcomes, like invading other countries without thinking too far ahead, as well as treatment, more treatment and even more treatment. Partly because of fears of being sued if they don't pursue all possible avenues, doctors and specialists want you to undergo every test known to medicine and advise you to have surgery at the sign of anything they believe needs fixing. My New York gynaecologist finally talked me into taking hormone replacement therapy (HRT) six months before the definitive study came out linking HRT with increased rates of breast cancer and blood clots. I stopped but other women, knowing all the risks, have continued with HRT because for them the benefits of feeling better outweigh the dangers. It's all about 'our bodies, our choices', and very complicated both of those are, too.

The best example of the snakes and ladders of women's health prevention and treatment is the mammogram, now recommended annually for women aged between fifty and seventy-five. But are they effective? Women's anti-cancer groups and doctors continue to argue for more and more screening programs. Others are saying that mammograms are 'hard to justify' when research findings indicate this screening does not lead to lower death rates for average-risk women in their forties and fifties. Or even worse: one in five healthy women, who would never become symptomatic or die from their disease, will be diagnosed and treated for breast cancer unnecessarily.[20]

This overtreatment exposes women to the adverse effects of surgery, chemotherapy and radiation, which can cause leukaemia and other malignancies. I've been trying to make sense of this material for years now and finally decided not to have my annual mammogram in 2014—a conservative response for someone who's had one every year for the last twenty years with no history of breast cancer in the family and no negative mammograms to date. Yet my doctor was shocked with my decision and I am now checking my breasts anxiously for bumps and lumps. We worked hard to make mammograms free and readily available, which makes it even harder to say maybe the cost is not worth the benefit.

There is big money to be made by drug companies and specialists in older women's health. Frances Reynolds and I were both prescribed Fosamax to strengthen our bones. After I read the two pages of small print that came with the packet warning me of possible ulcers, stomach perforations, abnormal heartbeat and jaw fractures, I decided to give it a miss. Frances' doctor must have eventually read the same small print as some months later he advised her to stop taking it because of potential side-effects. Right now our best bet is to find a good GP and an excellent gynaecologist. It's in our laps—we have to do the research, look at our histories and make our own decisions.

The two-year threshold

As we get older and creep into our fifties and sixties and seventies far too many of our conversations start revolving around health—or rather, ill health. That one has dementia, this husband a low-level leukaemia, those two friends are having knee operations, one a reconstruction and the other to mend a torn meniscus. Others have had strokes or breast cancer. The whole medical dictionary of diseases becomes overly familiar. We all have our aches and pains. For me it's been my broken wrist, my right knee from a whack on a sharp rock, then the snap of my left one from an awkward twist. We notice that our bits and pieces take months to heal and we extrapolate and think, if I'm like this now, what's it going to be like in ten or twenty years. My Pilates teacher rolls her eyes pityingly when I ask whether there'll be a time again when I won't have anything wrong with me.

Here's the thing I've noticed and had confirmed by the women I interviewed: a couple of years after you recover you hardly remember that you ever had anything wrong with you. Betty Walton says, 'I have been so fortunate with my health,' and replies 'no' when I ask if she's ever had anything wrong. It's only after I ask again she remembers, 'Oh, yes' she did have kidney problems but on her last visit her specialist told her, 'You are the fittest octogenarian I know.' More probing leads to her admitting, 'I have a half tablet each morning to slow my heart rate and I have a blood pressure tablet, and that's it.' Then there's the aneurism, the one she nearly died from. What does she want to say about that? 'I was playing tennis again in seven months,' and the surgeon said he had 'never seen such a complete recovery'. When her friend suggested that might not be the end of the problem and that 'you can have an aneurism anywhere', Betty put her right. 'I said, "Let's talk about Italian literature shall we?"' And when the friend wanted to talk about her own aneurism, Betty said, 'I don't care where you've had one, I don't want to talk about it.' As far as Betty is concerned, end of story.

If something is hurting or affecting our lives—Maxie's failing eyesight, Bertha's deafness and leg problems, Barbara Hamer and Margaret Barnett becoming shaky on their feet—it's at the forefront of our consciousness. Once we are cured, or used to it, who cares? When I asked Lady Flo whether she had had her hips done, she said 'no', but the question nudged her to remember: 'Oh, let's see. I have had operations on my knees. I have got artificial knees, they work pretty well I must say. I am pretty glad I don't have to oil them or anything, they sort of just go.' Her knees work and don't need attention so she never thinks of them.

It could be that socio-emotional selectivity that Professor Laura Carstensen of the Stanford University Center on Longevity identified where, as we age, we remember the pleasant and not the unpleasant. Only because she's explaining how she took up knitting heirloom rugs, does Margaret Fulton mention her quadruple by-pass surgery in 2005. According to Margaret, her daughter, 'Suzanne said, "Mum, could you knit this? I will treasure it for the rest of my life," and she got that weepy voice and I thought, "Oh my God, am I going to die," and I started knitting and then I got interested.' Margaret has no interest in telling me the details of her surgery but wants me to know about the great pleasure she gets from knitting these patchwork rugs using Shetland wool, the colours and texture of which evoke memories and musings of her childhood and Scottish birthplace.

This is very much my experience. I now remember the great trip and glorious hiking I did in China with my wrist in plaster and a sling and not the pain or frustration of missing the Castlemaine to Bendigo walk. Betty Walton and I agree that we don't want to spend the rest of our lives talking about sickness and death. It doesn't make us feel better to go over and over whatever is not quite right with us. Allow a maximum of ten minutes of talk with friends on any health problem and get it over with at the beginning of the conversation. There'll be friends who need more, especially if they don't have family to support them. Again you need to judge how much good it's doing either of you and if you'd both do better talking about Iranian movies or how to make good compost.

The exercise solution

It's the twenty-first century and exercise is touted as the panacea for everything that ails us. Mary Broughton and Flo Howlett credit their excellent health to walking and gardening. Jean Allison tells us to, 'just keep walking'. A leader with the Melbourne University and Alumni Bushwalkers, she tries to persuade people to stop being a rat on the treadmill in the gym and get out and enjoy nature and the beauty that's all around them. Dorothy Shultz and Beth Gott swim three times a week. Beth is sold on exercise: 'It's not just that it does things for the body but the brain too.' She believes regular exercise should be built into your life. 'Keep yourself moving. I have a great belief in the value of exercise. I remember my husband's mother, she used to spend most of the time in bed and she didn't exercise and in the end she just disintegrated. Her spine just gave way because she wasn't using it.'

Beth's mother-in-law sounds like one of the 'zombies' that Bertha Lowitt argues you'll turn into if you don't keep moving. Bertha is fervently committed to exercise. As well as her twice-a-week physical therapy, she does exercises every morning and evening, and on Tuesdays she attends an exercise class held in the building where she lives. On top of all this, using her cane, she walks every single day, no matter what the weather. 'And if it's raining I walk up and down the hall,' she tells me. 'Renata, you have to. I am telling you, or you end up a zombie, a nothing. And I have seen people younger than me who are. I am telling you otherwise you die, you might as well not be.'

Most of the women agree. Frances Reynolds does Pilates once a week to keep herself mobile, and makes sure she's active every day even if nowadays, at ninety, on her walk she needs to 'look for a seat to sit down after twenty minutes'. Stephanie Charlesworth believes that you need to work—and work hard—at being well. Regular physiotherapy and twice weekly gym sessions have helped her overcome and manage serious back and knee problems.

When I ask Dodo if she exercises, she quips, 'I eat.' But she's not sedentary, and although Koho Yamamoto, Kali Paxinos and Elisabeth Kirkby don't have exercise programs they live active lifestyles—walking, climbing stairs, taking public transport. Scouring the research, it's impossible to find an argument against moderate regular exercise. A sedentary lifestyle is more risky for women of all ages than it is for men, and in a study of over nine thousand adults aged seventy to seventy-five, the women who didn't exercise were twice as likely to die as women who exercised regularly.[21] Those with mobility problems like May Lowe, Margaret Barnett, Joan Lowrie, Barbara Hamer, Lady Flo and the others should definitely be in an exercise program. It won't do them any harm and will improve their mood and lower their chance of injury.

It is said that exercise helps those with Alzheimer's and dementia, heart disease, diabetes, colon cancer, high blood pressure and obesity. Regular exercise has been linked to improvements in blood pressure, diabetes, cholesterol, osteoarthritis, osteoporosis, and neuro-cognitive function. Whether or not all these claims hold up over the long term, I'm convinced that exercise is good for us. Ideally you want to mix some walking or swimming or other aerobic exercise, with strength training and balance and flexibility.[22] So get on your bike, put on those sneakers and let's hop to it.

Smoking and drinking

Rose Stone and Koho Yamamoto smoke. They know it's bad for them but they enjoy an occasional cigarette and they are both over ninety! I finally gave up smoking at forty-three, after having smoked for thirty years, with the promise that I could and would start again in another thirty years. My current thinking is I will have one token cigarette a day, although I can no longer stand the smell of smoke on others. But it is an addiction so I could get hooked all over again. I have five years to my Smoking Decision-Day!

Dodo's advice is to 'never drink alone'. Betty Walton loved champagne and then suddenly, in her early eighties, it made her faint and dizzy so she gave it up. As we age we become more sensitive to the effects of alcohol—it rots our insides, muddles our brains and badly affects our sense of balance. The highest recommended quantity for women that I could find was from the Royal College of Medicine in the United Kingdom: two small glasses of wine a day. Alcohol also doesn't make for a good night's sleep—you fall asleep okay but come 3 a.m. you're wide awake, sweating and tossing. As well, despite that initial feeling of relaxation, alcohol increases anxiety over the longer term. Here lies another hard choice: the sensible long-term good health solution or the short-term pleasure of drinking? With smoking and drinking and being well, I have to say don't do it—not at all or as little as you can.

Weight and diet

Frances Reynolds advises us not to be overweight, as this is the basis of many problems in later life. Until very recently this was considered as much gospel as not drinking and not smoking. Interestingly, weight is now a hot topic of contention. New research suggests that the thin die young. Even women whose weight is just right do not live as long as those who are on the plump side. It's thought that fat and a bigger waistline may be advantageous for the old, providing protection to better recover from illnesses and surgery. Several large-scale long-term studies have reached the same conclusions. Older adults who are overweight are less likely to die from any cause over a ten-year period, compared with those of normal weight. Those who were underweight are far more likely to die, while obese elderly people have the same mortality risk as those of normal weight.[23]

Such heresy does not go unchallenged. Preventative health experts like Dr Joanne Manson, a Harvard medical school professor, immediately shot back: 'There is a difference between survival and quality of life.' She argues that 'given all the adverse effects of obesity on health, it isn't biologically plausible that being overweight would lower mortality risks'.[24]

The authoritative Australian Longitudinal Study of Women's Health (ALSWH) findings are more nuanced. A normal weight is good for preventing diabetes and heart disease but being fatter 'may be optimal for osteoporosis and mortality'. The researchers conclude that, for women over seventy, carrying extra weight is not necessarily a bad thing.[25] At the current state of play, unless you've got diabetes or heart disease, don't worry about those extra few kilograms or the rolls round your middle. They're good for your bones and a longer life.

Beth Gott is scathing about diet fads. 'The so-called Neanderthal diet is absolutely rotten because all the Neanderthals ate was meat.' She advocates a hunter-gatherer diet where you exercise, eat mostly plant-based foods, and a little bit of meat and fish. This is much like the Mediterranean diet, highly recommended as the basis for living well after seventy, with less likelihood of chronic disease or physical and cognitive impairment.[26] More and more research links eating less animal protein (meat and dairy) to living longer and having a lower risk of getting cancer.[27]

If I wrote a book saying that you would live to be 101 if you gave up some particular foodstuff—pick any food—I'd be sure to earn big bucks. My inclinations are to recommend a plant-based diet, for which there's plenty of evidence about it being good for you. It has the added bonus that you won't harm any animals and be kinder to the planet. And if you feel you must, for whatever reason, eat animal protein, go for fish or for free range produce. The see-saw of what you should eat has come full circle to the latest studies finding no evidence that saturated fat increases the risk of heart disease.[28] I am still hoping that researchers will find that booze and cake are the healthiest diet for the old.

The way forward: goal shifting

At ninety-eight, Sensei Keiko Fukida became the first woman to earn Judo's highest-degree black belt, and she still teaches the martial art three times a week. But most of us are going to get slower and creakier. The remarkably well Dodo is aware of her physical limitations. 'Now it's different,' she says, 'I need help opening a window, a jar. At ninety-eight, your goals shift. Right now it's to have tea with somebody. They shift a lot and you're happier. I can't keep going. A battery stops, a clock stops, a car stops, I know my body.' That's why she stopped flying to Italy, and no longer has the energy to dance all night. When we met her goal was to do a song and dance at her grandson Scott's wedding in May 2013. She made it, performing 'The Bells are Ringing, for Scott and Michelle, in heels, though medium-sized instead of Ginger Rogers' stilettos. Her current goal is getting to her hundredth birthday in September 2014.

'I am sort of young up here but the poor old legs are going,' says May Lowe of her head and upper body. When I say that she doesn't seem too bad, May disabuses me. She knows her limitations but is not fazed or depressed that she can't get around as she once used to. 'Oh, yeah, I have got to have support,' she says, to walk from the dining room to her own rooms. 'I couldn't do that. I couldn't do it. You know at ninety-seven some things are going to go.' Objectively May's health problem limits her but subjectively she has dealt with this shift, accepting her new circumstances and still seeing herself as having 'good health'.

In various different ways the women agree that you need to shift your goals as you get older. Beth Gott says, 'I am not one of those people who demand that when I am ninety I should have the health of someone at twenty, there are things you have to put up with and I recognise that there are things I can't do anymore.' Betty Walton was in shock when she was told at eighty she had to stop playing tennis. 'I never dreamed I would ever have to stop tennis, that's how I always saw myself.' And yet soon she was walking instead.

Barbara Hamer says that, 'if you grieve too hard, you will be saying, "That was perfect and I want it back," and you can't have it back.' She advises not to lament what we can no longer do or have as we get older. Dame Margaret Scott agrees. Although she exercises and gardens and swims, her joints and body are 'not what they used to be' and she's aware that she's 'become rather slow'. 'Everything changes and changes at a different pace and if you do start regretting [these losses] then you become very miserable,' she says. This adjustment, 'is an ongoing part of every-body's life. You sort of give things away. Among the Africans they think as you grow older you're not dying you are just giving away your gifts.' Give away your gifts, like running and dancing, advises Dame Margaret Scott, without regret.

The goal shifting that Dodo and the other women describe is already happening. I'm fine about not being able to stay up much past 1 a.m. or pull all-nighters to finish projects, I can't swim the forty laps of the pool in thirty minutes any more, and hiking 15 kilometres a day is plenty for me now. We need to focus on all the wonderful things we can still do, continue to set our goal posts, and be flexible enough to know when to shift them.

A final word about health and longevity

We know that any kind of work, paid or unpaid, good or bad is good for your health and longevity. Even more surprising findings have come from an eight-decade longevity study, which discovered that conscientiousness is the best personality predic-tor of long life. The staid and sober, the worriers, the stressed and ambitious all live longer than those who are happy-go-lucky, cheerful and optimistic.[29] Perhaps if you're lucky and persistent you can get a job, at least a volunteer job. But in your fifties can you change your personality and become conscientious and sober instead of fun loving? And in your eighties or nineties is it worth giving up fags, booze and venison for an extra few years? Elisabeth Kirkby says, 'If you're fit you can do anything,' but she wouldn't say it's worth anything to be fit.

HOT TIPS For being well

➤ Don't take dramatic medical events as portents: a stroke or broken bone do not a cripple make. That wrist will heal, if not as quickly as when you were younger, and the Warfarin will keep your blood thin and flowing. Pacemakers will keep your ticker going and if your hip crumbles, you can get a new one.

➤ Goal setting and goal shifting: aim as high as you can and set goals for the year, week and day. When you can't do it any more shift that goal post to something you can do and enjoy, and do it with gusto.

➤ Don't lament what you can no longer do or be—let it go.

➤ Don't worry about forgetting names, people and dates—nothing is wrong with you except that you know too much to retrieve the data quickly.

➤ Stick to the ten-minute limit on talking about sickness (and death) with others, or you'll never talk about anything else. This rule can be broken on a one-time-only basis for family members and friends who really need to get that stuff off their chests.

➤ Don't smoke. You will not be the exception that proves the rule.

➤ Drink as little as you can or not at all. The maximum allowable daily alcohol is two small glasses of wine or one shot of spirits or one biggish glass of beer. Sorry, but you knew this already and didn't need me to tell you. Alcohol is bad for all the bits of you and makes you unsteady on your feet.

➤ Try to exercise—keeping mobile is good for you.

➤ Stop worrying about moderate weight gain or a few extra centimetres round your middle. Only do something about your weight if you're losing it, you don't like the way you look, you're obese or if the doctor says it's affecting your health and mobility.

➤ Don't worry about what you can't do anything about. So don't get tested for Parkinson's or Alzheimer's until it starts to affect your life and there is something you can do to treat the condition.

➤ Do have annual checks of your eyes, ears, heart and other things where there are aids and simple treatment that could improve your quality of life,

➤ Find a GP you can trust, one who is knowledgeable beyond the material provided by the drug companies.

➤ Keep up with women's health issues. There are difficult decisions and hard choices to be made and you'll need to be on the ball to work out what's best for you.

➤ And finally, enjoy being happier than you've been since you were eighteen.

4

Money Matters

I'M IN MY sixties, galloping towards seventy. I own my home, have a tidy sum saved in superannuation, and some other investments. I've done everything I can to make sure I'm financially okay in my old age, including putting assets in my name in case my husband runs off with a floozy. Still, I am worried. I could live another thirty years and how the hell can I predict what's going to happen in that time. I wouldn't have predicted that I'd get zero per cent interest on my US savings account and a measly 3.7 per cent—and still falling—for money I put into a fixed-term deposit in Australia. With inflation at around 3 per cent this is not a good investment. When I bought my first house I paid 17 per cent interest on my loan, and that was thirty years ago.

No wonder I'm worried, and the hotshot economists and bankers out there are no better at predicting the future than I am. They can't even tell when the property boom will go bust this time round. Meanwhile my anxiety is being raised to stress level by threats of cuts to the age pension, raising the age of eligibility, and the whole atmosphere of blaming us—the boomers—for more or less everything, and especially government deficits. We're being attacked as 'blood suckers', when the reality is that more of us have jobs than ever before, and even more would be working if there were jobs and less discrimination against employing us.

With only 40 per cent of taxes coming from people's wages there is a big 60 per cent of government income that has nothing to do with the ageing of the population.[1]

Even if the government stops using the over sixty-fives as their economic whipping posts, changes to the age pension, to super-annuation benefits, to interest rates, and in the ups and downs of the economy are inevitable and unpredictable. Our first lesson is that no matter what financial advisers and economic soothsayers tell us, there is no sure-fire, absolute security that will ensure us a comfortable or even adequate income for the next three decades. Anything could happen so we need to be prepared for change and insecurity. Thirty years is a long time.

Women and money

Meanwhile in the here and now many of my friends are already struggling financially. Alice has moved to the backblocks of nowhere—too far away for anyone to visit her—so that she can rent out her inner-city house and try to live on the difference between the rent she gets and the rent she pays. Another friend is shacking up, illegally—if Centrelink finds out she's cohabiting they'll cut off the part age pension she gets. If she tells them and the relationship doesn't work out, it will take months of paper-work and meetings for her to get back that part pension she can't manage without.

When you're widowed, the negative financial fallout persists over time, long after you get over the emotional trauma. A survey of four thousand women aged seventy-six to eighty-one found that because they weren't used to managing alone they stayed worse off financially. The report's recommendation was for financial advice to be made available in those first years of widowhood.[2] The death of a husband, a late-life divorce, a series of strokes or suddenly losing your job can all push you into financial no-woman's land.

What about the women now in their fifties and sixties who missed out on education and skills, never had or lost their home, and have little or no super because they worked cash-in-hand or casual jobs like taxi driving and house cleaning? Bad luck? Yes, partly, but also poor financial management. The sad fact is that most women are not financially literate—they have never been encouraged to understand money and have been happy to leave the finances to someone else to worry about. When I ask Betty Walton if she had any money worries at eighty-seven she says, 'Oh, no, I have never been interested in money, I am not materialistic at all,' which didn't actually answer my question. Many women share the view instilled into Betty by her Dad: 'My father brought me up to think it was distasteful to talk about money.'

Although I asked women about money, very few gave specific answers. Only Bertha Lowitt describes her income in actual dollars. The others talk about 'being comfortable', their answers often more vague and euphemistic than even the ones they gave about sex. Not talking about money is bad enough but women often don't think about it either, certainly not enough to plan ahead for retirement. They do not realise that they are likely to be retired for decades. And because they don't budget they have no idea what they spend their money on. On top of all this women are highly risk averse—probably because of their lack of confidence in money matters—and will keep any money they do have in bank accounts or fixed-term deposits. This financial strategy is especially foolish when interest rates are low, as they are now. After inflation is taken into account, they are actually losing money. At the least we need to be interested in money and know that we need financial education.[3]

We could be good with money. There is nothing innate about women being risk averse or less financially literate. Many studies have shown that financial know-how reflects income, assets and time constraints—not gender. High-end earning women are just as astute with their money, if not more so, than men.[4]

Bad stuff happens to good women

Although neither of them came from wealth, by the time they were in their sixties Lady Florence Bjelke-Petersen and Margaret Fulton were very well off financially. In 1987 Lady Flo earned an excellent salary as a senator in federal parliament. Her children were grown and she was married to the premier of Queensland, who also pulled in a high wage. As well as *Bethany*, their property near Kingaroy in Queensland, they had other large properties and investments and looked set for life. Five years later they were struggling financially and living on a small annuity that came from Lady Flo's superannuation: 'We lived on just a little bit more I suppose than the pension, but you have to be grateful I guess that we've got that.' What happened?

Sir Joh was ousted as premier of Queensland in December 1987 and in 1991 faced a criminal trial for perjury during the Fitzgerald Corruption Inquiry. The massive legal fees he incurred sent them broke. They had to sell properties and investments and took half of Lady Flo's superannuation payout as a lump sum, 'to help pay the bills to the bank. And they're still not paid of course.' In an interview in 1994 Lady Flo said that they would have been fine, with an extra 'million and a half dollars', if her husband hadn't refused to join the Queensland Parliament Superannuation Scheme because it 'was feathering your own nest'.[5] Fortunately for them both Lady Flo didn't follow her husband's advice. She made sure she stayed in the Senate for twelve and a half years, taking leave rather than resigning to be with her husband during the perjury trial. This was long enough for her to be eligible for her full parliamentary super payout.

Instead of a relaxing retirement, the Bjelke-Petersens had debt hanging over them in their late seventies and eighties. Some money came in from the busloads of tourists Sir Joh took around *Bethany* and for whom Lady Flo baked her famous pumpkin scones. In

1994 she said, 'We're managing all right but, there's no doubt about it, if you've got a little bit extra it certainly comes in handy.' When I spoke to her, nine years later, the bad times were over and she says, 'I have been blessed that my money seems to be coping all right.'

Margaret Fulton had built a wonderful career as Australia's best-known cookery writer and expert, and had almost paid off her home on Sydney Harbour. With the love of her life, she travelled overseas with no expense spared, staying in the Plaza Hotel in New York and shopping at Bergdorf's. And then she almost lost everything, including her beloved home. It started with $170,000 she was planning to use to pay off her mortgage. Her accountant advised that she 'should really be making money from it' and so she signed a document investing in the building of a retirement home, with the understanding that she'd get the money back in two years. Although she was a small investor in a big project, 'It ended me in an awful, awful lot of trouble because the thing went broke and then the banks wanted their money and they wanted my house, they wanted everything.' Margaret fought back and by 1997, after almost ten years of litigation, with compound interest and legal fees, she was being sued for 'close to three million'.[6]

These were years when Margaret says, 'for the first time in my life, I'm finding it difficult to smile. I'm finding it difficult to be carefree.' She says, 'that's my lesson in life, that even though you've always been, you know, everybody's darling,'[7] all of a sudden that can change and people want to knock you down. 'It was a near miss.' Margaret did keep her house and was able to rebuild her finances, despite losing her investment and paying a fair whack in legal fees. Her advice is not to sign anything until, 'You're sure what you're signing away.' Then you won't have to go through ten blighted years. She had no idea what she was putting at risk. 'I was misled, and yes, I shouldn't have signed it. But I got myself into a pickle.'

Margaret has very strong opinions about looking after your money to ensure a decent old age and they are not just based on her own experience. Her niece took out a loan on her house after seeing an advertisement asking, 'Are you asset rich and cash poor?' She borrowed the money for a trip to Scotland. It wasn't a big sum but eight years later, with compound interest, she 'was going to be turfed out of her home'. Her niece now lives with Margaret and rents out her home to service the loan. Margaret is very much against reverse mortgages and keeps a folder of cuttings with headlines like, 'How seniors can access up to one million extra cash.'

A reverse mortgage is not always a bad idea. It is a complex financial product that allows you to borrow money against the value of your home. New regulations since September 2012 mean that you can't end up owing more than the market value of your home. Be aware, though, that because the interest compounds, the debt grows quickly. If you borrow $50,000 that debt could grow to $232,000 after fifteen years and over a $1 million in thirty. Only do it as a last resort and wait as long as you can before you hock your most valuable asset—your home. Before you do anything check that the money you borrow won't affect your pension. In Australia, the ASIC website is very clear about the benefits and pitfalls and has a 'reverse mortgage calculator' to help you work out the most effective options.[8] Margaret advises you to avoid all get-rich schemes and tells me about her friends: B who lost everything in a Ponzi scheme, and C, who was caught up in a cult that left her destitute. Thankful not to have money worries as she nears ninety, Margaret Fulton wants others to learn from her mistakes and experience.

We've never had it so good

Surprising, for some women life after sixty has been more financially secure than ever before. Ironically, they are among the least well off: those who come from poor families, inherited nothing from relatives, and never finished high school. Koho Yamamoto is the poorest woman I spoke to. 'I have struggled all my life,' she says, 'this is the happiest time of my life' because 'I don't have to worry about making a living so much. I am saving a certain amount for my old age when I become old.' Koho is ninety-one and hoping to live to 110. She lives on US social security, which averages US$1293.83 a month and Koho is likely to be getting less because she contributed little during a working life of part-time, poorly paid jobs. She supplements her pension with what she gets from teaching but nowadays has few students. In the years before her sixties she was 'half-starved' and always worried about money. Now she's more comfortable financially than she's ever been, with the backup of some savings that grew from US$20,000 compensation she was paid by the US Government for being interned during World War II.

For Flo Howlett a lifetime of never having enough money dramatically improved in her sixties. Her sixties and seventies were one of the best periods of her life because, 'You do things you could never afford because up until you're sixty, you haven't got much money, not in our day.' Her five children were grown, and she was working in her brother's jewellery shop, bringing in some money for the first time since she married. Her husband stopped 'backing horses and drinking beer, he was quite content to be home and just do things together and that doesn't cost so much money'. Because her husband worked on the railways all his life, he retired on an excellent government pension.

Koho and Flo are not oddities. Their experience is supported by findings of the Australian Unity Wellbeing Survey conducted by the Australian Centre on Quality of Life at Deakin University, for which data is collected nationally through phone surveys of a random sample of two thousand Australians, at least twice a year. Having a low income—one below $15,000 a year—has a highly detrimental effect on women's wellbeing from the ages of twenty-five to fifty-five. After that a low income makes less and less difference. By the time women are aged seventy-six and over, the wellbeing scores of low-income women converge with those on high incomes of $61,000 to $100,000. This is an amazing finding because the overall study, when not differentiated for age or gender, finds that people with the highest wellbeing have an annual household income between $60,000 and $90,000.[9]

Stephanie Charlesworth has more money than she expected in retirement, a good deal more than her upper middle-class parents had, although her father 'had an executive position, he had super,' she says. 'I always assumed that it would be the same with us and that we would have to live a lot more simply when we retired.' She thinks they're the generation who have good super and, of course, Stephanie, unlike her mother, has worked for most of her life.

Many of the women have shares, properties and other investments. Maxie Meldrum is typical of the wealthy group when she says, 'I inherited quite a reasonable sum of money and that was sensibly invested. I have got pretty much as much as I need, if I need any extra money I can sell some shares. I am giving money away at the moment. I really am seriously giving money away.' For these women a combination of inherited money, good economic times and sensible decisions have set them up for a very comfortable old age. Others from poor backgrounds, like May Lowe, benefited from the economic boom of the 1950s and 1960s to build up assets and investments for their future. Bertha Lowitt and Margaret Barnett grabbed educational opportunities, worked full time as long as they could, and now have more than enough to live well in old age.

In a UK survey of 220 people aged over ninety, 71 per cent felt they had enough money, and 7 per cent said that they had more than enough money. The authors were surprised by these findings about money and suggest that responses are influenced by the fact that people don't want to identify themselves as poor, and the culture among this particular cohort of not wanting to complain or be seen as whingers.[10] Those ninety year olds were born in the final twenty years of the nineteenth century, whereas the women I talked to were born between 1913 and 1928, and yet the results are much the same. All the women say they have enough or more than enough income.

The generation divide

Before we start relaxing about our future happiness, we need to remember that women now in their eighties and nineties have come through the Great Depression and World War II. Their needs and wants were formed in hardier, thriftier times, as two of the women in our group who rely on the age pension epitomise.

Raising five children on very little money means that Kali Paxinos is used to making do. She says, 'When you get to my age money shouldn't be or isn't that enormous a priority. The way the pension is structured today I think if you own your own home you are quite comfortable.' Kali believes that how you live your older life depends on knowing what your real needs are. She would like a little more ready money to go to concerts and the theatre. But she is happy with her life. In the evenings she is busy undoing a jumper to re-use, knitting singlets, jumpers, ponchos and pants for vulnerable children in Europe.

Rose Stone loves concerts and the theatre and she's not about to give them up even though the age pension is her sole source of income. Her life is incredibly full and active. Her advice is to live frugally so that you can splurge when you need to and, like Kali, she says, 'The big question you need to ask yourself is, "Do I really need it?" If you really do, then buy it or do it. However, you'll often discover that things don't necessarily make you happy.' Rose has always sewn her own clothes and made her own hats and, although she treats herself to the occasional meal out, mostly she cooks and eats at home. Both Rose and Kali have given up their cars and Rose, like Kali, has never been well off. She grew up in a flat in Poland with no running water and just two rooms, one of which her father worked in and the other in which she, her parents and three siblings lived.

Even the wealthy women are frugal. None are living in vast homes with staff and luxury cars. Barbara Hamer says, 'A lot of people think I should be driving a Mercedes or something ... I just drive a little Honda Jazz because it's got a high seat and it's very comfortable, also extremely economical.' Frances Reynolds laughs when she describes her car: 'I got it for my seventieth birthday saying, this will see me out, and here I am twenty years later.' In some cases the lives of the wealthy women are no different than those of the poor ones. Unlike Flo Howlett, April Hamer has never had a worry about money her whole life. When she was five, she and her sister had a French governess. She attended expensive private schools and as a young married woman travelled overseas, leaving her children in the care of a nanny. But now her life is not that different to Flo's: both live in similarly comfortable but not glamorous aged-care homes.

Flo Howlett is not concerned about her own finances or those of her five children whom she describes as 'sensible'. But she is very worried about her fifteen grandchildren. Their spending shocks her, not only because it's so different to her own ways but because she can't see how they'll manage in the future. She says, 'How on earth can they afford it all the time? I couldn't afford to even go to Coles and have a cup of tea. When I was young that was what you made at home. You couldn't spend two dollars or something on a cup of tea.' It's more like $4 a cup in reality and my friend Shelley, who's scraping by on her tiny super payout, says she'll scream if she hears someone else say, 'It's only the price of a cup of coffee a day.' That's over $1500 a year!

Flo is outraged by the prices charged by the cafés where her grandchildren take her. One grandchild told her that, 'They went somewhere, three of them, and it cost $300 for three. That was just drinks. No wonder they are all screaming they haven't got enough money. Half of them wouldn't know how to boil an egg would they?' When her granddaughters tell her they spend over a hundred dollars at the hairdresser she says, 'For goodness sake, why would you work all that time and spend a hundred dollars just getting your hair straightened.'

Like Flo Howlett's grandchildren, I pay to go out to eat and drink and Flo would be outraged by my expenditure at the hairdresser, the florist and the bakery where I pay six dollars for a loaf of bread. Most of the women are not as frugal as Flo, Kali or Rose—they don't have to be. But the crucial fact is that not one has had to dramatically downsize her standard of living as she's gotten older. Either they're better off than they were in the past, or as well off as they've ever been.

Your own home

All the Australian women I interviewed owned their own homes. The Association of Superannuation Funds of Australia (ASFA), the peak industry body for the super sector, provides detailed retirement budgets. These budgets assume you own your home, and every financial advice column and book trumpets the same message: make sure you own your own home and are debt free when you reach retirement age.

For this generation of women, born in the teens and twenties of the twentieth century, especially the ones who started with nothing, owning their own home has been a great way of saving and an excellent investment. Although Beth Gott's husband had a commerce degree, 'He used to spend like a drunken sailor,' while she tried to make sure they lived within their means. She is financially secure only through the money she made selling her home. Not only was it an architect-designed house set on a generous corner block in a desirable area, but it was also, 'Next door to a block of flats that was going to be demolished anyway, which would have given them a really big block to build on.'

Not long after they turned ninety Flo and John Howlett sold the home, which they'd built for £3250, for $480,000. 'It was a pretty good profit,' says Flo. Like Beth Gott, she used the proceeds of the sale to move into retirement accommodation and still had money over to put into savings to supplement the pension. Beth and Flo feel they had the best of it: somewhere they loved to live while they were raising their families that became a valuable asset in their old age.

Jean Allison loves her house but, 'If things get really bad financially, I see there's some flats advertised very close that are only $380,000. Well, you see, I could sell my house and move to those flats.' Jean admits she hasn't been the best financial planner but owning her own home is a backup in case she tips over into not managing on her current income.

The experience of these women holds true for those of us born in later decades. We, too, bought houses that have rocketed up in value. Today's thirty-five to fifty-four year olds are less likely to be homeowners than previous generations. The home ownership of this age group was 68 per cent in 2010, a decline of 4.5 per cent over the previous ten years.[11]

Public housing waiting lists in Australia grow longer and longer and the private rental market tighter, and more expensive. Sadly you won't get a rent-controlled apartment any longer, not even like the tiny one Koho Yamamoto has in Greenwich Village, New York. Rent control and stabilisation programs no longer exist, not in the United States, the United Kingdom or Australia. And your chances of getting into Mitchell-Lama affordable housing projects, like the one Bertha Lowitt lives in, in Brooklyn, New York, are about the same as winning the lottery.

Close to home and among my friends, owning their own homes has been critical to their financial wellbeing. As Rose Stone and Kali Paxinos say, you couldn't manage on the age pension unless you own your own home. My friend Ellen is selling her home and plans to buy something smaller and much cheaper so she can invest the difference to supplement her pension. She is in a much better situation than Shirley, who is struggling to pay for her home, travelling across Melbourne to a part-time job that barely pays her mortgage. They are both in their early seventies. Having a home as an asset makes a big difference for a comfortable future. To achieve this important financial goal you will need to start on this mission a good twenty years before you stop working.

How much do you need?

Finance companies use income and actuarial models to predict how much money you need when you retire. The older you are when you stop work, the less you'll need. Most estimates are based on your final full-time salary and they range from a low of eight times your salary to a high of eighteen—quite a big difference. Taking a mean of eleven times your annual pay, if you retire at sixty-five, having earned $75,000 a year, you will need to have saved $825,000 to invest. Another method calculates that you'll need thirty-three times what you expect to spend in your first year of retirement. Using this measure, if you spend $40,000 a year you'll need a nest egg of $1.32 million to invest for your future.[12]

The ASFA retirement budgets are updated to reflect cost of living rises and shifts in government policy. As of May 2014, a single person needed $23,283 a year for a modest lifestyle and $42,254 to live comfortably. This comfortable lifestyle allows you to renovate your kitchen or bathroom at some stage, drink alcohol, eat out, have private health insurance at the top rate, and take economical overseas holidays. Both budgets assume you own your home outright and are relatively healthy.

More than half the retired people in Australia can't afford the modest lifestyle outlined by ASFA. In 2011–2012, 50 per cent of single retired Australians had an annual income of less than $21,700. And 1.8 million Australians rely on the age pension of $21,563 per annum. We've already seen that you can live on the pension, if you're frugal. You won't have the money to run a car, or eat out except for cheap takeaways. Forget about travel, or any type of alcohol except home brew. Without other savings or help from the kids, there'll be no budget to fix home problems like a rusty roof. And you won't have private health insurance. According to ASFA to have a 'comfortable' retirement, a single person needs $430,000 in retirement savings, to own their home and to be debt free.[13]

Some of us want a lifestyle above the ASFA comfort level. We want to travel less economically, to eat out and entertain more often, to donate to good causes and to visit our families in other states. Another $10,000 to $20,000 a year would do that. $1million invested conservatively will give you an income of $50,000 to $60,000 per year, as long as you own your own home and have no debt—mortgage or credit card.[14]

There's plenty of disagreement about how much you'll need to save for a comfortable old age. Some argue that the fearmongering and high figures are fuelled by the financial services industry's vested interest in encouraging you to save as much as possible and then invest those savings in their products. These pundits say that about 50 per cent of your working income will give you a very comfortable lifestyle in retirement, one where you can have plenty to fund all the things you enjoy doing. Those who favour this 50 per cent estimate base their argument on having lower expenses. You'll have paid off your mortgage, your kids will be independent, you no longer have to save for retirement and your tax bill will be far less. 'The amazing truth that many people fail to grasp: you can live on 50 per cent to 60 per cent of your working income when you retire, because that's exactly what you were living on when you were working,' says Malcolm Hamilton, a worldwide partner in Mercer, the benefits consulting firm.[15]

At the other end of the scale are those for whom the whole idea of living on less in your retirement is a myth. They argue that you're likely to spend more, just as you do when you have free time now. With a third of young Americans aged eighteen to thirty-one still living at home, and women having children into their forties, you could also still be supporting your children until you are much older than previous generations. And it's not unusual for someone retiring at sixty-five to have an elderly parent to look after.[16] The women I spoke to are not big spenders and fall near the 50 per cent end of the working income spectrum. But could this be because they are all very old?

Different decades, different needs

Looking at our adult lives from a financial perspective we can see definite stages. In your thirties and forties you are likely to be financially stretched with 30 per cent of your income going to pay tax, another 20 per cent for the mortgage and another 10 per cent in child expenses. This leaves you only 40 per cent of disposable income. In your fifties and sixties the mortgage should be paid off and the kids gone, so you'll have an extra 40 per cent of your income to play with, and even putting 10 to 20 per cent away for retirement, you should have more to spend.[17]

Our needs and wants don't stay the same over the last thirty years of our lives either. By our fifties and sixties we've all accumulated far more stuff than we need. Most of us stop or slow down on acquisitions. Our homes and shelves and cupboards are full to overflowing. Everyone is talking about clearing out, giving away, simplifying and downsizing. We eat out and travel, and spend as much as ever on entertainment, food and gifts. Many of my friends are hiking, canoeing and ticking through their bucket list of exotic destinations, feeling the pressure to do all these things while they're still fit and able. And when we stop work our travel budget will rocket up still further—we've got the time and hopefully have saved the money.

One school of retirement planning says that although people spend up big in the early years of retirement, their spending evens itself out in later years. They argue that even if you want to live it up in retirement, you probably only have to budget for about ten years of the high life. One such pundit advises, 'If you want to live large in retirement, split your savings in two. Think about how much you'll need for those once-in-a-lifetime things you want to do in your sixties, because once you reach your seventies, you'll just want to relax.'[18]

He must be in his thirties or forties to have this stereotypical view of people at seventy, imagining roomfuls of them in recliners in front of the television. But there are far too many once-in-a-lifetime things to fit into your sixties. And what's with this relaxing? For the people I know it means climbing Mt Kilimanjaro or exploring the Kimberley. And who is filling up those cruises to Alaska, and most of the seats at the theatre? People in their sixties, seventies, eighties and nineties. The women I spoke to describe their sixties and seventies as a very active time in their lives, when they were doing as much or more than ever. It is true that by the time they hit the second half of the nineties they are slowing down somewhat.

Apart from Dodo Berk—always the exception to the rule—none of the oldest women travel further than an hour or two from home. The wonderful Dodo still takes her annual cruise with her daughter and spends every winter in Florida. Mary Broughton goes with her son to their country place about an hour's drive away and May Lowe's sons also take her for drives to the country for lunch. Bertha Lowitt and Flo Howlett stick to the city and the cheapest traveller of all is Joan Lowrie, who tries her best not to leave her house. In contrast at the other end of the age range there's still a lot of travel expense happening!

Overseas travel is very much on the agenda of the younger old ones, those in their late eighties and early nineties who can afford it and are physically able to enjoy it. When I last spoke to Margaret Barnett she was excitedly preparing for a trip to Spain with her son and daughter-in-law. Dorothy Shultz was planning where next to go overseas with her husband, and Elisabeth Kirkby was not long back from Morocco, having attended the 34th Biennial Conference of the International Association of Women in Radio and Television. Jean Allison says about a trip that cost her $14,000, 'One of the things that I do not regret in the slightest but has caused a bit of financial pain is going to Antarctica.' And she's planning to attend the next World Anaesthetists Conference in Hong Kong, even if she has to sell her house to get there.

I'd advise against financial planning for the last third of your life that assumes you will need less money as you get older.

Money does make a difference

Although all the women say they are 'comfortable', their means vary enormously. Having more money does add to the pleasure and lifestyle options of older women and their families. At the top of the list is the satisfaction women get from being able to help their children. Barbara Hamer was able to pay for her grandchildren's private schools and support her son-in-law in establishing his business. Bertha Lowitt can ensure her grandson stays in the neighbourhood. 'He pays $2500 a month for a one-bedroom apartment on State Street. So I give him a thousand dollars a month. What does he get as a teacher after eleven years, $50,000? But he's got to pay that kind of rental, he's got to live. But that's what I do and I help out my kids whenever I can, for their anniversaries and their birthday I take them out very fancy. They pick the place and it's not a hundred dollars.'

Being able to take her children and grandchildren out for special meals and trips gives April Hamer the pleasure of having something to offer. This is important to all the women who can afford to help their children. Dame Margaret Scott says, 'I used to spend a lot of money on travelling and clothes and all that kind of thing, I don't anymore. Now I give it all to my kids. Money is such a pleasure, it makes me be able to do things.' For those who don't have much money, their children help them. Rose's daughter takes her out for meals and to concerts. Kali's kids insisted on buying her a new television, and Flo Howlett is enticed out to cafes and restaurants by her brood, all the while telling them she thinks they are wasting their money.

Being able to pay for extra health and medical needs is also important. June Helmer has Parkinson's disease and is wealthy enough to afford private carers and housekeeping help. Someone is with her twenty-four hours a day, on hand to drive her where she wants to go and help her have as good a quality of life as possible and stay in the home she's lived in most of her life. Fortunately for Joyce McGrath, once her local council told her that she needed more care than they could offer she had the money to pay privately for the help she needs now that she can't drive or shower herself. It's very expensive but she did have some inheritance. 'I invested it in a few stocks and shares, Telstra and Westpac and CSL, so I have got a bit of money in those, with that and the superannuation I have got enough to manage to do the things I want to do.'

As you get older Beth Gott says, 'There are things you need and that's why I am pleased to have private health insurance. You need eyes, you need glasses, you need dental work. I just broke a tooth and had a rather expensive replacement for it. So you are glad to be able to get some sort of recompense for dental work, for example, and the ears as well.' Beth considers herself very lucky that her second husband worked for Rio Tinto and Rio Tinto continues to pay her private health contribution.

All the women with money use it to pay for extra help around the home—to do the things they can't or don't want to do. Suzanne Simon has a woman come in three times a week to do the housework, shopping and to 'cook casseroles that can be frozen and I have them on the nights'. Most employ regular cleaners. Bertha Lowitt's two-bedroom apartment is spotless and neat. 'I have someone who comes in every single week. Every Wednesday she is here and does not only the cleaning but the washing and ironing.' And there are plenty of other jobs older women need to employ help for, like removing the dead tree in the tub on her terrace, that Barbara Hamer says, 'Wants to come out but I can't deal with that, I have to get somebody. I can't do that sort of gardening any more.'

Depending on where they live, the less well off can access subsidised services from their local council. Joan Lowrie, as a 'frail elderly' person has a council home-care worker who shops for her, does her banking, cleans and prepares meals. 'Domestic assistance', 'delivered meals', 'personal care' and even some gardening and home maintenance are paid for by the federal government under Joan's Department of Veteran Affairs Gold Card entitlements. Only Koho Yamamoto, Rose Stone and Kali Paxinos don't pay anyone to do their cleaning and washing.

Extra money means you don't have to rely on public transport; you can afford taxis and car services. Being able to pay someone to pick you up from home to take you to the train station or airport, and carry your luggage, does tend to encourage you to go places. In the managed blocks of flats where Barbara Hamer and Maxie Meldrum live, they can call on their caretaker to drive them places for a fee. But the eligibility requirement for half-price taxis in Victoria is pretty tough—a severe and permanent disability that prevents you from safely and independently using public transport, and proof of financial difficulty. A bigger barrier than money can be the Depression-era mentality. Parents of friends of mine, well able to afford taxis, still see them as extravagant. Instead they stay trapped at home or wait for their already over-committed children to take them to appointments.

Without a doubt money allows you to choose from a wider range of leisure and culture options. As you get older hitchhiking and the shoestring-budget options don't appeal so much—not to me anyway. It's great to be able to afford airfares instead of Greyhound buses, and economy plus or business class for that longer trip to visit the relatives in Perth, see Paris in the spring again, or warm your bones in Port Douglas in winter. Elisabeth Kirkby described a wonderful trip to Cambodia she did with The Art Gallery of New South Wales. You won't be able to afford these trips on the age pension. The cheapest advertised in 2014 is to China for $8500, including airfares, and the most expensive to Chile and Peru for $12,350, plus airfares.

And although there are wonderful free and cheap entertainments available, most theatre and concert tickets are expensive. Kali Paxinos would love to be able, 'To go to the theatre and go to some musical concerts, but I have looked at tickets for example and to go to see concerts it's quite expensive. So for me at the moment, yeah I have got the radio, so I will listen to the music on the radio, so you compensate.' Joan Lowrie loves musicals. 'We'd see every show in town. We used to go to the Westin and have lovely club sandwiches. We saw *Singing in The Rain*. And *South Pacific*. I heard someone say the tickets are about $200. We used to go to *Morning Melodies* whenever it was on—it used to be $6 and it's now $17.' Perhaps if she had more money or the tickets were cheaper we could entice Joan to go out.

Having heard how good for the mental and physical health of the elderly it is to have a pet I was surprised to find that only Margaret Barnett had one, her cat Jacques. They do cost a fair bit in food and treatments and vet fees. But it seems the women already knew that most of this research has been at the behest of pet food companies. An independent survey of 2551 older Australians shows that pet ownership confers no health benefits. They are more likely to be depressed and in poorer physical health than people who don't own pets.[19]

Probably the biggest single expense you could incur would be paying to move into a retirement, assisted living or nursing home. Although the Australian Government will ensure that you can get into some kind of home if you're assessed as needing it, you'll be expected to contribute to the cost of your care if you can afford to do so. The more money you have, the more you'll pay, but you'll also have a wider choice of homes.

Another wonderful thing about having more money is being able to support causes you believe in. Betty Walton may buy her clothes at Vinnies but she supports fourteen charities financially. 'Because I have money,' she says, 'I think of the blind, I think of the strokes, of African children with cataracts, and the money I have I like to spend on other people who have all these things.'

Women and super

Superannuation, also known as pensions or social security, used to be for men and single women because the concept of retirement was tied to full-time work. When I started work it was optional for female teachers to join the Married Women's Super Fund, which was far less generous, and therefore less attractive, than the compulsory male scheme. In July 1982 Victoria's women teachers were finally automatically enrolled in the same compulsory super scheme as the men. That year only 24 per cent of Australian women had any super so it's not surprising that most of the women I spoke to have none.

For the majority of women in their late eighties and nineties 'the man was the plan' for financing their old age. Flo Howlett's husband worked for the state government on the railways and, even now after his death, she receives 75 per cent of his pension. Frances Reynolds hardly worked after she married. She and her husband are self-funded retirees, and much of their income comes from what her husband accrued in super in his years working in the mining industry. And the same is true for most of the married women of her generation. They depended on their husband as provider before and after retirement. But not all of them, and not the single women.

Bertha Lowitt worked full time until she was seventy-seven, in unionised professions with good pension plans. Her social security of $3300 a month is more than adequate to meet her needs. A good super scheme is a wonderful thing. Lady Flo took half of her Federal Parliament super payout as a lump sum to pay pressing debts and still has enough to live comfortably almost twenty years later. Of her years in the NSW Parliament, Elisabeth Kirkby says, 'I was very lucky to get into parliament when I did because that means I have a parliamentary pension, that is adjusted to the cost of living. My pension is perfectly adequate for my life.'

The government schemes and the university one that Stephanie Charlesworth and her husband were in are generous. All are defined benefit schemes and you know exactly what you're getting when you retire. On retirement you were eligible for a pension of 60 per cent or more of your final salary with automatic adjustments for inflation. This pension continues until death. If you're in a defined benefit scheme, stick with it.

Since 1992 super has been compulsory for almost everyone who works. By 2007, 66 per cent of Australian women had some super, and although not as high as the 76 per cent of men, it's a big improvement.[20] Yet the average sixty year old Australian woman would need to work an extra twenty-five years to retire on the same amount of super savings as her male counterpart.[21] So why are women still missing out? The gender pay gap is the biggest factor. Women earn 17 per cent less on average than men and employer contributions are based on a percentage of your salary. Build in the years of halted and part-time work caring for kids and elderly parents, and women get to sixty to find their super savings are a whopping $121,200 less than the bloke who is sitting next to them at the office.

If Beth Gott had been a man she'd be rolling in super now. A brilliant student, she is a renowned expert on indigenous plants. Instead she gets nothing but a tiny bit of social security from when she taught in the United States. Beth worked part time or on soft money grants and contracts. 'I did have an appointment for a short period at Monash with teaching and I had a bit of super then, and I think I cashed it in or did something with it.' In the past, when 'our plan was a man' we took out the bits of super we had on leaving one job for another to buy a new washing machine or something else we needed.

Although she worked into her eighties, because Kali Paxinos started working late in life and always part time she has, 'Very very little. Because women didn't have super. It started I think towards the end of the time I was at Swinburne.' Even today women who work casually, like Rose Stone, or in poorly paid jobs, like artist Koho Yamamoto, will have little super or social security. And we are unlikely to be in a defined benefit scheme that guarantees us a cost of living adjusted income after we retire. Most people are now in accumulated super funds, where your retirement income depends on what you and your employer contribute and the investment return on these contributions. You can take it with you when you move jobs but there is no guaranteed income when you're ready to stop work. If the market collapses, as it did with the GFC, your retirement savings will take a hit.

Australia's super system is one of the world's largest and will continue to expand, because tax rates are attractive and compulsory contributions are large and growing. We've seen that it still

disadvantages women and is always at risk of changes in government policies and unpredictable investment outcomes. But we
need to be in it. You've got to have super to hedge your bets
because you can't depend on the age pension staying as it is or the
housing market either. Start building up more super in your fifties
with salary sacrifice or other income, and please don't leave it to
your partner or your accountant or anyone else to look after.

Who's looking after your money?

You will not be surprised that Betty Walton, who doesn't like
to talk about money, leaves its management to her husband.
Frances Reynolds does too. Husbands being in charge of the
family finances remains the norm to a surprising degree. It took
my friend Angela two years to sort through the finances while in
deep grief for the loss of her husband of sixty years. She had to
hire a new team of lawyers and accountants to untangle the mess.
With a very demanding job, Kathy had left day-to-day finances to
her husband. After he died, she realised that she would have done
a much better job.

Women remain far less engaged, aware or confident about
managing finances in general and for their retirement. No wonder
investment companies are saying, 'With women expected to outlive men by nearly five years, one lesson is clear: regardless of
their age, women must take the steps to educate themselves in
order to be an equal partner with their spouse in the key financial
decisions shaping their lives, now and in years to come.'[22] If you
are partnered, push through those hurdles of lack of confidence
and interest, and get on top of the money. Read all the documen-
tation and make sure that you attend meetings with the bank,
accountant and adviser. Remember that men are no smarter than
we are, and no better at managing money.

Sister Mary Gregory, a nun since she was twenty-one, has
never had to think about money. Now that she's in an assisted

living home, the Order is still managing her money. She does get the pension, 'but all the extras and you know the board and whatever it is, it's all done at a central level. But I have an account at the head office and can withdraw money to a certain amount.' This is 'an annuity' so she can buy her own clothes, 'have my hair cut and have coffee with somebody'. Most women seem to want someone else to look after the money. If you don't have the Order of the Good Samaritans, or your husband is dead, you've still got your kids.

Beth Gott describes her daughters descending on her 'periodically, every so often, and saying, "Right, now let's have a look at all this." They get very bossy about it, but I don't mind. I am quite happy for someone else to do it.' Dodo Berk says, 'My daughter looks after my money, I have no money worries.' At ninety-nine and with nothing wrong with her, it's not that she can't, but she doesn't want to, look after her money. Dodo wants to spend her energy and time on fun stuff. So does May Lowe, whose money is looked after by her eldest son, a retired bank manager. Although Mary Broughton successfully managed her finances for fifty years after her husband died, at ninety-seven she's not as competent as she used to be and has handed them over to her son.

Is it okay to pass your money management to your children? And if so, at what age should you do this? Think of what happened to King Lear when he gave up his assets. Look after your money, just as you look after your health and your appearance and your home—for as long as you can. And when you do let your kids take over, keep some oversight and get a financial adviser as well as this will take some of the load off them.

You have to look after your money whether you're rich or poor. True, the more you have the more complicated it is. Women on pensions and low incomes, and still living in their own homes, like Rose Stone, Kali Paxinos, Joan Lowrie and Koho Yamamoto, are more likely to be looking after their own money. As are single women. Jean Allison and Joyce McGrath have never had anyone else to palm this chore off to.

Since her husband died eleven years ago, Barbara Hamer has also been single. But she's been managing her own money for most of her life, and is the only woman who talked about actively being in charge and doing things with money. She comes from a wealthy family—her father was an industrialist—and says, 'I do feel that I have had a privileged background.' At eighty-eight Barbara is still running her own company. She spends a couple of hours every morning on her computer looking after her business ventures and investments. With some of her profits she's paid for her grandchildren's expensive private schools and financed a son-in-law's manufacturing business.

A number of women referred to their accountants managing their money. Bertha Lowitt, who has $500,000 with an accountant, says, 'I can withdraw, I can deposit.' Bertha is ninety-six and even if the accountant gambles it all away or does a Bernie Madoff, she'll be okay. But generally accountants are not the best people to be managing your money. Their job is counting money—making sure books are balanced, tax is paid and audit requirements met. Accountants are not qualified in how to make the most of your money. For that you'll need another adviser.

Managing our finances and saving for our old age is much more complicated than it used to be. Money does not grow by sitting in the bank. To make the most of your last thirty years your financial wellbeing is as important as your health wellbeing. You need a financial adviser or planner—a good one. Go about finding the right one just as you would a doctor. Of course, only consider qualified ones, those who hold an Australian Financial Services Licence. And get recommendations from your friends. Next, talk to two or three to see who suits you—the first consultation is usually free. If you're more comfortable with a woman, there are specialist services you can tap into. And be sure to ask about their fees—they usually charge by the hour. Everything else you need to know about employing a financial adviser can be found on the ASIC MoneySmart website. You've got no excuses. None of us can afford to be financially illiterate.

Where to from here?

When I plan what I'm doing it's at most a year or so in advance, whether it's being ready to leave that job, finish writing this book, or wanting to take a trip to Western Australia. But with money it's different, especially once you hit fifty. Planning for a year or two is not enough. We all need longer term money strategies because in five, ten or twenty years we'll stop earning a salary. And because there are so many unknowns when we look ahead more than a few years, we've got to hedge our bets.

The age pension is very important to Australian women: 73 per cent of those who receive the single rate of the age pension are women. No one knows how eligibility criteria for the age pension will change in the future so we must avoid relying on it alone to support us in old age. We can and should get involved in trying to influence government and superannuation providers to make fairer policies. I'm happy to support the raising of the pension age to seventy but only as long as there are jobs for all those over fifty who want and need them. I'm also fine about tightening eligibility criteria as long as they only impact the rich and the rorters. I see no hands raised in favour of keeping any free perks for retired members of parliament, who already get extremely generous super payouts. But I'm not running the country. Finance experts warn us that we'd be 'nuts' to expect to rely on a pension twenty or thirty years from now. And it's the same with super. Who knows whether the highly advantageous tax policies will survive or how the stock market will move. Ditto the housing market. The three-prong approach is essential: a debt-free home, a decent super nest egg, and the age pension as a safety net.

This brings us back to defining a decent nest egg. To start, decide what kind of person you are. Being comfortable in the years after you reach sixty depends on the lifestyle you've had before that. A survey of eight hundred retired women aged between fifty and eighty found that 81 per cent were happier in retirement, although 52 per cent have a less comfortable lifestyle. The authors note that despite their low incomes—77 per cent of the sample were reliant on some form of government pension—the women managed well because they were used to budgeting and being frugal.[23] If your lifestyle now does not require the upkeep of a large home, overseas travel, chic haircuts, and fancy restaurants, you're not likely to be doing those things all of a sudden in your sixties, seventies and eighties. Will you be like Kali Paxinos or Beth Gott or Rose Stone in your needs and habits?

If you do get the age pension you'll also get a pensioner concession card and healthcare card, which entitle you to bulk billing and other health refunds, a telephone allowance, free rail travel and other fare concessions, and a reductions in property rates, water, energy and car registration. But because of the risk to these entitlements and to have money for those extras, like fixing your teeth and mending the fence, please save some money. There will be unexpected needs and emergencies the pension will never cover. A little bit more may allow you an annual cruise.

If you have a holiday house, go to Leonard Cohen concerts or visit your daughter in London, you'll still want to do that and more when you stop working. Are you more like Margaret Barnett and Elisabeth Kirkby and still hooked on the adventure of travel? If you are you'll need to save that magic $1 million at the least. Remember though if you don't get to that magic number or even near it, you've still got your health, your family and your friends and you're likelier to be happier than you've ever been.

HOT TIPS For money matters

➤ Don't leave looking after money to anyone else—become financially literate and educate yourself.

➤ Attend any meeting about your money and read all the documents.

➤ Get yourself a financial planner and don't rely on your accountant for money advice.

➤ Don't sign anything without giving it time, care and thought.

➤ You've got to have a super plan, or a 401(k) if you're in the United States.

➤ Buy your own home, however small, and make sure it's mortgage free before you retire.

➤ Be debt free and don't buy stuff without asking yourself, 'Do I really need it?'

➤ Avoid taking out a reverse mortgage. Remember that the interest compounds—only as a last resort give up your home equity.

➤ Keep working for as long as you can—remember another ten years means you'll have more super and fewer years to fund in retirement.

➤ Don't worry too much about what you can't do anything about—like interest rates and the world economy.

➤ Join others to advocate and agitate for women-friendly and fair government retirement policies and programs and superannuation rules.

➤ If everything goes financially pear-shaped, remember that if you've still got your health, your family and your friends you're likelier to be happier than you've ever been.

5

Keeping Up Appearances

PICTURE A GROUP of six women sitting in the garden in the shade of an umbrella, or around a café table or . . . you choose the location. The women are good friends and all over fifty. Listen to their conversation about politics and books and children and lovers. Before much time has passed one woman says, 'I'm sick of having my hair coloured, going to the hairdresser every four weeks—all that time and money. What do you think about me going grey?' The two grey-haired women are immediately encouraging: 'Great, do it.' 'It'll suit you.' After a minute, a brunette says, 'Grey hair will make you look older.'

I cannot count the number of times I've had this conversation and hundreds like it about how we look and what we should do to improve our appearance, especially the parts of us that show our age. Why do we spend so much time discussing the details of our appearance—hair colour, body shape, weight, sunspots, veins and the rest? We're not airheads. But we do know appearance counts.

A mountain of research demonstrates just how much in life can be determined by the way you present yourself. Height, obesity and the symmetry of your facial features make a difference for both men and women but there are many ways women's appearance is judged that do not apply to men. It matters even more for women than for men. Women who wear makeup are ranked higher for competence and trustworthiness and can earn 30 per cent more than those who are not made up.[1] And having bigger or smaller breasts means the lecture you present will be rated lower by your male colleagues than if you gave that very same lecture wearing an average C-cup size.[2]

We all make irrational snap judgements, often in the blink of an eye but at most within the first thirty seconds of seeing a face, not just about age and social standing but also about qualities like attractiveness, competence, aggression, likeability and trustworthiness.[3] As we get older another whole layer of judging comes into play. Now it's not just about being a woman but about becoming an older woman. Hence, the going-grey-or-not discussion, which is a stark example of the double standard that affects the ageing experience of men and women. For older men grey hair is a signifier of authoritativeness, wisdom and distinction whereas women who don't dye their hair are seen as 'letting themselves go'.

Every woman I've ever known cares about how she looks. And nuns are no exception. Sister Mary Gregory says, 'I love to care for myself and I like my appearance to be good, you know.' The women I spoke to all believe firmly in 'looking good' though the ways they present to the world vary greatly. They talk about 'feeling attractive', 'making the most of yourself' and 'not letting yourself go'. The latter is seen as a sign that something is seriously wrong with you—most likely dementia or a mental illness, usually depression.

Hair and hairdressers figure prominently in their accounts of what they do to look good. Our crowning glory, its colour, length, texture and style, is one of the main ways we identify each other. From childhood, when we want to point someone out we focus on their hair: 'the girl with the skinny black plaits', 'the curly haired one' and 'her shiny cap of hair'. Together with clothing, and body size and shape, your hair creates that immediate first impression.

For my mother's cohort—the era of Margaret Thatcher and Nancy Reagan and the women in this group—looking 'nice' meant weekly visits to the hairdresser for a set, if you could afford it. Although for most women this has morphed into less stiff and sprayed styles, the weekly visit continues for a comb up or a blow wave. Among the women for whom this is routine are Dodo Berk, Barbara Hamer and Lady Florence Bjelke-Petersen. Lady Flo feels more attractive having her hair done and 'you might as well have it done properly. Every Friday I go.' Barbara Hamer visits a local hairdresser every week for a blow dry and for more serious hair events like perms and cuts she travels further to a hairdresser she's had for many years.

To grey or not to grey?

There is never consensus about the hair-colour issue for women. While looking good for Dodo Berk, Joan Lowrie and Margaret Barnett means having their hair coloured, others stopped dyeing their hair in their sixties. Margaret Fulton, Betty Walters and Joyce McGrath went grey because they believe the dye is not good for you and makes your hair brittle and thinner. Barbara Hamer stopped dyeing her hair when she was sixty-five, at her hairdresser's suggestion.

The majority of the group never dyed their hair. All Bertha Lowitt's friends coloured over their grey till the day they died but not Bertha: 'That's one thing I don't like in people, I don't see what's wrong with grey hair.' Maxie Meldrum has never coloured hers because 'I have never tried to look younger', and Suzanne Simon never dyed hers because both she and her husband liked the silvery colour.

I'm surprised that a majority never covered their grey hair. Last week I went to a wedding with two hundred people of all ages, including the grandparents of the bride and groom, and there wasn't a woman in the room with grey hair. This is not a generational shift. My mother and her friends were dyeing their hair into their eighties, and most of them into their coffins. And although it's cheaper to go grey, it's not necessarily the poorer of the women in the group who make that choice. What does make a difference is the norm of your milieu. Among my mother's socio-cultural group—Jewish immigrants from Eastern Europe—there was no question of not colouring your hair. I never saw my mother's original hair colour and I know that she had dark-brown hair only from photographs taken before I was born.

It's rare for women in public life to go grey. English newscaster Fiona Bruce caused a stir when she admitted, 'I dye my grey hair because age is an issue for women on TV.'[4] SBS newsreader Lee Lin Chin is the only female grey-haired newsreader I've ever seen, and I doubt that she would be employed on a commercial ratings oriented channel. There are no female politicians in the US Congress who don't use hair dye and so few women in the movies that we can name them individually: Diane Keaton, Jamie Lee Curtis, Helen Mirren and Judi Dench. Perhaps, especially if you're at the very top of the ladder, it's more acceptable in finance and banking, where we can look to Westpac's Gail Kelly and IMF head Christine Lagarde. These women certainly knock on the head the suggestion that going grey means 'letting yourself go'.

Meanwhile 'silver fox' models are hitting the catwalks. Silver—never call it grey, darling—haired models cut are in demand by designers. These include not only models in their fifties and sixties but also the likes of Carmen Dell'Orefice in the United States and Daphne Selfe in the United Kingdom, who are both over eighty. This trend is likely to continue as our age group accounts for an ever-increasing percentage of consumer spending. Older models are proud of being pioneers. 'The best part is encouraging other women. So many tell me they love what I'm doing and that I'm showing women over a certain age don't have to hide,' says 65-year-old British model Pam Lucas.[5]

Conceptions of beauty are social constructs, relative to a specific time and place—just think of those powdered white wigs popular among the upper classes in eighteenth-century Europe or the thick white face paint of a Japanese geisha. Embracing this physical symptom of ageing would be a feminist move. Grey hair only looks old on women because we've decided that it does. Most women start to go grey in their late thirties and early forties. If more younger women stay grey—and there is such a slight trend, especially among the health conscious who want to avoid the chemicals in dye—would that shift the paradigm that grey equals old? I agree with Anne Kreamer, author of *Going Gray,* that we need to be realistic, especially in jobs where youthful looks count. While her dream is that television personalities like Katie Couric and Diane Sawyer, and politicians like Hillary Clinton and Nancy Pelosi will start letting their hair go grey, she recommends that 'until that time, if you feel you must, dye your hair'.[6]

Earlier this year, sitting at the hairdresser's having the colour applied to my grey roots, I complained that here I was again, looking terrible, with that nasty re-growth showing, only three weeks since I'd last had my hair dyed. 'It seems to be growing back faster and faster. I can see myself having to come and live with you so you can do my colour every day.' Instead of joining in my joke, my hairdresser said, 'Why not stop colouring it. You've got curls. Grey hair will work on you and I can do it so that the transition is not too painful.' In a moment of bravura I said, 'Let's do it.' There was no self-interest in his advice as he stood to lose money from fewer visits and no colour.

For years I have been talking about whether to dye or not to dye. Slowly over the past six months, as I've been working up to writing this section, my hair is becoming more grey. I am free to go grey because I'm never going to apply for a job again— believe me, never. And yes I do look older because that's still what grey hair signifies. My husband is not crazy about it but he's adjusting and my friends are saying supportive things because they are my friends. I'm not sure that I'll stick with it but I want to see my full head of grey hair before I make a final decision. Perhaps by then I'll be used to it and to the extra time and money I've gained. The best part so far is not watching that telltale line of grey re-growth appear and knowing I have to do something about it.

Why we can't win

Warning was selected as the United Kingdom's most popular post-war poem in a 1996 BBC survey. It was one of my favourite poems. The poet predicts that as an old woman she will snub the conventions, wear outlandish clothes and behave outrageously to make up for the 'sobriety' of her youth. Jenny Joseph wrote *Warning* in 1961 when she was twenty-nine. I was about that age when I first read this revelation of the freedom that becoming old would bring me: to be anything I wanted to be, without any concern for how others saw me or what they thought.

Now that I am an old—okay, older—woman, I know it's bunkum, a fantasy. What nonsense to play into the myth that old women don't care about how they look. The women I spoke to would be aghast at wearing something that didn't suit them and behaving like naughty children. We'd be put away in the dementia wing if we started acting out and running amok. Bertha Lowitt may be ninety-six years old but she still wants to feel attractive. At home she wear jeans but when she goes out she says, 'I'm dressed.' Bertha wants to make the effort, to carefully put together an outfit that presents her to the world. Suzanne Simon also tells me, 'I love clothes, and I always try to look as good as I can.' They both care about what they wear and how they look because they are engaged with the world and other people.

Women notice others, too. Lady Florence Bjelke-Petersen commented that the then governor-general of Australia, Quentin Bryce, was 'always very well-dressed'. Rather than being free to dress anyway we fancy, the strictures of acceptability actually tighten as we move into and past our middle years. *Quelle horreur* should we wear anything that makes us look like mutton dressed as lamb!

We are criticised for caring too much about our appearance and for caring too little, for letting ourselves go and for wasting time on facials and manicures. We may feel that we can't win, and it's true, we can't. From one side there is feminist pressure to 'grow old gracefully' (whatever that means) and on the other the pressure to use the increasing opportunities to reject an ageing identity.

None of the women see themselves as dowdy or frumpy, or 'old biddies' or 'old ducks'. Like all of us, they want the way they present themselves to the world via their clothing, makeup and hair to express their personality. For special occasions Rose Stone wears a reddish pixie-cut styled wig to cover her thinning hair and when she's out she covers her head with a jaunty hat or cap. Some of the others dye their hair. Most wear make-up and lipstick. Elisabeth Kirkby calls it straight: 'As you get older and your face gets blotchy, it's just a question of trying to cover up blotchy because you are not really going to make much difference are you?' Although Koho Yamamoto stopped dyeing her hair because she 'decided to show my real self and, anyway, "Take it or leave it," I said to myself,' she maintains a demanding beauty regime. Every night she puts her hair in pin curls 'and then next morning I take out the pin curls and then it gets curly, only stays for one day'. She likes big expressive eyes and, as well as putting on eyeliner and mascara, she uses eyelash glue to glue her eyelids open to make them look bigger.

'Yes I always like to look nice,' says Flo Howlett, who is at the no-artifice-at-all end of the spectrum. She believes she's 'not very wrinkly' because I 'never plastered my face'. 'Oh, God, no,' she says when I ask if she used beauty creams—her skin is quite lovely. 'I was flat out buying lipstick. What for?'

My friends use age-resisting and defying techniques that go far beyond hair dye, make-up, clothing and diet. They have bags removed from under their eyes, eyelids lifted, wrinkles and spots lasered off their faces, mini-facelifts and fillers—and these are just the ones they've told me about. Partly the difference between them and the older women is that the pressure to conform is different at eighty-five than in your fifties, sixties and seventies. That is for ordinary folks, not the likes of US journalist Barbara Walters, who only retired from television at eight-four, or comedian Joan Rivers who said, when asked if she was a plastic surgery addict, 'No. I think I'm in a business where you have to look good, and it's totally youth oriented.'[7]

Older women in public life have a tough time. When Hillary Clinton ran for the presidential nomination, Rush Limbaugh asked on his radio show, 'Do Americans want to watch a woman get older before their eyes?' A photo of her wearing glasses and little make-up went viral when she was secretary of state and led to criticism that she looked 'tired and withdrawn'. Asked to comment she said she didn't care what people thought about how she looked. 'I feel so relieved to be at the stage I'm at in my life right now. If I want to wear my glasses I'm wearing my glasses. If I want to wear my hair back I'm pulling my hair back.'[8]

Although facelifts have been around for almost a century, it's only in recent decades that botox, liposuction, laser and many other ways to look better and younger have become widely available. When I describe how some women I know in New York look younger than their daughters, I get the 'it's unnatural' response. If you want to see me blow my top just try the 'we should age naturally' line with me. Sometimes, instead of the word 'natural', people fudge and say 'authentic'. Spare me this nonsense. If you believe in natural you have to give up all forms of birth control and probably have a baby every nine months. Our whole life is not natural. Growing old gracefully is just one more unattainable goal set up for women.

Women are judged harshly about age-appropriate behaviour, looks and appearance, damned if they show any signs of their age, and damned if they don't. Gossip magazines sell millions of copies with covers that feature celebrities with sagging breasts and bellies one week—'Stars who've let themselves go'—and the next week the focus is on shame—'Have They Gone Too Far?' 'Botox and Women who can't move their faces'. To do this or that to look younger or better is not a moral issue. It's women, not men, who buy these magazines. Why do we feed into this snap judgement of other women? We're willing participants in creating our can't-win situation.

Our ageing bodies, ourselves

In 2006 a paparazzi snapped 62-year-old Dame Helen Mirren in the now-famous red bikini and anointed her with sex symbol status. 'That bloody photograph—that will haunt me for the rest of my life,' says Mirren, who can escape no interview without being asked about it.[9] Time and again the actress responds, 'The truth is I don't really look that good, it was just a flattering picture. I am beyond the bikini-wearing age, really. I wouldn't normally wear one. I look like a woman in her 60s.'[10] Helen Mirren is now stuck with an unattainable image of herself and, unwillingly and unwittingly, has set an impossible standard for the rest of us.

In New York and Melbourne I work helping women choose clothes to assist them over that first interview hurdle—looking the part for the job. As I bring clothes to the dressing room for them to try on, nine out of ten women apologise to me for their bodies. Young, middle-aged, old; black, white, hispanic; fat and thin, and short and tall—I hear the same refrain. 'I've put on a lot of weight since I lost my job/had the baby/came to this country.' Or more specifically they castigate their flabby thighs, wide feet, thin arms, small bust, big bust . . .

Dissatisfaction with our bodies did not disappear with second-wave feminism and as we age it can curdle into disgust. Hatred of our bodies is fuelled by lifestyle sections of newspapers, magazine articles and television makeover shows that scream advice: 'Do not go sleeveless after forty.' 'Avoid low necklines.' 'Absolutely no skirts above the knees, and women over sixty should never, never, never be seen in . . . leggings.' The message is, cover up and don't reveal your disintegrating and decaying body. For some of us forty was a long time ago. Must we spend the next fifty years hot and sweaty in our de rigueur long sleeves, calf-length skirts and turtleneck tops just so others don't have to look at our crêpey necks and flabby arms

Psychiatrists report that in the past few years they have been treating more people over seventy who have anorexia and other eating disorders. Dr Alex Yellowlees, the medical director and a consultant psychiatrist at the Glasgow Priory Clinic, says, 'Today everybody is acutely aware of how they look, and our appearance has become a currency we trade on. That means we value old people less because they don't fit the currency of "youth".'[11] These psychiatrists are perhaps seeing a younger group of old people, or old people who would have had some other mental health problem if they weren't fixated on body ageing. The women I spoke to are happy with how they look. Joan Lowrie says, 'Sometimes when you look at old ladies and their skin is hanging, I look at myself and I don't look too bad.' The statistical data supports the women I spoke to and not the British psychiatrists.

The July 2014 US Gallup Wellbeing Index, based on interviews with 80,000 people, found that people over sixty-five feel better about how they look than any other adults. Even more surprising is the shift in ratio between men and women. In young adults the gap is 12 per cent—more men feel good about their looks than women. By retirement age this gap has narrowed to 4 per cent. At seventy the number of women feeling good about their appearance is still rising while more men are growing dissatisfied with how they look.[12] Like the women I spoke to, we will be happier about how we look as we get older. By the time we're seventy, we'll be happier with our appearance than we've been since puberty. Now that's something to look forward to.

Perhaps we'd be more happy with our appearance at a younger age if we had more exposure to older women's bodies—ones that don't look like Helen Mirren's. For a dose of hyperrealism that neither sets up an unrealistic physical ideal nor makes you turn away in disgust, take a look at artist Aleah Chapin's The Aunties Project. Her nudes are as you've never seen them before. They are lovingly painted. These older women's bodies say 'take us as we are', with our blotchy skin, weathered bodies, saggy breasts, scars and grey hair. There's something exhilaratingly different about seeing old women who look comfortable in their bodies, even though Aleah Chapin says, 'The Aunties Project is less about age and more about making paintings that fully embrace the real human body, this fascinating vessel that carries us through our experiences.'[13]

When Rose Stone saw a 103-year-old shot-putting world champion on television, she felt embarrassed for Ruth Frith exposing so much of her wrinkly old body. It seems we've internalised the standards that we apply in making judgements about how older women should dress. All the women I spoke to wear clothing befitting this image, clothing that covers their bodies. Aleah Chapin's paintings make me think that if we covered up less, we'd get used to seeing our necks and arms and legs. I'm not suggesting that we all start running around in the nude. Even if we can't see our ageing and old bodies, with all their imperfections, as beautiful, we might stop being embarrassed and disgusted by them.

Let's hear it from the men

How often have we heard that women dress only for other women; that it's women who are hard on other women, and set the rules on how older women should look and dress. Men, it's said, like curves and see past grey hair and wrinkles to our deeper selves. Well don't you believe it. And as a salutary reminder of what men really think, take the case of Mary Beard.

Mary Beard does not look like Helen Mirren but she does appear regularly on British television. A professor of classics at Cambridge University, Mary Beard hosts popular series about Pompeii and Rome on the BBC. AA Gill, the TV critic of *The Sunday Times*, hoed into her in his review of *Pompeii*, saying she had 'corpses' teeth', and that 'From behind she is 16; from the front, 60. The hair is a disaster, the outfit an embarrassment.' He upped the ante in reviewing *Meet the Romans*. As Mary Beard says, 'He suggested that I should be kept away from the cameras altogether and, in a topical reference, went on to imply that I belonged on *The Undateables*, a recent Channel 4 programme charting the dating difficulties of the disabled and facially disfigured.'

Mary Beard admits to being hurt and upset by his remarks but she's not one to cave into sexist stereotypes about women on television. 'I'm every inch the 57-year-old wife, mum and academic, half-proud of her wrinkles, her crow's feet, even her hunched shoulders from all those misspent years poring over a library desk.' She's proud of her years and what they signify. 'And I ask only one thing of anyone who chooses to condemn me for not quite living up to the stereotype Botoxed blonde Gill seems to want me to become: see my programmes for yourself and decide if it is worth investing your time in watching me, even with my grey hair, double chin and wrinkles. It's the content that's the thing.'[14] Her grey hair and wrinkles really set men off. More recently, after appearing on BBC1's *Question Time* she has become the victim of a torrent of 'truly vile' abuse online of the kind that would 'put many women off appearing in public'. Many postings were aggressive and sexual—even sadistic. One was a photo of her face superimposed onto a picture of female genitalia.[15]

There are many old grey-haired men on television. Older women are permitted into public life on sufferance. Once we stick our necks out or say something a man doesn't like, he doesn't have to argue with what we've said. All he needs to do is rant about some part of our appearance that veers off from the so-called perfect body, hair, skin and clothing. Watch out Helen Mirren. Stay away from controversy or they'll find your flaws too.

A question of identity

Kali Paxinos' mother, who died at fifty-seven, told her, 'there is beauty in every age'. Kali says:

> That had a very strong impact on me. I don't feel I need to dye my hair because I want to look younger. I want to be seen for my age and I feel proud I have reached this age, because I feel good about myself. I don't object to people dyeing their hair but for me I don't see that that's going to give me joy. I feel that I have got to be seen as I am.

There are many images of Kali online presenting information about schizophrenia. Her hair is pulled back into a loose bun with no make-up or lipstick. She's always well dressed, often with a pretty scarf or a colourful necklace to set off her outfit. The sense you get from Kali's welcoming smile is overwhelmingly of comfort. Here's someone who will listen and understand and wants to help you. How she looks expresses who she is.

'There is beauty in every age,' is also Koho Yamamoto's mantra. Koho says, 'I feel I look young,' and people are always asking her, 'How do you keep so young?' When people ask her, 'What is your secret?' she replies, 'Don't do anything against your conscience. We all have conscience, and I am not an angel, I am not a boozer but I tried not to do anything against my conscience, so my face is clear.' Like every woman I've spoken to, she says, 'I try to make myself as presentable as possible, why not?' Koho puts a lot more time and effort into her appearance than Kali. She loves jewellery and if she had more money, one thing she'd definitely do is 'get nice jewellery'. Koho is after all an artist, and with her eye glue and make-up, her clothing, her jewellery and the styling of her hair she presents herself as a living work of art.

She is one of the many stylish older women photographed on the streets of New York for the 'Advanced Style' blog and her picture is included in the book of the same name. Ari Seth Cohen, inspired by his grandmother's unique personal style, began his highly successful blog to celebrate the lives and looks of older women. There is now also a film, and a colouring book. Across the Atlantic in September 2013, BBC Channel 4 showed *Fabulous Fashionistas*, a documentary about six women with an average age of eighty, who love fashion and have broken through the stereotypes of how older women should dress. Most of the fabulously dressed women over sixty photographed for the blog, book and films are not actors or models nor do they have much money. What they have in common is a love of dressing up, expressing themselves through style. Their individual look reflects their approach to life, an approach not constrained by how old they are.

'Dare to be yourself' is not limited to older women with a passion for fashion and the desire to put a lot of time into achieving a particular look. Professor Mary Beard is also doing the same by not giving in to the abuse and being her smart out-there self. She too has cracked the age cage. Kali Paxinos and Koho Yamamoto and all the women I spoke to—each in her own way—express their identity in how they choose to present themselves to others.

They've achieved the style that we're all looking for when we dress: to present ourselves to the outside world in a way that most closely matches who we are inside.

Why is looking good important?

Unlike the fashionistas, the women in my group do not mention creativity or 'living the theatre of life' or expressing their identity through how they dress, although all agree, 'You should look the best you can look.' Stephanie Charlesworth is slimly elegant in red and black and definitely a candidate for the *Advanced Style* book. Dressing well and caring about her appearance are for her:

> A compliment to the people that you are with. I think that people who look shabby and down at heel and depressed, will wear their depression in their clothes, look indifferent to the people around them. I would feel annoyed say if someone came looking like something the cat had dragged in, I would feel a little bit confronted, but when they come in looking very nice ...

Making the effort to look good is a mark of respect to others. 'Oh you've got to keep up your appearances,' says Frances Reynolds. 'I think you've got to take a pride in your appearance.' She gets 'annoyed at ones who let themselves go. Usually they do take a pride in their appearances I think most people do. It's when they don't, well, then you worry about them, yeah because you know something's wrong.' Pride in your appearance is a sign of self-worth as well as how much you respect others.

For Dame Margaret Scott it's a habit. 'I wore make-up, I've always been conscious of clothing, and am always conscious of keeping a certain figure because that's habit for me now.' It's what she's always done, like brushing her teeth. Why would or should she stop?

People treat you better when you're well dressed, says Suzanne Simon. She describes how her husband had to go to hospital often in his last few years and, 'He would get ready and then I would come out and he would say, "We're not going to a fashion parade." I said, "Look, Alec, I have got to look well dressed, I think they take more notice of you when you are in hospital if I am well dressed rather than if I just turned up looking dishevelled."' Suzanne lovingly describes some tops she's bought to celebrate turning ninety. Many of the other women also love clothes but bemoan that there is not more choice available for them or places where they—women in their eighties and nineties—feel comfortable shopping and can find things they like.

All agree with Joyce McGrath: 'I just do my best to make myself look as good as I can.' This making the most of yourself means setting a personal standard, not one that can be judged by others. They believe that if you take the time and make the effort then you'll be rewarded with a sense of pride and self-esteem, and you'll make a better impression on others.

Becoming invisible

There's a certain time in a woman's life when her sense of pride and self-esteem takes a real knock. One of the ways older women describe the experience is in its most obvious sense: people don't see us. We go into cafés and shops and the staff—young people—look right through us, as though we have wrapped ourselves in cloaks of invisibility. One woman described sitting in a café and not being able to catch anyone's eye. After half an hour of watching everyone else being attended to, she dashed into the bathroom to look in a mirror to make sure she was actually visible. On the online site The Hoopla, Aidrie Grant wrote about not being served by the young men staffing the Dick Smith shop. In protest the fifty-eight year old turned off all the blaring televisions, sound systems and DVDs in the shop. She writes, 'I was quite blatant. I even turned off the flat-screen car racing in the middle of the store. Can anyone beat this record? Don't worry about being "caught". No one will even know you are in the shop.'[16] I wonder if she ever got to buy what she went in for?

We've all had this experience—many times. And it's not just us nobodies waiting to pay our bills, hands stretched out, watching the waiters walk on by. Actress Kristin Scott Thomas, who is fifty-three, says she also feels 'invisible'. 'I'm not talking about in a private setting, at a dinner party or anything. But when you're walking down the street, you get bumped into, people slam doors in your face—they just don't notice you,' she said. 'Somehow, you just vanish. It's a cliché, but men grow in gravitas as they get older, while women just disappear.'[17]

Not all women 'disappear' as they get older. Koho Yamamoto is determinedly against becoming invisible: 'I make noise so they will hear me.' When she was nineteen her art teacher in the internment camp told her 'not to walk so low' to 'walk tall and don't feel inferior' and so she does. Out there in the streets, on trains, in shops and public spaces Koho Yamamoto and the other fabulous fashionistas are wearing gorgeous and often outrageous look-at-me outfits. They turn heads and do not go unnoticed. What a wonderful antidote to invisibility. It takes a certain amount of chutzpah to be old and visible.

The women who talk and write about 'no longer being seen at all' are in their late forties and early fifties, the age of menopause. As Maxie Meldrum says, this invisibility is about feeling the loss of your sex appeal, or what Erica Jong, in her book *Fear of Fifty*, described as not being a 'babe' any more. We've all experienced it—that certain nothing where there used to be something. No flirty looks or smiles, no wolf whistles when you walk past building sites, and the immediate slippage away after a quick look when you enter a room. This disappearance of the male gaze is one of the reasons women get 'work' done. In a study of 2000 women in the United Kingdom, more than two-thirds of the women over forty-five experienced walking into a room and been 'completely unnoticed' by the opposite sex. By the time they reach fifty-one, many women believe they have become invisible to men.[18]

You'll be pleased to know that regret for this loss, if you have it, is a passing phase—you're over it by your sixties. And, by the time you get to be eighty-five, you will have long ago adjusted to not being a 'babe'. Frances Reynolds describes a different kind of invisibility: 'I get the feeling a little bit now that people know you're old and they're at a stage where they are going to be old like you shortly and they want to get more out of life, they're not, this sounds a bit mean I suppose, they don't want to be bothered with older people.' Middle aged and nearly old people often do not want to be around the old. They shun them because they don't want to recognise what old people represent: the inevitability of decline and dependence.

Many people of my age, those just starting on that last trimester, have expressed wonder at my interest in old 'ladies'. 'So depressing to be around,' they comment. This version of the invisible woman—and it applies to old men too—is more like Ralph Ellison's *Invisible Man*: the unnamed black man in the novel was not literally invisible but society refused to see him as anything but a stereotype. When you're old, people often only see and respond to a generic oldie—not you. What they see is an amalgam of their fears and prejudices of old women. And these are not pretty. To those who don't really see you, you might be a crone or biddy, old bag or old bat, old trout or old dear, a wrinkly—anything but an individual. This cultural revulsion was exposed and explored in Simone de Beauvoir's *The Coming of Age*, published in English in 1971. The women I spoke to, each in her unique style, show we've come a long way towards a happier old age than the abject misery described by de Beauvoir, not that there isn't still a ways to go.

If you're a woman over the 'babe' age I've got an experiment for you to try at parties: check how many men ask you anything about what you are doing? A couple of years ago my friend Marion pointed out to me that even men we know quite well, who are the husbands of our friends and who we see regularly at social events, never ask us anything about what we're doing. She is right. When the conversation isn't about a recent news story or scandal, some sporting event or a movie, it's me asking the man about his late-life crisis, his job or his trip or his grandchildren, and he always has plenty to say. I started introducing heavy hints—'I've nearly finished the second chapter of my book,' 'It was a rough week at work,' 'People management is the hardest for me.' Ninety per cent of my experiments get the response, 'Really, how interesting,' and then the man either moves off to talk to another group or continues on about himself. Note that this does not apply to all men—only 90 per cent of them. Of course, my husband says he isn't like this. But after making a conscious effort always to ask women what they are doing, he admits it's paid off for him. He's had many more interesting conversations.

Men tend to see the older woman as an ear to talk into and someone who wants to know stuff about their fascinating lives. Once you're no longer 'a babe' men don't have to pretend to be interested in you. But, when I asked Dame Margaret Scott whether people don't listen to her, she said, 'I have never experienced that.' Context and status make a difference in whether people, particularly men, listen to you and take you seriously. Being a Dame and famed for her work in ballet would make a difference. Margaret Barnett says that in surgeries and cocktail parties, 'I don't suffer that nearly as much as perhaps others in the community, once people find out I am a doctor.' It's less likely to happen in a work context, especially if you've achieved expert status like Beth Gott, who has no trouble being taken seriously in her field. It's not about how old you are but how powerful you are and the influence you can or might wield.

If you are being avoided and stereotyped, and not being listened to, then follow Dodo Berk's advice: stop making nice. Drop these people. Stay away from them at social events. Stick to people who are really listening to and seeing you—not some anonymous older woman—people who are interested in what you are doing and what you've got to say. Like so many messages about women, those about age and invisibility are mixed. It's more about how we are seen by whom and in what context. Being seen as a stereotypical old woman also brings a new visibility: people go out of their way to be good to you.

Maxie Meldrum says, 'I must say now I am invisible, except that people are so extraordinarily good to me, absolutely fantastic.' She describes how people help her to cross the road, and ask, 'Can I help you?' when they see she's having difficulty getting out of a car. 'I had a bad fall in Malvern and some woman came up and she went to a lot of trouble to take me to the next shop, and she said, "Look would you like me to drive you home?"' Other women describe similar good deeds and helpfulness. The women who appreciate this new visibility say that we need to accept this shift to some kinds of dependency. Even Dodo Berk—with one of her maxims being, 'Don't let anyone treat you like a shmatte', a rag—knows when she needs help to unscrew a jar or open a window, and asks for it.

Since I've been going grey, more people offer me their seats on public transport. Usually I wave them away although I try to be appreciative: 'Thanks so much but it's only a couple of stops.' Dealing with this new visibility is a challenge. I hope I wasn't too snappy with the usher who tapped my shoulder as I was heading for the stairs in the theatre and said, 'There's an elevator over there, ma'am.' And I tried to slough off the pointed laugher when I ran for the bus and heard, 'Hey, look at that grandma out running—watch her go!' This attention is new to me and not always welcome. I want to choose when I'm going to be dependent and when I'm going to be independent and not be trapped by stereotypes. Please wait for me to ask for help. I'll let you know if I want that seat or help with my luggage.

My experience is that the older I get, the nicer I have to be if I want good service. I can't be seen as a mean old crone. I'm not always able to stick to my own advice, which is when you're being ignored or overlooked don't get mad, get super sickly nice. When I do crack it, I know that I'm adding to those negative stereotypes. Another young person will strengthen their picture of crabby old women. Dodo Berk's advice is to always be interested in others— then you'll never be invisible. When I interviewed her, she took control and started asking me questions. She knows everyone in her apartment building and always has a question about their families. The gifts and cards she sends to hundreds of people on special occasions—graduations, births, deaths, birthdays, weddings and more—are expressions of her thoughtfulness and care. With one comment, one joke, Dodo breaks the stereotype wide open. You see Dodo, not a centenarian.

Many of the other women I spoke to have that star quality. People are drawn to Betty Walton's vivacity and want to talk to her. Koho Yamamoto is never invisible. She gets plenty of street attention and she's respected for her unique artistic skills. Margaret Fulton is always the centre of attention when she's in the room. No one could imagine Stephanie Charlesworth or Elisabeth Kirkby putting up with people not listening to them. These women don't feel invisible in most contexts—that's why they still care about what they look like and what others think of them.

As Elisabeth Kirkby says, 'I think what makes you feel attractive is if you are with somebody who is responsive and interested in you, is not just treating you like, you know, like a piece of furniture.' We must play our part now that we're fifty or sixty or seventy and look past the stereotypes, and fears, we have of women older than us. They're just as interesting and fun to be around, if not more, than we are.

HOT TIPS For keeping up appearances

➤ Be aware of how apt we are to make irrational snap judgements of people based on their exterior.

➤ Don't judge older women—your idea of 'growing old gracefully' may look like 'letting yourself go' to someone else.

➤ Don't feed into the can't-win trap: why shouldn't mutton be allowed a fashion frolic?

➤ Appearances do count, whether you are twenty or ninety-eight.

➤ We all care about how we look. Don't be ashamed or guilty about it.

➤ If you're an older women in public life or the media you'll need a thick skin as others will make a target of you.

➤ Know your milieu and then you can choose whether to conform, push the boundaries, or be a rebel.

➤ Don't agonise too much about the small stuff—hair can be re-coloured and re-cut.

➤ Practise how you'd like others to behave towards you when you are their age.

➤ Make yourself look at older women until you see beyond the stereotype—there is a real person in there.

➤ Agitate for a better representation of older women in all media. We are as knowledgeable, witty and smart as those old pontificating men.

➤ Make sure you support other women once they've put them-selves out there. Forget about political allegiances, and please stop commenting on Hillary's hairdo and Julia's bum.

➤ Provide opportunities for the non-voyeuristic representation of old women's bodies—flaws and all.

➤ Don't be afraid to be cool in summer—go sleeveless, wear shorts.

➤ Dare to be yourself and dress like a mouse, a witch or a diva, or even hide behind an exterior armour—clothes can be a great disguise.

➤ Making the effort to look good will make you feel better.

➤ Making the most of yourself will show that you are still engaged with the world and other people.

➤ Don't worry about losing the male gaze. The sense of loss will soon pass as you move on to a rich older age.

➤ If people aren't seeing you or listening to you, drop them. Find a more appreciative crowd to hang out with.

➤ At all costs avoid people who don't want to be around old people. You do not need the negativity.

➤ Show your interest and concern for others and they'll be inter-ested in you.

———————————

6

Home or a Home?

WHERE WE LIVE—OUR home—expresses who we are, perhaps even more so than how we dress. It's important in creating and sustaining our self-identity. Visiting my interviewees in the places they'd chosen to live, I find myself imagining living in new landscapes, buildings and rooms, weighing the consequences of one of the most serious decisions we will make: where to live when we're old.

On one of my visits, after driving an hour and a half from the centre of Melbourne on a miserably rainy day, I'm confronted by a squat grey block of a building in a treeless field of mud. Deep inside this building the woman I'm going to interview is waiting for me. In a more central location, some weeks later, I'm led through a foyer, wooden benches on all sides packed with old people staring into space. My interviewee takes me to her room, just big enough for her single bed, one narrow chair and a tiny bedside table.

First impressions are as powerful as the disinfectant used in homes for the aged. What's being covered up with a product so toxic it makes my eyes water and my nose run? This caustic smell feeds my stereotypes of what awaits us in our golden years if we can't stay in our own home. Even the smallest home I visit— Koho Yamamoto's minuscule two-room apartment in Greenwich Village, New York—is bigger than any room in those homes.

But it wasn't the small size of the rooms that disturbed me. In the leafier Melbourne suburbs are retirement homes with vast foyers where I'm an insignificant speck, making my way across expanses of marble flooring under atriums modelled on five-star Hyatt hotels—and just as impersonal. Every surface gleams, cold and hard except for the huge plush sofas I'm afraid to sit on—once I've sunk into them I might be trapped, not able to get out again.

After these visits I stomp about in shock and outrage. How could their children do this to them? How can anyone live in these places? My friends respond sensibly, calmly: 'The staff are wonderful,' 'They're not so bad,' 'The government mandates the room size.'

These aren't my first experience of homes—the word I use for institutional settings where old people live. When she decided she couldn't manage the flight of stairs to her flat any more, my friend Cyla and I toured several in Melbourne. We checked out the rooms and rose bush–filled gardens, and ate the grey food on fine china in wood-panelled dining rooms. I didn't like the places we visited but I wasn't churned up or angry. But this time around I'm twelve years older and the question is unavoidable: is this how I want to live?

The place we live can enable or restrict the quality of our lives in our seventies, eighties and nineties. Most of the women are happy with where they are living. They had to make choices, not all of which worked out. There's plenty to learn from their experiences—good and not so good.

Living with the children

Not one woman I spoke to is living with her children. Although Flo Howlett's mother lived in a bungalow at the back of her brother's place, she says, 'There is not one of my kids I would like to live with full time.' And she has five loving children. After the Howletts sold their house and were waiting for the old-age home they planned to move into to be built, Flo and her husband lived for three months with one of their daughters. Flo did not like it at all, and not just because, 'I wouldn't like to live in a house with stairs.' Flo describes how her daughter was out all day at work and didn't get home until 6.30 or 7 p.m. 'And then, of course, all my life tea-time was six o'clock. Not that we waited, we had our meal. It's not the same when you're living in someone else's house, not doing what you want to do, how you want to do it.' At the old-age home there are activities to join and people to chat to and have morning tea with, if and when Flo chooses, as well as dinner being served nice and early, as she likes it.

'You have to be in charge of yourself,' is Dodo Berk's forceful advice. After Hurricane Sandy wrecked the apartment building in Lido Beach, New York, where she's lived for over fifty years, she refused to move in with her daughter. Dodo's daughter would have welcomed her for the eight months it was going to take to make the building habitable. But Dodo's mantra is, 'Old age can be beautiful if you're living by yourself and you're happy and you're not living other people's lives.' Instead she chose to move to the empty apartment that had belonged to her dead sister on the Upper East Side of New York City with no television and little furniture, a feisty ninety-eight year old, happy to be on her own.

The women are part of a huge shift that has nothing to do with the selfishness of younger generations not wanting to care for their parents, or the breakdown of family ties. People like their privacy and this well-documented trend has far more to do with the old choosing other options once they can afford them. US data shows this trend very clearly. During the fifty years before the US Social Security Act of 1935, the living arrangements of elderly widows were virtually unchanged. Roughly 10 per cent lived alone, 70 per cent with adult children, and the rest in institutions or with other individuals. Beginning in the 1940s, the social security pension allowed people who were no longer working to maintain independent households. The percentage of elderly widows living alone rose from 18 per cent in 1940 to 62 per cent in 1990.[1]

In the land of Confucius, and amid expectations of filial piety, old-age homes are going up even faster than other buildings in China. Again, it's more about industrialisation and women working than the self-centredness of the younger generation. Children are living far from their parents, and daughters and daughters-in-law are working long hours. There's no one at home to look after the elderly parent however loved they might be.

Living with the children is still the norm within some ethnic communities and for those who need to do it for financial reasons. One side-effect of the economic downtown in the United States was a rise in multigenerational households. Over the past few years older parents have begun moving in with their adult children again. In 2008, 4.05 million parents were living with an adult child. By the end of 2011, the number had risen to 4.6 million—a 13.7 per cent increase.[2] I'm betting they aren't sharing bathrooms.

Flo Howlett expresses it perfectly when she talks about how we value our space and independence, and have our preferences and routines. I can't stay in anyone else's house for more than a few days without feeling grumpy and constrained by their rituals and habits.

Living in the family house

All the women have owned their own homes but not many are now living in the family home. Lady Florence Bjelke-Petersen and Margaret Fulton are among the few living in the homes in which they brought up their families. For both it's made possible by having their families nearby, as well as other supports and assistance.

Lady Flo lives on the family farm not far out of Kingaroy in Queensland, in a 1950s yellow brick house. She tells how her husband, 'built this house, sixty years ago now, and I have lived here all my married life'. Next door—a driveway's width away—is *Bethany*, the old homestead where her husband grew up. Now her son John, his wife and their five children live in *Bethany*, right next door to Lady Flo. Two of her daughters are five minutes' drive away and usually drop in every day. Lady Flo appreciates having three of her four children nearby: 'Well if you can stay in your own home it's wonderful, there is no doubt about that.' It helps that she has Meals on Wheels delivered three times a week, and a woman in weekly to do the washing and cleaning. Men who work for her son John on the farm also look after the upkeep of the large grounds surrounding the house.

Pointing out the plate-glass picture window she says, 'I am very blessed to have that. My place here, where it's lovely to look out on this all around and look at the nice green grass and think well it's lovely here. When you go over to the window you can see the town and the district and the background and see the lights there at night time.' From this prime spot she can look up from reading her book and watch her grandchildren jumping on the trampoline or playing in the dam.

Margaret Fulton bought her Balmain house with 'the best view in Sydney' forty years ago. Her cosy home is filled with loved objects and furniture collected over a long life. Windows and French doors bring light into the woodsy kitchen that's more country farmhouse than high-tech stainless steel. Best of all are the views of Sydney Harbour and the bridge from the back windows and deck. Just like Lady Flo, Margaret has her family close by. 'I always thought I needed my family around me,' she says. 'My daughter lives two doors down and my granddaughter lives in a flat I bought with just the same view as me.' Margaret says, 'I love being here,' and feels safe and happy in her known environment with her family able to pop in easily.

Kali Paxinos, Dame Margaret Scott and Frances Reynolds also still live in the family home and each has someone living with them—Kali with her son Peri and Dame Margaret and Frances with their husbands. You can see why Frances and John Reynolds haven't considered moving from the home they've lived in since 1970. Having been built as a 'model' house, it's very light and bright. Being on a battleaxe block means there is no big garden to maintain; instead they have all the benefits of the beautiful park that backs onto their property without any of the work.

Joan Lowrie is a stayer. Born in the front room of a house in St Kilda, she has lived all her life in this suburb, and almost ninety years in this house. 'We came here paying rent of 2 pound 5 shilling a week.' When the owner said he was selling and they'd have to move out, the whole family got together the deposit to buy it for £3500. Her father and mother, and her husband, died there. Once there were aunts and cousins living nearby but now there's just Joan. Her Victorian cottage is in a suburb once known for sailors and prostitutes. Now it's gentrified with Joan probably having the least renovated house in the whole street. Except for a brief visit to hospital in 2013 to have a melanoma removed, she hasn't been away from her home for decades. There's no central heating and Joan stays in bed on days when it's really cold. She tells me about her neighbours, away on holidays in France and Italy—places she's never been.

When I first met Joan in 2012 she wasn't living alone. She had taken in Marie, a dithery woman in her sixties on a slow slide into alcoholism and dementia who had previously lived across the road. 'I'd be too frightened to stay here on my own now. I wouldn't like to stay on my own,' Joan told me then. Two years later, Marie is in a home and Joan, at ninety-four, is living alone in her home and intends to stay there. Joan can do this success-fully because she has the supports she needs, and she also found that she's not nervous at being on her own at night. Her cheerful carer Rosie comes on four days of the week to do anything Joan wants—cleaning, washing, banking, organising repairs, cooking and shopping, which includes picking out new clothes. Rosie is provided through the government-run Home and Community Care program (HACC) and, because Joan has a Department of Veterans' Affairs Gold Card, all these services are free.

Joan's close-knit neighbourhood is as important as this formal support. A few years ago the ceiling of Joan's kitchen collapsed. One phone call mobilised the neighbours and the local electrician made the house safe, others took her food home to store, and a cleaning bee had the kitchen spick and span in two hours. Joan is happy, busy with the comings and goings of friends and loved and well looked after in the 'hood'.

With the right set up you can stay in the family home for as long as you like. You'll need to have someone living with you or people very close by who care about and for you. At some stage you will also need others to help you with the shopping, cleaning, cooking, gardening and home repairs—all the many things that looking after a house requires. Whether staying in the family home is the best option for you is another question.

Location, location, location

The search for the perfect place to spend the years when you're no longer in paid work has led people to move large distances. Hundreds of thousands of retirees have packed their bags and left homes in England to move to the South of France and the Caribbean, to shift from Chicago to Arizona or Florida, from Melbourne to Queensland, and from Los Angeles to Mexico. As we've got wealthier our horizons about the golden lands where we can live out our golden years have expanded to take in the whole world.

Moving to a new town or state is more the norm in the United States than it is in Australia. You only need to spend one winter in the north of the United States or Canada to understand why people flock south. For months you can't get out of the front door without shovelling snow, only to then battle the sleet in your face, below freezing temperatures and, should you actually make it onto the street, black ice for you to slip on and break your bones. Once you're no longer spending your week inside working, good weather becomes more important to you. As well as warmer weather, people are looking for lower taxes, which vary from state to state in the United States. Other factors that count are cheaper real estate, lower crime rates, the quality of health care and the availability of part-time work.[3]

One person's heaven is another person's hell. In this case, mine. Florida, for example, is usually hot and very humid. Spending most of the year inside with the air conditioning blasting is not my idea of fun. And much of the state is covered in high-rise buildings and freeways and, around Miami especially, very smoggy. People moved from Sydney and Melbourne to the northern beaches of New South Wales and Queensland to escape the dirt and noise, the hustle and bustle of urban life. The irony is that because of these population shifts, initiated by retirees, the places they moved to have become more and more like the places they left.

Not one woman I spoke to ever considered moving permanently somewhere warmer or interstate. They chose the known over the unknown. If you want new adventures, dream of Byron Bay or a house in the woods then go for it. But do a test run and rent for six months before selling up permanently.

Moving near the kids

One reason women are less likely to move far is their deeper and wider connection to their children, grandchildren and siblings, the mother-daughter bond being the strongest of all.[4] Of the women who have moved away from their family home and suburb, some have done this to be nearer to their children. And although no one wanted to move in with the kids, being nearer to them was important, especially for widows when they sold the family home. But there's a warning story, which you may have heard, of the retired parents moving from Sydney to Perth to be near their daughter and her family. Two years later the son-in-law's job was relocated back to Sydney but the elderly parents could not afford to move back because of the huge difference in house prices. Before you go moving your life across the continent make sure your kids are staying put.

On the surface this is also April Hamer's story. She lived her married life—sixty years—in a large two-storey house in Kew in the east of Melbourne. After her husband died the house was too big and too much work for her alone. Her son-in-law suggested she move to a house being sold opposite them in Alphington. But family circumstances and needs often change and, a year after April moved, her daughter and her family moved to St Andrews on the outskirts of Melbourne, 35 kilometres away. But April Hamer loved the small, liveable, light-filled house, in 'a very nice strip to live in', close to a shopping centre and public transport. She also says, 'My darling niece, my only sister's only daughter, lives a couple of doors down the road, just by chance. I didn't even think of that or weigh it up [when moving in], and she's been very good.' Despite not being nearer to her children, where she is has served her needs well for ten years after her husband died.

When I asked May Lowe if there's anything she regrets, she tells me that she would have loved to have stayed in the area she grew up and lived in until she was eighty. 'I really love that area down Port Melbourne and Albert Park, it's a lovely area, but that's not possible now because I have come here because I am closer to my family. They are all closer to me, whereas down in Albert Park I didn't see them much because I was too far away from them.' When May moved to Kew, she was a widow whose big house was too much for her to look after, and her only daughter had left

Middle Park for Brisbane. May moved within a few blocks of one son, and much closer to her other two sons. She has never driven a car. Every day until she was ninety-two, and no longer mobile enough, May caught the bus from Kew to Port Melbourne—a 45-minute trip each way. 'I do miss Port Melbourne but there's no good drooling about it because I can't go back.'

What a hard choice: stay in the area you love and where you have all your connections and networks and not see much of your children, or move nearer to your children, to a part of the city where you have no roots and know no one. Why didn't May find a small place in Port Melbourne and take taxis to visit her sons regularly? On the good side, May has coped well with losing Port Melbourne, and has made a new life for herself on the other side of town.

For Beth Gott moving nearer her daughter has been a great success, mainly because it was only one among a number of reasons for moving to her current home. Beth sold her family home in St Kilda and like May moved to the other side of the city and the river, to North Carlton. In North Carlton she is closer to her daughter and they spend each Saturday together food shopping and having lunch out. Beth already knew the area well from attending, and teaching at, nearby Melbourne University. More importantly, close friends 'had come down from Canberra and they were moving in here, and they were very enthusiastic. They thought it was good here and I was rattling around in my house. I thought maybe I will settle and move in here and it's been very good.' The area is very well served by public transport with nearby shops, and it's a short tram ride to the cinema and the city.

Both April, fortuitously, and Beth, with planning, had other people apart from the children who lived nearby. As well, the places they moved to were well located for transport, shops, recreational and other needs. This meant that their location shift worked even if the kids moved away.

Moving near your family

After working for twenty-five years in Hong Kong, Jean Allison decided to come home. She'd seen the poor choices made by her expatriate friends, the widows and the single women. Either they ended up in nursing homes in England, where they knew nobody, or in the less than salubrious China Coast Hostel in Hong Kong. She says, 'You should go home when you are about sixty, when it's not too late to adapt to going home, and when you can adapt to realising it's not home anymore but you've got to make it home.'

At sixty-six Jean came back to Berwick on the outskirts of Melbourne, where some years earlier she'd bought the house next door to her sister, and had rented it until she was ready to move. She had thought it all through carefully. Three years later she left Berwick. 'I couldn't stand living there,' she says. 'It was just so quiet, I couldn't sleep.' Jean adds, 'I just didn't fit in,' and describes, 'how all the people living there were my age or older and I wasn't used to associating with old people.'

Living next door to her sister was not enough. Instead, Jean has lived since 1996 in centrally located and lively South Yarra, where she designed and built the perfect house for a single woman. Once you see Jean's house you'll know that she's not at all the conventional old lady she may appear to be. Although two storeys, everything Jean needs is downstairs—a large open-plan kitchen and living/dining room with a study alcove to the side for her computer and office. Also downstairs are her bedroom and bathroom and the laundry. Upstairs, for her friends who come to stay or the carer she might need in the future, are another two rooms and a bathroom.

Like Jean we need to be flexible enough to know that, however carefully thought out, Plan A might not work. So far Jean's Plan B is going well but should her finances take a dip or her health deteriorate she will adapt to Plan C. Other older people in

Australia and the United States are also leaving the suburbs for the city. They are trading in their lawnmowers for proximity to transport, restaurants and culture.

Moving your kids near you

You can have it all—a location you know and love, and your family—if your children move near to you. This can be an attractive proposition to them, as they love and feel responsible for you, and because it's pretty handy to call on you for grandchildren minding and school pick-ups. For some years, definitely in your sixties and seventies and perhaps even longer, you can help your children out and spend time with your grandchildren. Later, you may be the one who needs help and it's easier to keep an eye on an elderly parent living within walking distance.

A friend recently bought a flat in the same block as her parents who are in their nineties. The thrilled parents will move to the newly bought two-bedroom flat on the ground floor while their daughter and her husband will take up residence in their three-bedroom flat upstairs. It's a happy solution all round, especially for the elderly parents who fortunately live in an area that is seen as desirable by the younger generation. I am unlikely to achieve this enviable state. My children have determinedly moved north of the city, close to where all their friends live, and interstate. Margaret Fulton was prescient, and wealthy enough to plan ahead. As she said, she always wanted her family near her and decades ago organised for her daughter and family to move into the same street.

Bertha Lowitt has lived in Brooklyn, New York, almost all her life. For the past fifty years she has lived on the sixteenth floor of an apartment building right next to the subway and one stop from Manhattan. Her daughter and son-in-law live on the twentieth floor of the same building and her grandson on State Street, within walking distance. It's also only a short walk to shops and restaurants. Bertha loves her neighbourhood. The restaurant where she has lunch every Thursday and the one she dines in each Friday, 'treat me as if I was the Queen of Sheba,' she says.

She also loves the building she lives in: 'The building is wonderful, the staff. Now especially when they see me coming in they come out to help me.' She describes her spacious two-bedroom apartment with its panoramic views across the Brooklyn Bridge and over Manhattan as 'gorgeous'. Bertha plans to die right here. As well as having her daughter upstairs, the building has everything she needs—lifts, someone to open doors and collect and carry parcels. She has her cleaner, her exercise group, and her book club, and she is surrounded by people she knows from the half-century she's been living here.

The choice of where to live is wide open for a single woman without children or siblings like Joyce McGrath. Because of her disability, Joyce wanted somewhere she didn't have to mow the lawn. As soon as she saw the house that backed onto the golf course she fell in love with 'this beautiful little house'. Very sensibly, Joyce planned ahead, renting the house out for ten years until her loan was paid, 'and then I came to live here and it's been heaven on earth ever since'. Good planning, though, as Jean Allison will testify, can go bad.

Now that Joyce can't drive or walk far, she can't get out of the house without help. The responsibilities of home ownership are weighing on her, especially the hole in her ceiling made by the possums. Would it be better for her to move to a more central location—a retirement home or unit with lifts, doors wide enough for a wheelchair and staff to get taxis for her when she needs them? 'I really would like some regular card players,' she admits, but knows nobody nearby who she could invite over. If she lived in a complex like Bertha's or Beth's, she'd have plenty of card players on tap.

Joyce has weighed up her options and is not going to move until she absolutely has to. 'I am quite happy here,' she says pointing to the greenery and bush she can see through her big windows. 'It's lovely here, I have all sorts of birds; I have lorikeets and cockatoos and rosellas.'

Someone living with you

Bertha's plan to stay right where she is includes hiring someone to live in and care for her if that proves necessary. This is an affordable option in the United States, where cheap carers are easy to find. In Australia choosing to be cared for full time in your home, like June Helmer, is only for the wealthy. There are award wages and overtime to be paid and the costs will skyrocket if you need someone overnight with you as well. Among the very old, those older than ninety, people say they are less content and that they find life more difficult if they live alone. Having other people around is important for a sense of wellbeing.[5]

Barbara Hamer has always had someone living with her, usually 'people I have taken under my wing because they were needy'. When she lived in bigger houses she needed people to look after the garden and the dogs as she was often away. 'I've always had people round, never allowed myself to be totally alone.' At the moment she has someone living with her who she 'got through Wesley Home Share, and she was vetted before she came to me so she is not a needy person'. Joan Lowrie was also in the habit of caring for people: her mother, her husband, her next-door neighbour and, most recently, her companion, Marie. I have several friends who've taken in students and later refugees. It brings in a little money and you don't come home to an empty house. For this option to be viable you need to have the room in your home, to enjoy sharing your space with others and want the company.

Downsizing

When my youngest turned eighteen, we moved out of the family home and it was all my idea. I was more than ready to say good-bye to the big house on the large block of land and the suburb we'd lived in for twenty years. The too-quiet house, with its neat, empty bedrooms sighing for daughters who'd once reigned in them chaotically, gave me the creeps. I couldn't and didn't want to spend every weekend in the garden. Those days were over. My back hurt after an hour's weeding, and there was always more weeding. Enough already I said and on my fiftieth birthday dragged my husband kicking and screaming to a much smaller house with a tiny garden by the sea. Fortunately he loved it too, once he got used to it. Eighteen years later I see that I was a typi-cal empty nester, downsizing.

That's also what most of the women did. They moved into smaller places, lighter and brighter, with lifts, closer to transport and with little or no outside space to maintain. Like me, Jean Allison and Barbara Hamer wanted a change of scene. Barbara gave up the burden of an 'enormous family mansion' and in 1992 chose to move to South Yarra, the suburb where she'd gone to school and where she feels a sense of home and belonging. 'It's lovely, I've been very happy here', she says, about her upper-storey sunny flat.

This is not change for change's sake but a recognition that your capacities and your needs are changing. After thirty years on ten acres on the Bellarine Peninsula, Dorothy Shultz and her husband were very sad about leaving 'the most beautiful old house'. Because it was an hour and half's walk from any public transport, 'we decided to do it before we had to'. Their children live in various locations so they chose Queenscliff, a country town not far from their old property, with restaurants, shops and services within walking distance, plus a bus service to Melbourne. The Shultz's also have a pied-à-terre in the city where they usually spend one night a week and go to the theatre or art exhibitions, and visit friends and family.

Most common of all among the women—and a hot current trend according to real estate agents—is staying in the same area. Betty Walton, Maxie Meldrum and Stephanie Charlesworth are among those who chose to stay in their local communities, downsizing from a large family home to a single-level apartment. They got rid of the burden of maintenance while remaining close to the networks and relationships they'd built up over the years.

Maxie Meldrum has always lived in the Malvern-Toorak area of Melbourne. About her move to the flat she says, 'It was a brilliant thing to do. Every twenty years the house needed to be redone, it was getting old and the garden was getting beyond me. It was too much. We were old you know.' Maxie was in her mid seventies when she moved to the corner top flat, 'thrilled with this lovely view and all this light'.

'We lived in an enormous house,' says Betty Walton, until her husband said, 'I'm sick of fixing the back door.' Encouraged by their son, they moved to something more manageable, and now live in a flat not far from their former home and one block back from the beach. Pressure from their children finally convinced Stephanie and her husband Max Charlesworth to move from their home of thirty years. Their children felt, 'you needed to move to something simple while you could still manage, with a lift'. Like Betty and Maxie, they've stayed in their neighbourhood.

Retirement home living

For years my friends have talked about moving into a block of flats together or buying something we can renovate to suit our needs. The trouble is we can't even agree on the suburb we want to live in or when to make this move. It's a big financial commitment for something that may not work out if we don't get along. And perhaps it's unnecessary. There are many existing options for independent living. Bertha Lowitt, Maxie Meldrum, Barbara Hamer and others don't live in retirement homes, they live in blocks of flats with lifts and a caretaker or concierge. So what's the difference and why choose a retirement home?

Frances Reynolds sounded wistful telling me her husband 'wouldn't think of' living in a retirement village. Her parents had lived in one happily and so does her older sister. 'She's got her own house that's as big as this, and her husband died two years ago, and I think it's very good. She does everything for herself, but if he fell out of bed, she only had to get on the phone, someone came and got him up for her. Things like that.'

A major reason for moving into a retirement home is the desire to feel secure. Your flat or house could have an excellent security system that allows you to vet people getting in but it's unlikely to have an alert button in each room. Nor will there be 24-hour help on hand to respond. In the home you'll have buzzers to press and sensors set to detect lack of movement so that if you fall, someone will phone and raise the alarm if there's no response.

May Lowe and Margaret Barnett both live in the same retirement home in the eastern suburbs of Melbourne. This home's motto is, 'Independent living in a lifestyle you're accustomed to.' Living here is promoted as being 'like membership in a private club'. It's certainly very quiet. In the thirty minutes I spent in the foyer with its beautiful light fittings, I saw three people. This quietness and lack of activity is something Betty Friedan also noticed on visiting hundreds of specially designed retirement communities across the United States.[6] Once past the impressive foyers the décor standard usually drops, with the corridors and flats themselves being comfortable and well appointed rather than glitzy.

Margaret Barnett chose this home because it's close to where she lived 'in her big family home'. Even after years she hasn't quite adjusted: 'I feel a bit sort of closed in here.' The payoff for losing the space is peace of mind: 'I get very anxious when I am by myself,

I don't like it.' Pets are welcome and she has her cat Jacques to keep her company and has furnished her flat with her antiques and her collection of Australian landscape paintings, 'so now it looks a bit like a gallery'. Margaret only occasionally cooks for herself because, 'We can go downstairs and have lunch and dinner provided on five days a week.' There's a group of people she sits with for meals and 'we all mix together in the lounge room'. Margaret appreciates being able to walk out and just leave the flat when she travels, knowing everything is safe and will be looked after.

May is ten years older than Margaret, and the oldest resident at the home. After deciding that the stairs to the flat she lived in a few streets away were getting too much for her, she chose this home for herself and says, 'I love it.' 'I am well looked after, I have got some nice friends and two of them in particular, they are old enough to be my daughters.' May enjoys Friday nights when they have fish and chips 'and all we talk about is football'. As far as May is concerned the home she is in is perfect. 'They have got a beautiful kitchen out there. I feel as though I have done everything I want to do, I am just happy as I am going along, just glide along.'

Like most people who move into retirement homes, May and Margaret are single and looking for security and company but not wanting to move to anything that smacks of an old-age home. Facilities and services are among the reasons people give for moving to 'luxury' retirement homes with their indoor heated pools, in-house cinemas, gourmet catering, libraries, bars and coffee shops, well-equipped gyms, and wellness centres. Homes like the one May and Margaret live in are not cheap. In May 2014, in one such home, the prices started at $550,000 for a one-bedroom flat going up to $1million for a top-floor three-bedroom one with large terraces. You pay a weekly maintenance fee that covers basic services like meals, staff, heating and lighting. Extra fees are charged for cleaning, serving meals to your room and similar 'extra services'. Retirement homes also charge a departure fee, so watch out for this in your financial calculations.

A central characteristic of retirement homes has been catering for one age group: the old. Today this covers an enormous age range from fifty-five to over 100. And the age range is going to widen even further as more young families and professionals choose to move into complexes that are exactly like retirement homes. American friends have bought into Kensett Darien, a development perfectly suited to them as local residents, when they were 'looking to downscale while maintaining their connectivity to the town and providing enough bedrooms for visiting family'. Kensett Darien will have a sixty/forty mix of empty nesters and younger families and professionals. 'Families today often have two working parents or one working parent that works long hours and commutes to New York,' says the developer. 'Those families are not necessarily look-ing for a large yard and the work associated with a larger home.'[7]

By my standards these are very large homes, some with four bedrooms and five bathrooms and lifts to the three floors. When Kensett was launched in 2012 prices started at $US1.3 million. The appeal for my friends, who are leaving an even bigger house on acres of land, is getting rid of the responsibility for any grounds, plus maintenance support for their house, especially in winter. As well, there's the train to New York City five minutes away, a top-class pool and gym, plus a conservation area all around with wooded walking paths. And my friend has already bagged one of the vegetable gardening plots on offer.

Beth Gott chose a multi-storey newly built home because of its location and because she had friends there who recommended it highly. She'd been on the waiting list for an older home in a nearby suburb, where she also had friends living. On balance she chose the one that offered more space, especially for all her books. 'I love being on the top floor,' she says, where she has a wide terrace full of plants and three bedrooms, one of which she uses as a study. 'I also have a small balcony off my bedroom, which is devoted entirely to geraniums.'

Although there is no swimming pool—Beth swims at the local baths three times a week—and it is less glamorous and with fewer facilities than other homes, what Beth has found here, and what she appreciates, is the community. 'It's been a good decision because there are lots of people here who I can communicate with. I thought I am not going to go anywhere where I cannot communicate and there are a lot of university people. It's a good atmosphere and it's run well and there are panic buttons and things.' Beth cooks meals for herself and she goes down for morning coffee every day. 'There are all sorts of people you can talk too—we have got a book club going and lots of people here who are at my own level.' When I spoke to her she was looking forward to a Christmas in July.

If you are looking for greater security, facilities and services on the spot, and a built-in community, then the retirement home option may suit you. They exist at all price levels, in a wide variety of designs and environments, and for specific ethnicities and language speakers. You can find them in cities, suburbs and country towns all over Australia and the United States. The big difference in Australia between retirement homes (independent living) and aged-care homes is that no government subsidy is provided for retirement homes. You pay your own way entirely.

Aged-care homes: low or assisted care

Aged-care homes, providing respite, low, high, and dementia care, are Commonwealth Government approved and registered and receive government funding. You can't just decide that you feel like moving into an aged-care home. To be admitted you need an assessment that you are 'at risk' or not able to manage on your own at home. You will also need to make a full disclosure of all your assets so the government can determine how much you will contribute to the costs of your care. People move into aged-care homes for much the same reasons they choose residential homes. Often it's to ease the burden on children.

'I am really happy here,' Flo Howlett says about the aged-care home she's been living in for four years, 'but at the same time if you look around, it gets the kids off the hook.' The experience of watching her daughter-in-law deal with supporting an ageing mother at home convinced Mary Broughton that she didn't want to put her children through this. 'My poor daughter-in-law, her mother wouldn't go into a home, and she didn't like people coming in.' Mary put the interests of her children first. 'I don't think I really wanted to come here,' she says, 'but it's a good idea for my family. I have a son and a daughter, I think it's fair for them.'

From my observations it's much more likely that you'll stay in your own home if you don't have kids. Because Flo and Mary care about their children, they are taking their children's needs into account, as well as their own. If Joyce McGrath had had children, she'd be unlikely to still be living at home. There are risks you can take for yourself that your loved ones will not be able to handle.

Often the catalyst for deciding to move into an aged-care home is a fall or a medical problem that can't be managed at home. After sharing the burden of looking after a good friend reduced to 'immobility and incontinence' and then getting a bad enough flu to 'be reduced to helplessness' herself, the writer Diana Athill put her name down for a room at an old people's home. When the letter arrived offering her 'one of their best rooms, with big windows looking out over the garden and a balcony large enough for several flower pots and a chair,' she went into shock. 'The extent to which a personality depends on the space it occupies and the objects it possesses appeared to me at that moment overwhelming. How could I perform an act of what amounted to self-destruction? The answer was: I can't! I can't and I won't. I'd rather die.' To make this move, Diana Athill would have had to divest herself of almost everything, pare her life to one room that 'would hold a single bed, a desk, two chairs plus a desk chair—and that was that'.[8]

Diana Athill is not alone in finding it traumatic to reduce her life to one room and a bathroom. Ten years ago an aged-care home had three beds to a room, whereas now the single room with en-suite is the norm. Standards have improved greatly and the aged-care home market is as competitive as that for retirement homes. Some of the newest aged-care homes offer two- and three-bedroom suites, with most of the facilities of the five-star retirement homes.[9]

Increasing options mean that you can find a home without having to move from your neighbourhood. Flo Howlett can look out her window and see the chimney of the factory where she started work, now a Bunnings Warehouse. She prides herself on knowing this patch, which she's lived in for ninety years. Sister Mary Gregory's home is not run by the Catholic or any other church. 'I chose to come here myself because I have a network of friends and I am involved in things and groups around here.' The policy of her Order 'is now that we stay somewhere we feel at home'.

All the women in aged-care homes were over ninety. Unless they have dementia, people are not going into aged-care homes until they are very old and frail. The average 85-year-old woman will spend about a year and a half in an institution.[10] Homes now offer 'Aging in Place', or as the women bluntly name it: 'Until Death Do Us Part.' Flo Howlett says, 'Well we know we're all in here till we die so I'm very realistic aren't I?' For Mary Broughton it is very important to be 'somewhere where they will look after me until the end'. Modern aged-care homes provide the extra care you need in your room or elsewhere in the same building or complex.

Meanwhile there is plenty of living still to be done, with the security that you'll be well looked after when the time comes. Flo has blossomed in the home. She runs twice weekly armchair exercise classes, once weekly word game sessions, sings in the choir and participates in most activities. Here, she has found the community that she feels she lost as her Coburg neighbourhood changed. Flo is knitting a baby jumper not for a grandchild but for one of the nurses. 'I help the nurses clear the tables. It doesn't hurt you, it's only five minutes,' Flo says, when she takes me into morning tea and introduces me to her friends.

You need to choose something that suits you in an old-age home and April Hamer did just that. She visited a number of homes and on seeing the luxury versions in the eastern suburbs told her daughter that 'not in a blue fit' would she live there. She chose a small home with wonderful staff in the suburb she's come to love. Her daughter says that because April responds to having people around, she is so much happier in a home than she was on her own.

Your past life will make a difference as to how well and how quickly you take to living in a home. Sister Mary Gregory has lived communally since she joined the Order of the Good Samaritans at age twenty-one. Within six weeks she's quite settled in and avails herself of the exercise classes twice a week. She explains just how ready she was to move. 'I feel much more relaxed. It's extraordinary. I was at home and I was answering the phone and directing people, and getting involved in things. I enjoyed cooking a meal and that kind of thing. Though I must say that became more of a burden as time went on, but I don't have to worry about any of that here. I am much more relaxed, I am enjoying life.' Sister Mary is used to sharing her space, having her meals at set times and making the compromises that living in a home require.

Mary Broughton, who has been in her aged-care home for about the same amount of time as Sister Gregory, says, 'In a way I'm quite sad I came.' Having lived alone for fifty years, Mary is not used to communal living. People already have their set groups in the dining rooms for meals and so far she hadn't found a niche there, although she's been assured that 'the next person who comes into the home, I'll get someone brought to my table who I can talk to'. For Mary Broughton the sudden loss of independence was a shock. 'It's very difficult to get used to people doing things for you.'

Diana Athill wrote about finally divesting herself of almost everything she owned and after a very stressful period moving into the home. 'I knew that it was going to suit me. And sure enough, it does. A life free of worries in a snug little nest (my room really is charming), good friends among my neighbours, freedom to do everything I'm still capable of doing, and knowing one will be beautifully looked after if necessary: what could be better?'[11]

Dependence and independence

Each of us gives different weight to the freedom to do what we want to do versus a life free from worries. From mid April to December each year Dodo Berk lives in her apartment at Lido Beach, an hour's drive from New York City. In her home of over fifty years, she knows everyone and everyone knows her. She's their beloved icon and guru. The other months she lives in Five Star Senior Living in Florida. This retirement community has everything you could possibly want with bells and whistles, but Dodo doesn't like it. Dinner is at 4.30 p.m. because the staff need to leave at 6 p.m. But, even worse than the regimentation, there's no company for her.

Dodo says this alleged independent living home is full of people who are 'sick'. Most have carers, walkers and wheelchairs. Dodo won't mix with them and won't eat with them because all they do is complain. This lively centenarian doesn't want to spend her time with the whiners. When she attends the entertainments she nicks out five minutes before the end to avoid the wheelchair crush and having to listen to grumpy, rude people who are not engaged in life. Their complaints drive her crazy.

She is fiercely independent. She doesn't want to be told when to eat, or what to eat, or what to do but she does recognise that she is dependent on others to do many things—drive her places, open jars and windows, fetch and carry. Those New York winters are very harsh and Dodo knows she would be trapped in her apartment. I interviewed Dodo not long before she was leaving for Florida and she said, 'I hope I can find a friend there this time.'

Even more fervently opposed to living in a home than Dodo is Bertha Lowitt. 'I refuse ever to go into one of those living places. I had some friends who lived in those places and as nice as they were—they have their own apartment, their dinners and their meals were there—but no, not for me. I will stay here, as long as I can.' Bertha likes to cook and shop and do things for herself, even though she is seriously deaf and can't walk far or up stairs. What she really hates, at the age of ninety-six, is to be with old people. 'Most of the people who go into these places are you know—old. The minute you meet someone, this hurts me, that hurts me, I just had this.' She wants to be with her younger friends. 'They're wonderful. I mean they look up to you with respect, and in a certain sense love, and it's a wonderful feeling to have young people around. And you become part of what they're doing.' Bertha plans to employ someone to live in if need be in her second bedroom. 'There are many people in this building who have home attendants.' She'll be dependent on this person for almost everything but what counts for Bertha is that she will be in charge.

Even though Maxie Meldrum's husband was happy in what she considers was 'the best nursing home', she certainly wouldn't be. 'Some people are prepared to do it, I am not. I would have no one to talk too,' she says. 'I mean people in a nursing home they chat about the football, and I don't care about football. I have got no one that wants to talk to me nor that I have got anything to say to them. I suppose I am an intellectual snob but I just can't be bothered. It's boring, for God's sake.' Maxie understands that she may have to go into care 'if I get less able to do the things that I am interested in, if I become incontinent'. Like Bertha and Dodo, Maxie doesn't want to live communally, to have to be nice to people she doesn't care about, and to abide by imposed rules and schedules.

The future

We can look forward to greater diversity in housing for our old age. There'll be more choice because in future we'll demand more options and the clout of numbers and money means that we'll get them. In Australia the demand for community care will continue to grow—more and more people who are old want supports to help them stay in their own homes. This is also a much more affordable option for the government, which through service provision, bed subsidies and the pension, pays for 80 per cent of the costs of aged care. Providing integrated and affordable care at home will help us live independently for as long as possible. Technology will be part of this future and will support independence in the home.

The prediction is that only the severely demented and the very old and frail will be in aged-care homes. There'll be care in your home and high care. Low care like that now enjoyed by Flo Howlett, Sister Mary Gregory and Mary Broughton will disappear. 'Ageing in place' is not only a cheaper option, it's the preferred one. People want to live like Joan Lowrie and Rose Stone—at home. Rose is still independent at ninety-two and able to enjoy all the familiar delights of her lively multi-ethnic, multi-generational area with its busy street life, excellent transport, shops and restaurants. Not far away is Joan, who though housebound and dependent on a daily care regime, is still in charge. Joan can eat what and when she wants, see who she likes at all hours, and raise the volume on her television sky high.

Resort-like homes will be there for the super rich and for special groups. There'll be more lifestyle-focused homes like those being built on college campuses, with the pitch: 'Live like a senior, feel like a student.' With more people living in flats and units there'll be more NORCS: naturally occurring retirement communities. The first NORC was the Penn South complex in New York City, which like Bertha Lowitt's block, was built as middle-income housing in the 1960s. Forty years later it was full of old people and the board partnered with a welfare agency to get services provided on site, which included medical, recreation, nutrition and education. A NORC has at least one paid staff member and can be a block of flats or a suburban street of ten to twenty houses.

Apartments for Life is the planned version of this model. This vertical village for old people was pioneered in Rotterdam by Dr Hans Becker of the Humanitas Foundation. Highrise buildings in lively parts of the city are built around a village square with gardens, shops and cafes open to the broader community. There's also a fitness centre and key support services like a nurse, doctor and social worker. In Sydney's Bondi, the Benevolent Society is building such a village with 40 per cent of the units targeted at financially disadvantaged local people, mostly local renters who couldn't afford the price of a unit. Sale of the expensive units on the upper floors subsidises the overall project. A key aspect of the NORCS, and Apartments for Life is that old people are able to stay in their communities, and live in mixed age and mixed income environments.

The village concept, by encouraging volunteering, recognises and appreciates how much old people thrive from having someone to look after. All Joan Lowrie's life she's been someone who cared for others and just because she was ninety didn't stop her taking Marie in, to save her from becoming homeless. It can be very lonely in your own home in the Australian suburbs. As a teenager my daughter did deliveries for the local chemist. Most calls were to elderly women living alone in sprawling three-bedroom houses, desperately wanting to chat. We want independence but not isolation and loneliness. Housemate-matching schemes like Wesley Home Share—used by Barbara Hamer—are on the increase. These have formal contracts. In return for a bedroom and sharing her home, Barbara gets companionship, practical assistance and the security of a presence at night. As well as such formal matching services, which exist in many parts of the world, thousands of older people are choosing to share their homes with relatives and students.

Among people in their sixties and seventies co-housing is a popular option. They are living my fantasy of communal life. In these 'intentional communities', a group of like-minded people develop a property, live in units or flats clustered together, and share some weekly dinners, outdoor space and facilities.

With the push for, and appeal of home-based care will there be any need for institutions, what we used to call nursing homes? Many states in the United States offer the alternative of Elderly Foster Care programs, where typically one woman cares for three or four old women in her home. As well as providing meals, doing laundry and organising transport, she looks after their medication and helps them with eating, dressing, bowel and bladder care, personal care, walking and getting out of a bed or a chair. Obviously you need emotional as well as physical stamina to take this on. Unlike Family Day Care for children, the elderly do not go home at night and it's seven days a week. I'd choose a well-run home with properly paid staff working eight hours a day over living with an unskilled, overworked and underpaid woman.

At the core of the debate about the future of aged-care institutions is the independence-dependence pendulum. Critics argue that you are giving up too much, trading off autonomy and community involvement, by walling yourself in with the same age group.[12] Surely it depends on how much agency and ability you have. No matter how much home nursing and home medical care is provided there will always be a need for institutional care for people who are a threat to others, or have deteriorating conditions like muscular dystrophy, Parkinson's and dementia, needing constant and 24-hour attention.

It is true that institutions are overly concerned with risk and liability. Did the home need to take away Mary Broughton's Panadol? In future more homes will support residents in having all the 'usual rights of an adult', and let them keep their medications while they're capable of taking them properly. We must fight against seeing an old person as a passive object, which is more likely to happen in an institution. You may be old and disabled but you're still *you*. We can set-up systems in institutions that discourage paternalism and over protection. Better staff training with an emphasis on old people's autonomy will encourage their self-reliance.

Choosing for ourselves and making decisions is good for us however old and sick we are. 'People able to take control of their lives can get better, people who buy into the medical model—I'm old, I'm sick, aging means being a sedentary vegetable, being taken care of—they stop moving, they don't do well,' said Dr Carol Winograd of Stanford University. 'It's important to stay in control and make the decisions for as long as you can.'[13]

If you do need to go into an aged-care home, look for a smaller one where the nurses look after the same group of patients, and where you're supported in making personal choices—even unhealthy ones. My friend Mark was in a very expensive home. For as long as he could, he manoeuvred his wheelchair into a lift to go downstairs and outside for his only remaining pleasure—smoking. In his last months he couldn't get out of bed. What harm would it have done for the nurses to put a cigarette in his mouth for a puff. It's that kind of flexibility and care I'd be looking for in a home.

You'll need plenty of money to access the full range of choices. Full-time private care at home or in a luxury home is only for the rich. Most aged-care homes are run as for profit businesses. Dodo in Florida pays $3500 a month. In Australia, to get into the most desirable homes you need a bond of $500,000 plus, on top of which are weekly payments that vary according to what you can afford and the level of service you require.

The best choice of where to live at seventy may not suit me at eighty or ninety. Ideally, I'd like to live like Lady Flo and Margaret Fulton—in my own place, near my children and family. I also want to be within walking distance of shops and street life, cinemas and transport options. To achieve this I'd have to move across town, give up my sea view and my local networks.

Having visited Beth Gott, I've shed some of my prejudices about homes. Her place would suit me fine—excellent location, plenty of space and light, terraces for plants and sitting out in the sun and, best of all, a community of like-minded people. I could be happy there. The time for me to make those decisions has not yet come. My home is perfect: not too big, on one level with three trams at my door. Everything I need is within walking distance except a cinema. When I can't drive or walk as well or if I'm on my own, I'll reassess.

You'll know when it's time, when you can no longer look after your beloved garden or are finding that flight of stairs too much for you. The only advance planning you can do is to make sure you've got the means to access a range of choices.

HOT TIPS **For home or a home?**

➤ Stay in control of the decision-making about where you live for as long as you possibly can. Allay your family's fears and don't let the desire to save them from worry dictate your decision.

➤ Don't assume you'll live with your kids, or your sister or brother, in your old age. It may happen—and could work out well—but you'll need to plan for other options.

➤ Are you independent or do you need security to thrive? Knowing this will help you decide whether to move or stay.

➤ Are you looking for adventure and new places and new faces? Give it a shot but make sure you've got a fallback position so that you don't get stuck.

➤ Is your home a haven that enables you to live the life you want, or a prison? If it's a haven make sure you get the supports in place that will help you stay there. Get out if it's a prison—there are lots of other options.

➤ If you love your neighbourhood and the big house is getting too much for you, buy something smaller around the corner. More and more smaller dwellings that suit older people are being built.

➤ For making decisions about where to live timing is critical. Don't wait to be carried out on a stretcher and don't give up the place you love until you know you gotta go.

➤ Before moving ask yourself whether you want to be near your family or friends or both? If you move near to family or friends check that the location has more than this proximity going for it—they may move and you'll be stuck there.

➤ Perhaps encourage your kids to move near you. Help them to buy a place if you've got the funds and offer them as much childminding support as you can.

➤ Be sure to check the transport, support and lifestyle options of any place you are thinking of moving to. That remote farmhouse 50 kilometres from the nearest doctor is not likely to suit an eighty year old.

➤ Most importantly, make sure you can change your mind and don't get stuck in Perth or Berwick.

➤ Before signing on for co-housing or shared housing be sure that you want to live with others rather than on your own.

➤ You should look at retirement homes or independent living options if you:
  – are concerned about safety and security
  – want meals and other services provided
  – want in-house facilities like a pool and gym
  – like to have things done for you rather than doing them yourself
  – like the feeling of being looked after
  – like social activities organised for you.

➤ Remember to try and have a trial run before you commit to buying into a home.

➤ When choosing an independent living place to move into, consider:
  – location: if your priority is sailing or golf, that will dictate where you live and being near transport is always a good idea
  – affordability: stick to your budget—you could live a long time and watch out for that departure fee
  – design and atmosphere: the home needs to be to your taste and the options are there from the most glamorous and glitzy, to the more homey
  – facilities to suit your needs: will you use the pool and the gym or would you rather have garden space to stroll in? If you're a keen cook you'll want a good kitchen, but not if you're going to mostly eat in the communal dining room. Is a study important to you? Choose a home with facilities that you're going to use
  – and, most importantly, work out the community you're looking for: is it committed golfers, people of your sexual preference, religion, ethnicity or people you can talk to at morning tea time.

➤ If you do need to go into an aged-care home look for one:
  – in your community, close to where family and friends can visit and take you out
  – that's small enough for people to be able to get to know each other
  – where the same group of nurses will look after you and get to know you
  – where value is placed on residents having rights
  – with the atmosphere, facilities and people that will suit you.

➤ Remember that your Plan A move may not work out. Even if it's a great decision when you make it, it may no longer suit you ten years down the ageing track. Be prepared to implement Plan B, and if circumstances change again, Plan C.

7

Technology

W̲HEN I TOLD my grandson that I lived before there was television, he asked if I'd seen any dinosaurs. The coming of television remains the most dramatic technological event of my life, quite likely because it came to Melbourne with great fanfare along with the 1956 Olympic Games. Pushing my way through to the front of the electrical goods shop, I watched Betty Cuthbert run like stink to win gold for Australia. Sharing the exhilaration of the screaming whooping crowd around me and the excitement of all those inside that wood-panelled box, I've been hooked ever since.

Unlike my stumbling and grumbling with recent technology, television was pure pleasure and excitement. Was this because everything and anything new is grist to a ten year old? It was my parents who took responsibility for mastering the knobs that stopped the picture zigzagging frantically, and the medium of moving pictures—if not the machine in our lounge room—was familiar to me from my weekly visit to the cinema.

Those of us born after World War II in Europe, Australia or the United States take electricity and telephones, flush toilets, cars and planes for granted. Rose Stone remembers the day electricity was connected for the first time to her shtetl in Poland in the 1920s. When she came to Melbourne in 1938 she marvelled at water coming out of a tap in the kitchen. My other technological milestones include the shift from ice being delivered by the man with the heavy hessian sack over his shoulder to the shiny pastel pale-yellow Kelvinator in our kitchen, and the arrival of the twin-tub washing machine that signalled the end of my mother wielding the thick stick to stir the copper of steaming sudsy water. Take a trip to remote parts of Africa, South America and Asia and you too can experience life before electricity and sanitation. The radical change is that in that village where they are still pushing ploughs by hand, accessible only by a tough eight-hour hike, every adult now has a mobile phone.

Betty Friedan's challenge to the myths and stereotypes of ageing, *The Fountain of Age*, was published in 1993. This thorough 670-page book has no chapter on technology and no index items for internet, cell phone, computer or world wide web. Common use of the internet only began twenty-five years ago, so Betty had never sent an email by the time her tome was published. She did not foresee the wired world we live in. In the past thirty-five years society has gone from the invention of the personal computer to 78.9 per cent of American households owning one. Only twenty-five years after the invention of the world wide web, 75 per cent of people have the internet at home. The first commercial mobile phones didn't hit the market until 1983, and thirty years later more than 90 per cent of the population has one.[1] Australians may have been a bit slower on the uptake but we've more than caught up as a digital nation with 92 per cent of all Australians over eighteen using a mobile phone and 90 per cent accessing the internet at least once a week.[2]

The women I spoke with were already in their sixties and seventies when personal computers came into use. When I ask them about technology, not one mentions ATMs or credit cards, or electronic programming on their washing machine. They talk about computers, the internet and mobile phones—the dramatic and defining technologies of our time. Did they embrace this technology in the same way they'd taken to television and washing machines and the many other innovations that had improved their lives? Why some did and others haven't will help us understand what we must do if we want to harness future technologies to make the most of our old age.

Facing our fears

Every day I'm forced to learn something new. My oven and washing machine lights glow and flicker with programs and settings that mystify me. The bank has changed its online interface when it feels only yesterday I mastered the old one. I'm terrified of losing the scores of passwords and user names I must have to access everything from booking theatre tickets to paying my debts. Plus it's all done on machines, machines that I don't understand and have no idea what to do with, except that switching them off and on again often does the trick. There's a loose connection on the umbilical cord that connects my laptop to the power supply and I'm keeping an eye on its little green unsteady light. If it goes off my battery will not last two hours despite the all day claims made by the maker. What time does the computer shop close and will it have my cord in stock? It's a huge change from running out of ink for my fountain pen.

All over the world people aged sixty-five and older use computers and the internet less than younger people. Among these younger age groups there is little difference in usage between men and women. With the over sixty-fives, women are significantly less likely to access the internet through a computer than men. In Australia 73 per cent of women over this age have never sent or received an email.[3] This gender gap is no surprise. The computer-techy world is overwhelmingly a male one—think Steve Jobs, Bill Gates and the Google guys. How many women do you know with a roomful of computer parts they love assembling and pulling apart? There are still very few women in the field. Data from the

Australian Computer Society shows women made up just 28 per of Australia's information and communication technology workforce in 2013,[4] and the figure in the United States is the same at 27 to 29 per cent.[5] For most of us, the new technology was intimidating—it was male. Computers and printers and scanners were alien machines; they were from Mars and we were from Venus.

On her desk Barbara Hamer has a laptop computer and a printer. 'My batteries died and I didn't know what it was, and I am not very good at looking up all the little symbols and things that tell you, you have a dead battery.' Her printer also refused to cooperate. 'I had to rush down the street in order to print that off for you today because the jolly thing wasn't working. I got myself covered with ink.' Barbara and I are having the kind of technology conversation I have with my friends. Recently she acquired a touch screen phone and she's struggling with that. 'I am having trouble at the moment knowing exactly which button to push when somebody rings me. I have only had it a week or two, I am getting there. I am good at taking photographs.' Learning to use and using these machines is difficult and Barbara feels she has no choice. She needs the computer to write the memoir she's working on and the internet for running the finances and managing a farm and her own company. It's an integral part of her life. Every morning, 'I have a look at the computer and see who has sent me emails and things and I reply to them. I take my messages off both phones and I deal with any business issues.' And she's active on Facebook to keep up with what her grandchildren are doing.

Even the highly computer literate Elisabeth Kirkby says, 'It makes me scream,' and tells me how on a final read through of her PhD thesis she found that 'on one line of each page was spacing that had gone haywire'. Anyone who has used a self-publishing program knows how common this is and how crazy it makes you.

Learning and using new technology can be stressful and difficult but you cannot do a PhD without it.

Although only 9 per cent of women aged fifty-five to seventy-four use the internet daily compared to 18 per cent of men,[6] this gender difference is going to disappear. You'd be hard pressed to find anyone under fifty-five who has never sent an email. More surprising is that older people—those sixty-five and over—who aren't computer and internet users have no interest in using them in the future.[7] I am shocked that my contemporaries are choosing to stay out of the wired world even when access and training is offered to them. The internet is now the preferred method of information delivery of government and other agencies and organisations. I work with a poorly funded community organisation that has many elderly members without email addresses. Sending a letter or notice by post costs 70 cents for the stamp plus the price of the paper and envelope per person, whereas I can email it for nothing. Qantas charges you an extra $30 for each booking by phone. The world—me included—wants you to go online.

I can hear you under sixty year olds out there saying, 'We're not like that. We're internet and computer savvy and staying that way.' But it's not about the technology we already know and love, even though it gives us headaches. It's about what we don't know and could be just round the corner, waiting to ambush us. Why some women took to the computer, internet and mobile phone will provide clues for what to do when that next big thing hits us.

Embracing technology

For women already in their sixties and seventies at the time, their uptake of new technology is remarkable. Partly this is because the group is largely well off and well educated, both factors that make it more likely that you'll be using the internet, a computer and a mobile phone when you're over sixty-five.[8] Taking up new technology is not about how old you are. Bertha Lowitt is fully wired at ninety-six.

Bertha has worked her whole life. Until recently she was working in the education department of the Museum of Jewish Heritage and she wouldn't have been any use to them without computer and internet skills. Luckily Bertha has no fear of technology. Those war years she spent working complicated machinery at the Bausch & Lomb factory in Rochester, New York—her Rosie the Riveter experience—gave her the know-how and confidence. Going to college in her sixties, and teaching office skills until she was seventy-seven, meant that Bertha was up to date with the latest technology. She has a laptop and is an active emailer and Googler. She has a Kindle e-reader and swears by her iPhone. 'This is what I hear with,' she says, about the pendant-like device she wears around her neck. 'If the phone rings this lights up green and that's what I hear with. Oh it's wonderful.' Show Bertha what technology can do for her and Bertha will learn to use it.

Age in itself is not the barrier. It's the women who did little or no paid work after marriage who are the ones least likely to be online. Their level of education is another important factor. Flo Howlett and May Lowe left school early and neither has the interest or desire to take up new technologies. Family members have tried to get May a mobile phone but she doesn't want one. 'I have no interest in those sort of things,' she says. Flo is quite direct about it: 'I don't like technology.' Everything is laid on for Flo to be able to access the new technology with an up-to-date computer room available on site. She enjoys playing games on the computer but refused the offer of being taught to use the internet. 'I don't want to,' she says. 'Why do I want to be sending messages out to people for?' Flo feels that that it's all too much, and doesn't want to adapt. 'I am old-fashioned in my thinking,' she says. 'I think they've gone ahead too quick for us oldies. It just used to be on an even keel and all of a sudden it's gone up there. Now you've got all these different things that show photos when you take them.'

Among those aged ninety-five and over, Bertha is exceptional in how determined she has been to stay engaged with the world of work. None of the others in that age group worked after marriage. She is also the only one in that age group who went back to study. Her work experience and her education have given her confidence and the skill set—both the technical know-how and office skills—that has enabled her to sail into the new technological world. Needing to learn to use the new technology is the big difference between those, like me, who were propelled kicking and screaming into the digital age and those who said, 'No, thank you, it's not for me.' For most of the other full adapters, those who use a computer, mobile and internet, that push came from their work.

Although what she says about her computer skills is, 'Oh very simple on the computer, not quite as good as some,' Beth Gott is email and computer savvy. She has to be to have created and be continually updating the online databases of indigenous plants that she is in charge of, and to write articles and connect to colleagues and other researchers. The computer and internet are central to Beth's work, which involves handling large quantities of data and making this information accessible to everyone, all over the world, at any time. 'I will always check my email each day and do anything that needs to be done from that. I have got the writing of this chapter going on and I try to do something for that every day.' Email becomes part of our daily routine. For Beth, there'll be queries from botanists and students as well as the usual personal emails. She has a mobile phone and is thinking of getting an iPad. Age is no barrier to Beth adapting to new technology and, as botanists never retire, Beth will continue learning new software and improving her hardware.

The youngest of the group, Dorothy Shultz, has a computer, a tablet, and a smart phone. In her work as a trainer she had no option but to learn the latest technology. 'I see myself being part of the instant world whether I like it or not,' she says. Personal computers came into universities when Stephanie Charlesworth was teaching. She is the only woman who expresses real enthusiasm about keeping up with technology. 'I enjoy it. I have done quite a few computer courses. I have got an iPad, I have got a Mac Air, I have got an iPhone, and of course I am using very very good software for my genealogy.'

For Joyce McGrath, technology makes her life possible. Because of her stiff right hip, she can't drive and she can't walk far either. Joyce spends most of her time at home. Computers came into libraries in the 1960s and, as a trained librarian, Joyce has been using them for about fifty years. Having access to information matters to Joyce and via the internet she can do this from home. After she had a non-Hodgkin's lymphoma treated and removed, she checked the internet 'and I found that there had been some studies done that showed that if you dyed your hair a dark colour for more than twenty years you were more likely to get a non-Hodgkin's lymphoma, so I decided to stop getting my hair dyed.' Online she's able to keep up her contributions to the Bibliography of Australian Art and her voluntary work with the Victorian Artists Society, where it's her job to answer all the email queries they receive. Thanks to the internet, Joyce says, 'I am continuing what I was doing and I can maintain all the contacts that I had.'

And looking beyond information and communication technology, when Joyce takes delivery of her electric wheelchair, and gets electronically opening doors, she'll be able to get to her studio to paint and tootle up the street to do some shopping. We see more elderly people scooting around the footpaths of our city because of the improvements in wheelchair design and mobility and the invention of other personal motorised vehicles that help us get around when some of our body parts can no longer do it for us. In the future Joyce may even get FRIEND, a robot built on a wheelchair base that you sit on and that does everything you can't do. It will open those doors for her and prepare and serve her meals.[9]

You can't have a job or run a business or volunteer or do any kind of work if you aren't online. When she was sixty, Jean Allison bought her first computer. Twenty-eight years later she uses her computer and the internet for writing, research, playing Freecell, and storing and sharing her photographs. Recently she joined GetUp, a progressive online campaigning organisation of more than six hundred thousand members. At first she signed petitions calling for justice in the treatment of refugees, a cause close to her heart from when she worked in refugee settlements in Hong Kong. Her concern for the environment led her to graduate from online involvement to handing out information at the Sustainable Living Festival. What Jean has taken advantage of is the ability of the web to connect us to like-minded people across age, race and gender barriers, and its potential for political action.

This potential for broader social engagement also appeals to 90-year-old Sister Mary Gregory. One of the younger Good Samaritan Sisters has set up her tablet for her. Sister Mary has some computer experience, has used email and is looking forward to connecting to the causes and organisations she is part of, like Aboriginal reconciliation and the Mygunyah Camden Aboriginal Residents Group.

Mobile phones are different

Most of the women do have a mobile phone, though these are often switched off or put away in a drawer. Few use their mobiles for accessing the internet. This makes them a highly unusual group. Smart phone penetration among Australian adults was at 88 per cent by the end of 2013 (up 12 per cent in one year), and is projected to reach 93 per cent within the next nine months.

Considering that five years ago only 17 per cent of us had a smart phone, we've really taken to them.[10]

There's nothing gendered about mobile phone usage. By mid 2011, over half of the smart phone owners were women. In contrast to the computer and the internet, the mobile phone is an egalitarian technology, equally used by both genders and the whole population across age, income, education and ethnic origin. So why is that two highly competent computer and internet users do not have a mobile phone?

One reason is that Jean Allison and Joyce McGrath don't have children or grandchildren. Many of the women with mobile phones were talked into having them by their children, who see it as a safety device, making their mother contactable at any time and any place. The children and grandchildren are used to texting and 'hooking up' at very short notice. Mobile phones have completely changed the way we run our lives. Once we made complicated arrangements for when we'd get together, and how we'd recognise people we hadn't met before, and exactly which corner and what spot we'd meet. Now we say, text me when you get there.

Mary Broughton, ninety-eight, has had a mobile phone for some years: 'My first mobile phone was an antique thing, which was very handy. I used it in the car in case of emergencies and on a couple of occasions I had to use it.' Now she uses it to call taxis and ring her children and grandchildren. 'One of my granddaughters, there is no phone in their house, they both have mobiles. My grandson, he only has a mobile.' Like Mary's grandchildren, my contemporaries and younger people are ditching their landlines.

Making the move from a phone you could lift from its cradle and carry out to the garden while you were pruning the roses to one that you could carry everywhere was fairly seamless for most of us. You didn't have to learn anything new as you'd already been using a push-button system on the fixed phone. It was far less intimidating than sitting at a desk to front an alien-looking machine and blank screen. The less you get out and about, the less you are likely to need a mobile phone. Joyce McGrath and Joan Lowrie spend most of their time at home and don't have children. They have portable home phones they can take from room to room with them.

You don't have to be computer literate to use a mobile phone. Dodo Berk certainly isn't. She says, 'I'm a tremendous caller. I'm calling until 10.30 at night to different people.' Dodo likes to be able to ring her family and friends from wherever she happens to be—New York City, Long Island, Florida or places in between. Dodo does have children and grandchildren and lots of younger friends who want to chat to her, to find out what she's been up to, ask her advice and invite her out. Her phone rings constantly.

Mobile phones are not about work although they are for getting in touch with people in a hurry, which is what Elisabeth Kirkby uses hers for. It's so easy now to let someone know that your plane has been delayed so they shouldn't worry. Women take to mobile phones more because it's women who take responsibility for staying in touch with family and friends. We are attracted to technology that connects us to people. A phone is light and fits easily into your handbag. You don't need a high level of education or to go to special training programs to learn how to use them. Being user-friendly has helped the speed with which they've spread so quickly throughout the world. And the easier they become to use the more they become an extension of ourselves.

A friend of mine describes her mobile phone as her brain enhancer. You don't need to remember that phone number or address—it's all in your phone. The phone beeps to let you know you've got an appointment with the doctor and rings loudly when you need to be somewhere. I can monitor my heart rate by pointing my phone at my forehead. And if I'm lost I turn on the GPS. My nifty torch app is handy for reading menus in dark restaurants. Need a footy score, the name of that film, where to find Thai food—no problem. All this is only the beginning. The phone has grown from being something you make calls with to being a valuable communication and information device.

The smart phone has become irresistible. In your hand you hold instant access to, everything. My friend Nomi read *Middlemarch* on her phone, while travelling the New York subway to work.

Don't be a regretter

It was after I interviewed June Helmer that I decided to buy a smart phone. June loved her work preparing the audio-visual content for the exhibitions at the Jewish Museum of Australia. She was instrumental in helping the museum find a bigger and better home. Sadly, June remembers, 'The new museum had new technology and technology isn't my forte. I gave up.' Thinking about it some more she says, 'That was my really big mistake, not to keep up with technology. You don't get a second chance.'

June's regret at having missed this critical moment made me realise that I needed to keep up with smart-phone technology, even though I couldn't see its immediate advantage. At that time, with my simple mobile and laptop, I could do everything I needed and wanted to do. June's experience was pivotal in my understanding that I needed to learn to use the technology of the smart phone even if I didn't want the services and, more importantly, that I could not judge what it had to offer if I didn't give it a go. You will not be surprised to learn that I now love my smart phone and can't imagine being without it.

What June teaches us is that you need to take each step along the path or the space between those technology steps will become too wide for you to jump.

When I ask the computer- and internet-using Jean Allison, 'Do you have a mobile phone?' she throws her hands up in disgust. 'Don't talk to me about a mobile phone!' she says. 'I have got a fairly modern one and I have never gotten around to reading the instructions and I usually forget to switch it on.' Jean feels that she should keep up with technology and says, 'I sometimes feel envious of my friend Mary who is in her nineties and has an iPhone.' Koho Yamamoto's students bought her an iPad and created a Facebook page to promote her classes and work. 'I am not so good [with technology] but I don't want to be left behind but I've got an iPad,' she says. Koho sends occasional emails to her students, who have also paid for her to get one-on-one help at the nearby Apple Store. 'But I never go. I hate these things,' and she repeats fiercely, 'I hate it.'

I know exactly how she feels. Many times I've wanted to kick my computer and throw my phone down the toilet. Like Jean and Koho, I don't want to be left behind, but there are so many things that come more easily to me than learning new computer programs or working out how to use apps.

The rejectors

I understand the women who passed on using computers. I resisted them for as long as I could too. Friends of mine were using computers in the 1960s and 1970s, taking their punch cards into the computer room at the university to feed into that huge machine. Among the women I interviewed, most of those who have avoided using computers did not work after marriage. If they did work then their work didn't involve writing, financial management or crunching data.

Not all innovations strike us as necessary. Take the dishwasher. Doing dishes is not hard work and it can be fun standing at the sink gossiping while we do them together. After living in the United States in 1973—where dishwashers were already standard—I've never had a kitchen without one. I discovered that the machine does a better job, uses less water and saves me time. It's useful but not necessary. When I'm on my own, creating few dirty dishes, I don't use it, and if it breaks down, I don't go into panic mode like

I do when my computer dies. Some technologies matter to us more than others. I don't have a microwave. In the three years I had one all I used it for was heating coffee and making popcorn, which wasn't worth the space it took up in my kitchen.

For those women who didn't need it the computer was the equivalent of the dishwasher or microwave oven for me. Because they hadn't had to learn the basics of word processing and computer use, the gap between the known and the unknown became wider, as they got older. 'I have no technology,' says Dame Margaret Scott and explains. 'I don't have enough to do on one [a computer]. I mean, one doesn't need to as an eighty or ninety year old. It sounds silly but there are other pleasures, you don't have to be connected.' Dame Margaret is in agreement with all the other older people who are non-users—they are not interested because they perceive it as irrelevant to their lives.[11] Among the other total non-users is Margaret Fulton, who has no internet, computer or mobile phone. Lady Flo Bjelke-Petersen has a computer and, although she says 'I could still use it if I had to', it sits unused. She has never used the internet and doesn't have a mobile phone.

It's not that they reject all technology. Women who feel a little shaky on their feet have all taken to canes and rolling walkers to help them get around. Suzanne Simon says she is 'hopeless' with technology and when her youngest son gave her a tablet for Christmas, said, 'Don't give me one please, I don't want one'. Suzanne had no problem getting the latest and best in hearing aids and spending the time and effort it takes to adjust to these complex devices. Because she can hear better she's prepared to make the effort, to persevere. When we see the immediate improvement that an innovation brings, we will make the effort to learn to use it.

May Lowe, Flo Howlett and Joan Lowrie have full and enjoyable lives. Because they aren't active in the world beyond their family, friends and locality, they don't need the internet. Margaret

Fulton is still a player, publishing books and appearing on television and in advertising campaigns. How did she produce all those magazine pages without every having laid a finger on a computer? Easily: 'I have always had secretaries.' For all the new books coming out, her daughter and granddaughter do the computer work 'and they send it to me and I go through it'. Lady Flo Bjelke-Peterson was able to avoid the internet and mobile phone. 'I didn't have to use it. See, I mean, the girls would—I had very good staff while I was in the senate, so I was very lucky to have those.' The women who don't have staff, have husbands or children to print things out for them and keep them connected to what's going on around them.

Frances Reynolds and Betty Walton learned that I was looking for interviewees because they use their husbands' email addresses. Frances has a mobile phone and an e-reader. She is a science graduate and not a technophobe. Since he retired her husband John has 'got a room of his own with a computer and exercise bike'. John is on email and has been using a computer for twenty years. When I suggest that she might enjoy a tablet, Frances says, 'I know if I had one who would use it? I think I could probably use it if I had it all to myself. You would have to buy two, dear. You would only want to use it all the time,' she says to her husband. Perhaps by now both Frances and John have bought one.

Asked how she is with technology Betty Walton answers, 'Terrible I have no interest in it. I just have no interest in it.' She is so allergic to our instant world that she says, 'I think sometimes it would have been lovely to live in another century and then I think I like modern dentistry and modern medicine.' She doesn't even have a computer: 'Tom has and that's enough so that's how I got your email.' About the mobile phone she says, 'No, we have one but we never use it.' Betty ran a language school in Italy, taught French at Merton Hall and, more recently, taught Italian for five years at the U3A. She is still teaching theatre there. All these organisations communicate with their teachers and students by email. Tom must be very active on the computer and internet on Betty's behalf.

Why is an intelligent, educated woman like Betty Walton a technophobe? The crux is how she sees herself. 'Oh, I loved study, but I am hopeless at maths and hopeless at science, I am just good at languages, and tennis and drama. I love learning.' Like Suzanne Simon, Maxie Meldrum and several of the other women, Betty has an outdated view of scientific and mathematical ability being needed to master computers and the internet. This misconception has created a wall around her so that, even when being online would make her life—or at least Tom's—easier, it's too tough a barrier and too late to break through. And Betty revels in her persona: 'I write a lot of letters.' And she does. I get beautiful cards and snail mail from Betty in response to the emails I send Tom.

Margaret Fulton is not alone in relying on her children for online connections. Dame Margaret Scott says, 'I have got two sons that do it all for me. They go, "Oh, come on, Mum".' According to Rose Stone her children are happy to be her conduit to the online world: 'Janey loves doing it for me. Norm will do it for me. So why would I bother?' Rose has an antipathy to computers, the internet and mobile phones. 'I've let technology pass me by and I don't miss it,' she says, and, 'Yes I have a mobile phone but I hardly use it.'

Rose is, and prides herself on being, up-to-date in her social attitudes and opinions. She is very much out there in the world, still involved with the Union of Australian Women, going to the theatre, belonging to two book groups and playing bridge regularly. Her life is very different to that of Flo Howlett, Joan Lowrie and May Lowe. But like them, Rose had little formal education. 'I'm never going to be able to print things out,' she says. There's a fear of failure involved. Rose is a smart woman who has learned many new things in her life, including a whole new language and culture. So why not this? It's very hard to convince a ninety-two year old that the new technology is no longer about computers and that it's female friendly.

What I'm most shocked about with Rose and Betty and the others who say, 'No, thanks, we don't need it', is how they've dismissed these innovations without even trying them. I don't have a microwave but I did try it for a year before I made the decision I didn't want one. And one good meal cooked in one would have convinced me to give them another go. I would encourage them, and others of like mind, to borrow a smart phone or tablet and play around with them. For those, like Rose and Betty, who do want to stay connected to the wider world—to get notices of events and meetings, to be in touch with their family and friends interstate and overseas, to exchange photographs—it's risky to depend on others. Your husband might die and your children move away. Even staff won't always be there when you want them to be. Looking back, I'm pleased that my husband and my children wouldn't do it for me. Even now the children will show me once and then they say, 'Look it up on YouTube, there's a video that shows you how to do it.' And grumblingly I do.

Are they missing out on anything? Would moving into the digital world enhance the lives of women who aren't interested in the world beyond their family and friends and locality? Is it worth them making the effort to learn this technology? I can't see that any of the women need computers—certainly not desktop ones, unless they are planning to write their memoirs. But the internet, that's another story.

Dodo is an avid mobile phone user but hers is not a smart phone. All those months that Dodo spends in Florida in the retirement home, where she pines to find a 'soul mate' to talk to, she could be on Skype or FaceTime with her friends and family back home. Dodo loves being connected and would enjoy it even more if she could see the people she was talking to. She is a big fan of Broadway musicals and shows of all kinds, and I picture her watching her favourites on YouTube, trying out new dance steps and belting out tunes with Ethel Merman.

May Lowe misses her daughter Brenda, who now lives in Brisbane, and I'm sure they chat on the phone regularly. Her grandsons and some of her great grandchildren live in Japan. On Skype or FaceTime she could see her loved ones. Skype and FaceTime are especially good for getting to know the little ones who may not have a lot to say to you but can display what they made at kindergarten and school that day.

Reading is one of Flo Howlett's favourite pastimes but her eyesight is deteriorating. On a tablet or e-reader she could increase the size of the font and adjust the brightness of the text and back lighting to make it easier. Flo could take a lesson from Maxie Meldrum, who says she's a confirmed technophobe. Maxie, like Flo, has macular degeneration and she has taken to a tablet because it's easier for her to read using this device.

For each of the non-users of the internet there's something they love doing and could do better if they were connected to the web. But they don't need it. I think of everything they've learned and adapted to in their nine decades and I tell myself to butt out telling them how they can improve their lives. The non-users have chosen not to be part of the world that the rest of us now inhabit. Opting out is okay for those who are already ninety-five, but I'm less comfortable about the younger group having made this decision.

Nowadays, people who aren't online are a shrinking minority, even in Rose Stone's age group. She would have such fun downloading programs to improve her bridge game, looking up reviews of the books, and researching the Shakespeare readings she goes to. If Rose was online she could be more politically active, and join GetUp like Jean Allison has, and she'd be Skyping her granddaughter in Alice Springs. But Rose poo-poos my advice: 'Why should I spend my time sitting in front of a computer when I could read a book or go for a walk to the beach.' I'm still trying to convince her that she's rejecting the greatest invention of the last thirty years. If Rose and Betty and the others had given it a go, and knew what they were missing, I could accept their decision to have no part of it.

My ambivalence about their rejection is fuelled by selfishness. I can't get in touch with them by email or text, the ways I now use for communicating with everyone about almost everything. Rose wants to be in the loop—to be informed about concerts and films and folk dancing and all the other things going on in the world—and she is making it harder and more expensive for the rest of us to keep in touch with her. They are healthy, active women who could live another ten years or more and so surely want to be connected in the easiest way possible.

We who are now the age they were when they said no thanks to computers and the internet should not use getting older as an excuse to avoid and reject the new. We should give every new device a go and keep a growth mindset ready to take advantage of what's to come. Admitting our fears and accepting that it might be difficult are good first steps. Historically older people are later adopters of new technology but that could change when so many of the innovations on the horizon are going to be of great benefit to us. Although no one knows what the next big thing will be, there are innovations out there—ready to use or almost ready to use—that will make our old age radically different to that of previous generations.

Because there are hundreds of technological innovations already available or just around the corner, I can choose only a few strands to highlight in this brave new world. Making the best of any and all of them requires us to take some risks. How would you feel about jumping into a car where there's no driver?

The driverless car

'I want to drive forever,' says Suzanne Simon. That's what Beth Gott, June Helmer and Mary Broughton wanted too. But they've had their cars taken away from them and are very upset about it. The big loss for Mary Broughton was not being able to get to her country place at Shoreham when she wanted to. 'I used to go down there, but then I had my car taken from me.' Now she is dependent on her son taking her.

For June Helmer not being able to drive signalled the loss of her independence. 'That's the worst thing that can happen to anybody. You've been driving your whole life and they take your licence away because you can't see properly, you can't drive properly. If you have to wait for a taxi here, or depend on others to drive you around, you fade away.' Her advice is: 'Don't give up your licence. Fight for your licence. Even if you're a menace on the road. Take lessons, do something.' When I asked whether she'd rather be able to read or drive, June unhesitatingly said, 'Drive!'

Not being able to drive has made Beth Gott's life much harder. Before she had her licence taken away, Beth was driving to work at the university on four days of the week. 'I was forbidden from driving. They wouldn't let me drive anymore. I am perfectly capable of driving—haven't had an accident.' Some years earlier Beth thought it would be a good idea to have regular driving tests every five years and, 'It came back to bite me,' she says. 'They kept testing me, and you are not tested in your own car, you are tested in one of these new cars that work differently and also I can't help feeling that to a certain extent they looked at my age and said you shouldn't be driving.' Not being able to 'take off to areas where I knew the plants were and have a look at them', is a real limitation. It takes three times as long for her to get to Monash University by public transport so Beth now only goes twice a week. She says the worst thing is not being able to carry plants for the Aboriginal garden she cares for on public transport. And it's not just her work. Without a car she has to rely on others to drive her to her favourite pool if she wants to swim. Certainly for Beth, a self-driving car would be the answer.

In May 2014 Google launched its driverless car. It looks just like the bubble car of the future, a more stylish version of a Smart Car but with no driver, no steering wheel, no brake or accelerator. The only driver controls are a red 'e-stop' button for panic stops and a separate start button. You don't need a licence. On YouTube you can watch children, the legally blind and the very old using the car and praising it for giving them back their independence and being 'incredibly empowering'. You book the car with an app. It collects you and drives you to your destination, all done without human intervention, using software and sensors. The system is so sophisticated that it can 'recognise objects, people, cars, road marking, signs and traffic lights, obeying the rules of the road and allowing for multiple unpredictable hazards, including cyclists. It can even detect road works and safely navigate around them.'[12] By early 2015 Google will have 100 cars road-ready. Although Google won't say how much they'll cost, they will not be in the reach of the average motorist as each has $150,000 in equipment, including a $70,000 light-radar system.

Apart from price, the biggest hold-up to the cars becoming a common sight on the roads is legislation. A number of states in the United States, including California, have passed laws permitting autonomous cars but questions around liability are going to take a long time to sort out. Fully tested self-driving cars are at least five years away and it'll be more than twice as long before you can buy or hire one yourself. While this timeframe may be too late for 91-year-old Beth Gott, we should be able to benefit and keep driving to the places we need to go even after our vision and hearing get worse and they take our licences away from us.

The internet-of-things

We 'talk' to each other via the internet, with texts and emails, voicemail and Skype. Objects and machines can also connect in this way; they talk to each other. This internet-of-things will make our old age very different from that of our parents. If you drink too much or take a sleeping pill you could sleep through your smoke alarm when it goes off. In the future, that smoke alarm will be able to send a message to the motion detectors and, when no movement is detected, the signal goes straight to the fire brigade, who will dash in and save you and your house. Fall detectors, thermometers (for hypothermia risk), flooding and unlit gas sensors, all will be able to trigger alerts and send a message. Your appliances and your environment will communicate with each other and with outside service providers to make life safer for you.

Have you ever forgotten to take your pills? You'll like Glowcaps. The caps of these pill bottles light up when you don't open them and if left unopened for even longer they'll send an alert email or text to remind you. Self-monitoring healthcare devices will be part of the internet-of-things, providing you with instant personal data. These telehealth systems monitor chronic conditions like heart failure and diabetes without you needing to go to a doctor, and can eliminate the need for expensive tests. For heart problems an unobtrusive heart monitor is implanted in your arm. It's powered by your body's thermal energy and constantly monitors your heart. If anything's not right, the monitor sends a message to your phone telling you to get yourself to the hospital right away. Similarly, people with diabetes use a blood-glucose monitor to provide accurate and instant measurement so that they can adjust their diet and exercise regime accordingly.

Soon, when you leave hospital you may wear a layered bandage on your arm that houses sensor modules to transmit data by wireless. As reported in *New Scientist*, 'The heart rate is measured through electrical activity at the skin surface, temperature through a contact thermometer, and physical movement using an accelerometer. Sounds are gathered through a contact microphone: the researchers say that the sound patterns from internal organs can be used to assess the wearer's health.'[13]

The current must-haves are 'wearables' like Fitbits. The Fitbit Flexi wireless activity monitor is a slim stylish wristband available in lots of designer colours and it tracks the steps you take, distance you travel and the calories you burn, as well as your sleep quality, and waking you in the morning. This fitness gadget and others like it have the potential for much wider health and safety uses.

Regenerative technology

While we've a long way to go before anyone can create a new heart or lungs or kidneys, you can already get a new bladder grown from your own bladder cells. These cells are grown in a lab and then placed on top of a bladder shaped mould that's made from material that breaks down in the body. This is then 'baked' in an oven-like device and inserted into the patient. Amazingly, it works.

Even more exciting than eliminating one of the indignities and discomforts of old age is being able to see well. Most old people already have new lenses implanted, often one for distance and one for close up so that you don't need glasses at all. Since 2012 surgeons have been doing retina implants for people with retinal diseases such as retinitis pigmentosa or age-related macular degeneration. Maxie Meldrum, Flo Howlett and Mary Broughton are probably not going to benefit from this as the eight-hour operation is considered too stressful for those over ninety. But in this operation an electronic retina is implanted into the back of the eye and the power supply for it is buried under the skin behind the ear, similar to a cochlear implant. People who've been blind for many years learn to see again with their new electronic retina.

Not so long ago cataract operations were considered tricky. Perhaps retina implants will also become a standard day procedure.

Electromechanics, cyborgs and robots

Engineers are building electronics-based systems that use pulses of electricity to act on the neurons in our brains. More than a hundred thousand people with Parkinson's disease have electrodes implanted in their brains to stop their shaking. Deep brain stimulation (DBS) is also being tested for treating chronic pain, and serious depression.

According to the scientists, we have the electromechanical knowledge but don't yet know enough about the brain. Professor Thomas Berger at the University of Southern California is working on building a memory augmenting prosthetic. He sees a future where people with Alzheimer's can have a prosthetic device—a memory chip—implanted into their brain.[14] Sadly, this not going to be developed any time soon—not in time for us.

Electronics-based systems are mostly being developed and used in advanced prosthetics. Bionic limbs can do pretty well everything—chop onions, juggle, run fast, climb mountains and knit. They are being utilised by amputees, including at least two celebrity chefs. At the moment the price of prosthetic limbs containing electronic components can be tens of thousands of dollars. They will get cheaper, just like televisions and other electrical goods that were once more expensive. With mass production and competition, we'll be able to afford them and in our old age—the cyborg age—get prosthetic knees, hips and other parts as ours wear out.

Technological innovations that will help us as we get older can be small, like a spoon that uses camera stabilising technology to counteract hand tremors so you can feed yourself more easily. Sensors in the handle detect a person's tremor, and the spoon responds using motors to move the spoon in the opposite direction. That way the food stays in the spoon all the way to your mouth, without spilling. At the other end of the spectrum is the 'robot butler'. In 2012 Toyota 'unveiled its 130-centimetre-tall Human Support Robot, which can be trained and controlled by a tablet computer to fetch objects and pick them up with a mechanised calliper or suction cup at the end of its robotic arm'. The robot butler finds what you want and brings it to you while talking to you about what it's doing.[15] I'm very much looking forward to one that will unscrew jars, open my stuck sash windows, turn that heavy mattress and look after all my physical needs just like Jeeves did for Bertie Wooster.

Scary, alien, disturbing, demanding—the nature and speed of technological change is all of these and more. I can't see any alternative except to embrace it. At the very least we need to assess what's being offered carefully and ask what this technology can do for us. We're unlikely to pass up new retinas if they stop us from being blind. But there'll be trickier decisions to make that none of us are able to predict, as yet.

HOT TIPS For minding the technology

➤ Don't be intimidated by machines and gadgetry—remember that technology is for women, too, and definitely for older people.
➤ Don't be afraid, it's not going to be as hard as it looks, or scary—think of all the difficult new stuff you've learned already.
➤ To find out what it can do for you, ask five people and read three articles to get a wide view before rejecting it, regretting it or accepting it.
➤ Ask yourself: do I need it? Technology should make life easier for you.

➤ Ask yourself: do I want it? Technology should make life better for you.

➤ Don't be intimidated if you didn't get in on the ground floor, even if others may have been using it for ten years or longer—better later than never.

➤ Although it's not going to be as hard as you fear, it may not be easy. Be prepared for a steep learning curve.

➤ Don't be ashamed to ask for help learning new technology if you need it. Set up a support person you can call on for advice and to help you with malfunctions.

➤ Get some training—there's plenty on offer these days to choose from.

➤ Do not let other people do the whole process for you, not unless you are absolutely sure that you will never need or want to do it for yourself—like at midnight or on Christmas Day.

➤ Think about the Amish—you can stop the technology clock at any time you like and hunker down with your horse and wagon, but there will be a price to pay. And why choose that moment in time to be frozen?

➤ If you think you don't need and don't want it, do not reject it without trying it first.

8

Sex and Remarriage

Rose Stone loves to discuss sex. In my first few interviews, I didn't bring it up. Then along came Rose who insisted that we break the taboo about old people and sex. She talked about what gives her pleasure and how to make sure a man looks after your sexual needs in the kind of detail that made me squirmingly uncomfortable. For Rose, embracing women's liberation in her fifties brought with it sexual liberation, and she's been enjoying it ever since.

Even after Rose's pep talk convinced me it was ridiculous not to talk about sex I was too gutless to ask the former senator and wife of the ex-premier of Queensland, Lady Florence Bjelke-Petersen, about whether she missed sex with her husband Joh, and if she still had sexual feelings. I should have. Lady Flo wouldn't have been embarrassed. Older women seem to talk about sex honestly and easily.

A different era

Joyce McGrath and Sister Mary Gregory have never had sex. Both had romances with men. Sister Mary describes the 'lovely friendship' she had before she made up her mind to become a nun. That was in the 1940s. As Catholics, both Sister Mary and Joyce McGrath were raised to believe that sex should be between a husband and wife for the purpose of procreating children. Joyce had many offers: 'I have had other people wanting to be sexually active with me and making me aroused.' These romances and love affairs never progressed. 'I was always afraid to think about getting married because I didn't think I could do what you had to do when you were married, because my hip was stiff.' Joyce never contemplated 'sinning' and having a sexual relationship outside marriage. 'I was frightened, you know, if I got married and it was unsuccessful I would feel terrible, having ruined somebody else's life, so I didn't.'

In a later era, one of her admirers might have encouraged the very attractive Joyce to give it a try, to overcome her fears, without needing to commit to a lifetime together if things didn't work out. Probably things would have worked out just fine. Today, people with greater physical disabilities than Joyce enjoy sex, have relationships, get married and have children. There are sex and disability websites and helplines, as well as role models, like Paralympian Hannah Cockroft, a 20-year-old wheelchair racer whose message is: 'As long as there is a will, there is a way!'

Joyce is now much more disabled than she was a few years ago, and can no longer drive or get far on her own. Had I met her ten or twenty years ago I would have been tempted to encourage her to pursue some options, although that would be a chutzpah considering what a full and rich life she has created, without sex. Unlike Sister Mary, a young Catholic woman growing up in Australia or America today would probably give sex a try before becoming a nun. Society and its pressures have changed which is not to say that they are better. Being free from the pressure to be sexually active can be liberating. One of the great things about getting older is that you can give it up if you want to.

An opportunity to give it away

In our sex-soaked society you will find more advice and information than you can possibly handle on what old people should do to restart, rekindle or spice up their love lives. 'Sex tips for

Seniors' is a boom industry and it means big dollars for advice columnists, psychologists and online pundits. Following on from the megabuck success of Viagra, drug companies are working on one for women—Lybrido, which is supposed to hit our bedside tables in 2017. Viagra solves a mechanical physical problem: making the penis erect. What will arouse women to want sex? Lybrido combines a Viagra-like chemical with a substance that more directly targets the brain.

Do older women actually want to have sex, or more sex? The answer is that it depends on the woman and not her age. Gloria Steinem, at eighty, declared that her dwindling libido frees a woman's mind 'for all kinds of great things'. Responses to her comment in *The Guardian* newspaper ranged from totally in agreement to 'are you crazy?'[1] Some of the women I spoke to were with Gloria, thrilled that because they are now widowed, or their husband's sex interest has waned, they can happily give up something they had never enjoyed or, at least, not for some decades.

Sex stopped being part of Flo Howlett's life after her husband's big operation and she didn't miss it in that last quarter of her married life. As she so pithily puts it, 'After seventy it's very downhill—"I've got a headache tonight".' Or, as Maxie Meldrum says, 'It wasn't much fun for me. It was just something I didn't particularly like that I did because I loved my husband, but I don't think I have ever been highly sexed.' Betty Walton was never keen on sex, but she made an effort for her husband. 'I had to act a little, and I hoped I did it well. Every now and then I liked it, and I thought it's a pity I don't like it more.' She's relieved she doesn't have to pretend any more.

The results of the most comprehensive study ever undertaken of sexual activity among people aged fifty-seven to eighty-five were published in *The New England Journal of Medicine* in August 2007. Just as I did, the researchers found older people willing and comfortable to discuss taboo issues. That's why we know that half those aged fifty-seven to seventy-four and one-third of those aged seventy-five to eighty-five gave and received oral sex—who would have guessed? Sexual activity and interest do fall off in the over seventies, and women in all age groups were less likely to be sexually active than men. The researchers put this down to the fact that women lacked partners; far more were widowed. Only 13 per cent of men but 35 per cent of women said sex was 'not at all important'. Among this 35 per cent must be quite a few of the women I spoke to.[2]

UK data supports this male–female difference in sexual activity and interest. The 2013 results of the Third National Survey of Sexual Attitudes and Lifestyles, the first to survey people aged up to seventy-four, found that 42 per cent of women and 60 per cent of men aged sixty-five to seventy-four had sex in the past year. They were the age groups having the least sex—2.3 times a month for men and 1.4 for women. The most newsworthy aspect of these results was the overall decline in sexual activity in the whole adult population since the previous survey in 2000. Too many other things to do or the stresses of modern life were the somewhat vague explanations offered by the researchers.[3]

Unlike the need for keeping up appearances there are fewer pressures on us to have or not have sex any more in the last third of our life. If you've got no interest in sex, you can give it up.

The one and only

'I had a belly full of it,' is how Margaret Fulton describes her feelings about sex. Margaret had two husbands and plenty of sexual partners before meeting the love of her life, Mike McKeag, a film producer. 'When I was in my sixties, it was the best time of my life,' she says, 'the best love affairs', great travels and wonderful times. After he died in 1988 Margaret was seventy-four and she lost interest in sex. She believes, 'the more sex you have the more you want, the less you have the less you want. It's just as simple as that.'

Margaret's use-it-or-lose-it view is not without some basis. More frequent sex stimulates circulation to the genitals and this enhances lubrication and the elasticity of vaginal tissues—both of which go a long way toward boosting a woman's enjoyment of sex. There's a psychological component too. You may stop wanting sex if you go a long time without it. This is partially because 'turning off' helps you avoid feelings of sexual frustration. Margaret says, 'I found I had enough. When Mike died I felt I had tried sex and that's it. I finished with it.' But sex is never just sex. For Margaret, and all the women, the physical is tied to the one they love. It was Mike McKeag she loved and wanted to be intimate with.

After more than a decade as a widow, Bertha Lowitt is still angry with her husband for dying: 'How could he deny me? Because the sex was fantastic and I miss it very much.' Bertha believes that we should forget the taboos and talk more about older people and sex. She and Julian had sex three or four times a week, 'And if he wasn't feeling well, so it was a little less or it lasted less, whatever. Boy I miss that very, very much.' Bertha still has sexual desires. 'Oh, yes,' she says, and she looks at men. But it's not any man or any sex that Bertha wants. 'I do look at men and say, "Boy, why couldn't Julian be walking that way".'

Stephanie Charlesworth wants to be absolutely clear with me. Sex is still part of her life and not a diminishing part. 'Why would it be?' she says. 'I can't talk about sex in that sort of a way as if it was something separate. It's more who you are and what your commitment is and what you are about.' For Stephanie, physical intimacy is enmeshed in her sense of self, her husband Max and a broader belief system. Stephanie and Max brought the Catholic couples' movement, Teams of Our Lady, to Australia, which works at strengthening Christian marriage. Married couples support each other through the highs and lows of their personal and religious lives.

Though they may not have as conceptually integrated a view on this issue as Stephanie, for the other women with husbands it's also all about the relationship with that one special person and not about the sex. The physical is the expression of their feelings for one another and their life together.

Cuddling in bed

'Seniors still frisky', 'Sexed-up seniors do it more than you'd think', and 'Don't for a minute think we older women live in some sex-free zone', is how newspaper headlines report results of surveys about older people and sex. The women I spoke with are older than any surveyed in these 'landmark' research studies that cut out at seventy-four, or, at the oldest, eighty-five. Does this mean the researchers can't imagine anyone over eighty-five having sex?

From the research to date we know that sexual activity diminishes as you get into your seventies. But that doesn't equate to the myth of the sexless grandmother. Not so long ago the accepted view was that after menopause your libido vanished and your vaginal juices dried up. Looking back, you wonder who those male scientists were talking to. It's completely untrue that all older women lose interest in sex after menopause. If they have a partner, the women do still have sex, and other women would like to if they could find someone.

'The intimacy was an important part of our marriage,' says Suzanne Simon. And in hard times, such as when their youngest daughter died, their physical closeness brought consolation and comfort. 'Really, having Alec helped me tremendously and, I dare say, I helped him when Jenny died. Because we could just lie with each other and talk and console each other and cry if we wished and it was a great help.' Sex is an important part of being close. It is a bridge to intimacy, physically and emotionally connecting two people, and that's why we keep doing it, whatever age we are.

I'm no Dr Kinsey or even Masters or Johnson, and I didn't press anyone for the actual details of what sex was like for those over eighty-five. Some of the women would have been honest with me if I'd asked—more honest than I'd be. I did discover, though, that if you have a partner you're likely to be enjoying a close physical relationship into your nineties.

That sexual activity changes as we get older is undeniable. Married to John since 1950, Frances Reynolds was the first woman I interviewed who had a husband. Having heard widows say that they'd still be having sex if they had a husband, I asked Frances. 'Well, how much of a sex life?' she responded. She told me that sex for her tapered off, especially after she had her aorta valve replaced. 'After the heart valve, the mechanics of it became more difficult. There is the inclination but not the carry through. Does that make sense?' She still has the closeness, 'That's why we still sleep in a double bed.'

Other women also talked about these inevitable changes. Dame Margaret Scott said, 'I love the intimacy with my husband. I don't expect to be a sex kitten—I think your physiology changes it for you. You go through a normal ageing sort of physiological thing which changes it for you, it's not a case of making a decision.'

More couples over the age of seventy are having sex than among previous generations. Better yet, they are enjoying it more. Researchers at the University of Gothenburg in Sweden interviewed seventy year olds in 1971–72, 1976–77, 1992–93 and 2000–01 and found an increase in sexual intercourse among both married and unmarried men and women over this thirty-year period. The greatest increase was among married women, from 38 per cent to 56 per cent. There was also an increase in women reporting orgasms and being highly satisfied with their sex lives. This was true even when sexual dysfunctions are present! That sexual pleasure increases with age is confirmed by a survey of

1400 people in the United States, and those older people inter-viewed by American sex expert Shere Hite.[4]

By the last third of your life, if you have a partner, you are likely to be having sex more often than your parents and grand-parents did, but probably less frequently than you did in earlier decades, and you'll be enjoying it more. Sex is about intimacy, touching and being close. As couples age they are more likely to engage in erotic experiences described as outercourse, meaning 'everything but ... it's lovemaking without penetration, but that involves kissing, nuzzling, hugging, oral sex ... It's pleasuring each other with sexy talk. Perhaps it's erotica or sex toys. It's play-ful and comes in quite handy as you age.'[5]

Without the external aids, outercourse is how Kali Paxinos and her husband maintained their 'loving warmth'. Kali 'had a very satisfying sexual life' until her husband developed a 'bad heart'. 'He was just on seventy and we had quite an active sex life up until about that time but after that we still had a loving warmth within each other without actually going through the whole sexual act. This is normal as you get older anyway,' says Kali, who believes that age is no barrier to physical intimacy.

'For a long time we had good sex and that's very important at that age. I can't imagine living without sex,' is the gospel accord-ing to Rose Stone. 'If Fred was alive, we'd pop into bed now for a cuddle. If it worked, it worked. If it didn't, we weren't worried.' That same advice comes from all the women who have partners and enjoy sex. You're going to be able to be close and get physical pleasure as long as the two of you both shall live.

None of these women's husbands were taking Viagra and there is as yet no Lybrido. We younger ones may want to try them but it seems, without taking any drugs, intimacy and female orgasm will always be available to you. If you have a partner you'll be able to pop into bed for a very satisfying cuddle and some hot inter or outercourse, no matter how old you are.

Finding someone new

But what about women—now on their own—who are not one-man women? At seventy-one Jane Fonda said she was having the best sex of her life, despite living with pain from hip and knee replacements and a back operation that put an end to her running. She was also planning to climb the Himalayas! Does she really remember sex at twenty or thirty or forty? And why does it have to be the best? Good or satisfying would do. Even the most energetic of the women in their late eighties and nineties aren't planning to climb even one Himalayan peak or work their way through the Kama Sutra.

Two years later Jane also told us she'd been taking testosterone to improve her libido. She has been divorced three times—she is no one-man woman. Neither are Rose Stone and Elisabeth Kirkby, also divorced women who found new partners. Rose was in her late fifties when she and Fred Lester got together. When he died, Rose was eighty-eight, and says she was too old and tired to start up with a new man. She would be too embarrassed by her old body. Rose still fancies men but is not prepared for the hard yakka you need to put into those early stages of any new relationship. If a good-looking, young man made the running, Rose could be interested. That's what happened to Marjorie McCool.

Marjorie met Kyle Jones when she was working in a Pittsburgh bookstore in 2009. She's now ninety-one and he's thirty-one. He only likes older women and is also going out with a sixty-eight year old. Marjorie told a journalist that he 'makes her feel alive again ... The physical side of the relationship is wonderful. I amaze myself and he amazes me ... I sometimes feel like he's another son, until we hop in bed. Then I feel different.'[6]

He doesn't seem ghoulish or a con man and, although there are not many Kyle Jones out there, it's cheering to read that he finds wrinkles, natural hanging skin and 'platinum' hair attractive.

Elisabeth Kirkby has had three long relationships since she was sixty. 'I have never been able to develop beyond those sorts of relationships because the individuals concerned were married. And that's just unfortunate.' Although she is almost twenty years older than Jane Fonda, Elisabeth has not lost her sexual desires. Her current relationship 'is moving on to a non-sexual relationship but he is still a very involved friendship.' Elisabeth would like to be more sexually active but men are more likely to develop late-life medical conditions that limit sex, and the men's problems then limit the women's sex lives. 'You can still have orgasmic dreams,' she says.

After her husband died Barbara Hamer 'wouldn't have minded' finding someone else. The ones she got reasonably close to 'made it quite clear that they weren't in the market for that kind of relationship, because they had had their prostate out'. Barbara was then seventy-four, now she's over it. Perhaps the if-you-don't-use-it-you-lose-it syndrome has kicked in. If I'd known Barbara earlier, I might have introduced a discussion of outercourse. I sense that Beth Gott knows all about it, having lived for many years with a husband with a serious heart condition.

Being ninety doesn't mean that Beth Gott is past sex. 'I don't think that vanishes, I still have sexual feelings and I think that if Ken were here we would still be having sex—and there are a couple of men around here that I fancy.' What attracts her is, 'Where I feel there is a meeting of minds.' Beth knows what she's looking for in a new relationship and it's the whole package—body and mind, sex and good conversations. These women do not believe that sex before or outside marriage is a sin. They live in a cultural and social milieu where people have affairs and get divorced. If an interesting and interested man came along, a bit younger and reasonably healthy, they'd be game to give it a whirl.

But stop! Do not rush into sex with a new partner unprotected. Across the United Kingdom, North America and elsewhere scientists have documented a rise in sexually transmitted infections (STIs) among fifty to ninety year olds. Most vulnerable of all are women past menopause, not worrying about condoms because they can't get pregnant. Before you get into bed with him, make sure that man is wearing a condom or risk getting syphilis, chlamydia, gonorrhoea, genital herpes or even HIV. Evidence from North America, Australia, China and Korea shows clearly increasing rates of many STIs in the population group aged fifty years and older.[7] In Australia, single people over fifty-one are more likely than other age groups to have unprotected one-night stands or sex on the first date, leading to this dramatic rise in sexually transmitted infections among older women.[8] Be warned. There are new dangers out there for an older woman in a new relationship. Insist on a condom.

This warning, though, does not apply to those women who want the man but not the sex. A 91-year-old friend wrote to me about what would make her life better: 'First of all having your husband or a lover at your side is the most important thing. I have always enjoyed the company of men and although there is no question of a romantic connection at this point, I like this idea of a male presence.' That's what Margaret Barnett and many other older women want, including Alice who lives in New York City. At eighty-nine Alice wanted male companionship: a man to go to dinner and the movies with her. One of her potential dates 'was only interested in one thing'—sex. Alice was sourcing her dates through an online dating site so she crossed him off her list.[9]

Love on the web

Among the group I interviewed not even the more technology savvy women had tried online dating. It was her children who encouraged Alice to try online dating and recommended that she lie about her age—the online Alice instantly became eleven years younger, seventy-eight. Two of the men she responded to had 'the ultimate attractive quality in an older man these days: they drive at night'.

If America's most famous home design-and-style guru Martha Stewart can do online dating then we can be sure that it has lost any stigma it may once have had as the last resort of weird losers hunched over their computers in dark basements. In April 2013 on NBC TV's *Today* show she very publicly joined Match.com, an online dating service with websites serving twenty-five countries in more than eight languages. Martha Stewart is just one of thousands of older women looking for a man online. The over-fifties are the fastest-growing subscriber group to Australian sites like RSVP, Match and Oasis, with reported growths in their numbers of 30 per cent annually.[10] With a 40 per cent increase, the over fifties are also the fastest growing group in the United Kingdom, where the internet comes second only to being introduced by a friend as the best way to meet a new partner.[11]

These Australian and UK figures use data only from people who join online dating sites. Surveying the adult population as a whole, the picture is also one of growth—though not as dramatic. Between 2005 and 2013 in the United States, online dating increased by 13 per cent among the sixty-five pluses and 9 per cent for the fifty to sixty-four age group. The fastest growing group of users are actually the eighteen to twenty-nine year olds, who are less likely to be looking for a long-term partner.[12] Even discounting the hype, and the hyperbole about 'foxy fifties' and 'silver surfers', boomer online dating is booming. The main reason for the increase in numbers of older people using sites is that boomers, who make up 35 per cent of the adult population of the United States, are getting older. That one is a no-brainer.

Online dating suits widows and divorcees who are unlikely to have been in a milieu with single straight men. We are intelligent enough to realise that going online is better than perching on a bar stool, hoping someone will pick us up. Online dating lets us see who's out there, beyond our small circle and, because there are more potential mates, there should be a better chance of a happy outcome. We can sit comfortably at home, in our spare time, and send out data and a younger photo of ourselves—apparently that's what most women do, whereas men tend to lie about how tall they are. We've got hundreds of sites to choose from. Companies know we're out there and there is money to be made—it's a $2 billion-plus business. Some sites charge for their services, some are free, at least temporarily, and some survive through advertising. They take different approaches to matchmaking. There are those that require long and detailed psychometric tests that take hours to fill in. Others start with immediate video hook-ups or let you know who's nearby for a quick get-together.

If you're looking for that special someone there's a niche site for you: gay, lesbian, Jewish, Muslim, and even if you're a dog. My Lovely Parent, where the children of single parents in their fifties recommend their parents for dates, is just one of many sites for the older age group. An Australian entrepreneur has launched a site that is 'on a mission to eradicate social isolation for mature adults'. Focused on interests rather than appearance, it's 'for those who are looking for more than just a date ... for those who are looking for true companionship'.

There are more women than men using sites for seniors and older daters spend more time looking at the sites than younger ones—they also go on more dates than any other group. They have the time and prefer talking and meeting people to the snappy back and forth of digital chat. On OurTime, the biggest of the US fifty-plus-specific singles sites, both men and women list 'Nature and Outdoors' as their number one interest. For men, this is followed by sports and then fitness, whereas for women it's family and friends and then travel. Don't imagine that for the older crowd it's all about interests: 87 per cent of singles aged fifty to seventy vote physical attraction as essential.[13]

The popularity of online dating for older women gets a boost from news stories like, '90-year-old Weds Beau Met on Match. com'. Computer savvy Molly Holder was a former journalist and poetry buff looking for love. She told a reporter that she went online because 'I knew some prince on a white horse wasn't going to ride up and sweep me off my feet, so I had to do it myself.' After emailing back and forth she took her 41-year-old grandson with her on her first date with 82-year-old Edward Nisbett, 'to make sure everything was on the up-and-up'. Nine months later they married. Heart warming isn't it? The message is that online you might find your soul mate at any age.[14]

But things didn't work out so well for Martha Stewart. After *Today Show* host Matt Lauer helped her comb through thousands of suitors, she went on dates with two divorcees, Larry and Stan, both sixty-eight. Her profile is still active online and she's still looking: 'I'd like to have breakfast with somebody. I'd like to go to bed with somebody. Sleep with somebody.' The reality is that the odds of finding a partner on the internet at her age—seventy-two—are tiny, even if you are as rich and attractive as Martha Stewart. Just 1 per cent of those aged sixty-five and over, and 3 per cent of the fifty to sixty-four age group met people they are in long-term relationships with on the internet.[15]

It's not the fault of the online dating sites. Demographically finding a new relationship is going to be a challenge. When you're fifty to fifty-four, there are equal numbers of single men and single women. By the time you're sixty to sixty-four, there are close to 2.3 single women to every single man. When you get to seventy the ratio is four to one.[16]

You are not without other options for finding both sexual chemistry and emotional commitment. If what you're looking for includes sharing a bed and reading snippets of the morning paper to each other—being part of a close and loving couple—then perhaps you should look for a woman. That gets you over the demographic disparity. I'm thinking of sharing this piece of advice with Martha Stewart and I can point to a swathe of celebrities who've switched to women. Taboos are slowly crumbling and sexual orientation, especially in women, is no longer seen as something fixed.

'Sexual fluidity' is a new way of understanding sexuality and it is more common in women than men. Women are more likely to fall in and out of love with men or women at different times in their lives. For many women it's about the person, not their gender.[17] Qualitative and anecdotal data is supported by an experiment at North Western University in which women became sexually aroused when they viewed heterosexual as well as lesbian erotic films. This was true for both gay and straight women. In contrast, straight men were turned on only by erotic films with women, and gay men by those with men.[18] Gender lines are blurring and social attitudes shifting. It would not surprise me to see a rise in women to women relationships among older women who are seeking that deep emotional connection and letting their attraction to women override whatever heterosexual orientation they had.

Not every woman with an interest in sex wants a lover or mate. We've known since 1974 that if it's orgasms we want then we don't need anyone but ourselves. That was the year The Hite Report on Female Sexuality came out, and Shere Hite showed us that masturbation was the best way for most women to orgasm easily and regularly. Women who want sex without the ties that bind are now likely to go shopping and buy themselves a vibrator, perhaps their first. As Iris Krasnow wrote, 'Vibrator sales are huge. I can tell you that a big chunk of that industry is sales to women over sixty.'[19]

As Elisabeth Kirkby says, 'you can have orgasmic dreams' at any age and there are many women who enjoy being single and sexual. By the time you are in the last third of your life there is no stigma in being single. None of the women I met would ever be thought of as 'old maids'. By the time you get to their age, being a woman on your own is the norm.

Being single

Mary Broughton obviously enjoyed being single. Otherwise, how could she say, 'It never entered my head,' when I asked her about remarriage. We know that the happiest years of her life for Joan Lowrie have been her single ones, after she was finally rid of the terrible burden of her alcoholic husband. Already in her late seventies, and after an experience like that, Joan did not rush out looking for another man to oppress her. For most of her life Koho Yamamoto has been single and loving it: 'Being single is wonderful, I don't have to cater to anyone, I can do whatever I wish. This is the happiest time.' About sex she says, 'I don't crave for it,' and explains, 'some say, 80 per cent of art is sex. So this is like a sexual act, that's what my former husband said one time, "You know they say 80 per cent is sex. It's like making out."' Despite not having been in a relationship for over thirty years, she is open to change. 'If I fall in love with somebody I think I could be sexually active. I haven't met anyone but I'm not dead yet.' If she does meet someone he'll have to live somewhere else.

Koho is like a lot of women I know who are happily single. They are not actively looking, but would be open to having a relationship if they met the right person, but it would definitely not be a live-in relationship. Jean Allison never married but did have lovers or 'gentlemen friends'. All proved 'unsuitable' because 'they were either married or not the marrying kind'. She lost interest 'with the menopause' and compares herself to her younger sister, who also never married but has always been in a relationship. Her sister, 'had a gentleman friend and she was devastated when he died, fairly young. She met another man, a widower.

And they are very good friends, but she's not going to give up her house, she might get another place of her own, nearer her friend.'

Widows, divorcees and single women get used to being in charge, running their own lives, not looking after someone else and not being looked after. Independence has its price but once you've acquired the taste, it's hard to give up.

Remarriage

Although none of the women I spoke to remarried, other older women do, and not only the Jane Fondas and Elizabeth Taylors. True love and old age are always newsworthy—with the subtext that 'while there's breath there's hope', plus a touch of the prurient: 'Just look at what these old folks get up to!' The oldest recorded bride is Australian: Minnie Munro, age 102, who married Dudley Reid, eighty-three, at Point Clare, New South Wales, on 31 May 1991.

Rose Pollard and Forrest Lunsway met thirty years ago and have been hiking, kayaking and ballroom dancing together ever since. Rose had no intention of remarrying and airily promised she'd marry Forrest on his hundredth birthday. And she kept her promise. The wedding made every news service and internet site in the country.[20] In the reporting of centenarian weddings there are detailed descriptions of the bride's dress, jewellery and flowers, the venue, and the guests, but no one asks why?

As with Forrest and Rose, it's the man who usually wants to get married. Hazi Abdul Noor, 120, was quite clear what he wanted and asked his children to find a new wife to look after him. His children didn't find it easy to find a bride for such an old man but six years after his first wife died he married Samoi Bibi, sixty, who said, 'I will try my best to take care of my husband.'[21]

Religious and cultural beliefs about sex and marriage motivate most of the weddings of people who would not contemplate sex outside marriage. In a Catholic ceremony at the Rosewood

Health Care Center in Bowling Green, Kentucky, where both of them live, 100-year-old Dana Jackson married 87-year-old Bill Stauss. Her fluffy white wedding dress was tucked into her wheelchair and he leaned on his walker. The telling fact is that after the wedding they moved into a room together! No doubt there are rules at the nursing home about people not living together in sin.[22] Needing to conform to social codes of behaviour also pushed James Mason, ninety-three, into a quick proposal. Even though he visited Peggy Clark, eighty-four, with an elderly neighbour as chaperone, 'people were starting to gossip'. To stop the gossips he proposed to Peggy three days after they met at a day-care centre, One month later they married.[23]

Despite the headlines proclaiming that it's never too late to find love, and the desire of most men and some women to marry, there are very few remarriages among widows. In Australia it's predicted that 3 per cent of widowed women can expect to remarry.[24] Remarriage rates tell us little about the new relationships women form. Fewer and fewer of us are worried about 'living in sin'. The generation now coming into the last third of their lives—the boomers—were part of the sexual revolution. They don't need marriage to sanctify the sexual act.

What older women want

There are patterns I've observed in women who are widowed or divorced in their sixties, the age when that male to female imbalance kicks in. After they get over the initial grief and shock of their loss, they put themselves on the market. A little bit of work on the face, a different hair colour or style, some new clothes or moving to a suburb with a more singles-oriented lifestyle and demographic.

Janet joined a singles walking group. Sandra reconnected to an old boyfriend who she knew was single. Ellen started to travel with mixed groups to exotic places like Mongolia and Georgia. Their friends asked them to dinners and outings, inviting any single male they knew. Annie tried internet dating. A few years passed. Those who haven't found anyone settle into a rich and full life of work, close female friends, children, grandchildren, book groups and film clubs. They enjoy living alone and being independent. Whether they are sexually active or not I can't say. They could be self-pleasuring or, like Koho, not craving sex but not closed to it if the right person came along.

A few—perhaps one in five—find a new man. Most of them do not live together, although the new lovers often pressure them, and offer enticements of a larger house in a better suburb, and the fact that two can live more cheaply than one. They do have sex, exactly how and what I do not know, but probably satisfactory physical intimacy or why bother. They stay over at each other's houses, two to three nights a week, go out together as a couple and go on holidays together. Their families—children, siblings, grandchildren—get together on special occasions but otherwise they run a separate family life, finances and household.

What's the difference? Mainly it's wanting a man more and therefore putting more effort into finding one for longer—being determined and persistent. My mother's friend Genia won't say how old she is but we can guess from the fact that she went to university in 1943. Genia is a very smart and sexy woman who likes men. Since her husband died she's had a number of long-term male friends, one who lived with her for about ten years before he died, and others since. Genia looks great and is fun and interesting to be with. Available men are attracted to her vitality and sex appeal. It's not a case of her taking any man who can walk and talk—she's ended relationships that haven't pleased her. For a woman of her age, about ninety, she is very unusual. None of the women I interviewed want a man enough to go to this much trouble.

It is more likely to be the younger older women, women in their fifties and sixties, who still want both the physical and emotional connection enough to start again with a new person. They have the last third of their lives still in front of them and the time, all being well, to get to know a new person and make a new life together, even if they choose to live apart. These women will need to put time and work into their quest. Going to the football, taking up drag car racing and other activities where men outnumber women is a way to start. You need to put that light bulb of availability on, and give out a clear signal. In some circles women have been known to slip a piece of paper with their phone number into the pocket of the grieving widower at the cemetery. A widower's refrigerator usually overflows with casseroles from women who believe that the best way to get a man is through his stomach. Now that online dating is available, though, it's probably a better option than all that cooking.

A few women want to marry. The only women I know who married in their fifties and sixties had been looking for a relationship for many, many years, had never married or that marriage had failed decades earlier. None of these women had children and all acquired step-children and step-grandchildren, who they've become close to and involved with.

The future

What I've learned from talking to women and reading about what sex can be like as we age is that we need to talk about it more. Most of us are ignorant about the experience of other women and we believe the myths of a total loss of libido after menopause and the inevitability of the decline of sexual activity and pleasure. We need consciousness-raising groups, not to promote more sex but to learn from each other in an atmosphere of acceptance, where it's okay never to want sex again or to learn to use a vibrator.

In these groups we could read more about our sexuality and discuss the clitoris and why it's been denigrated in the past as the site of sexual pleasure. For instance, did you know that the clitoris contains at least eight thousand sensory nerve endings, compared to about four thousand in the penis? It also keeps growing throughout our lives so that after menopause, the clitoris is about seven times larger than it was at birth. Not surprisingly, then, women report increased sexual satisfaction as they get older. Unlike the male sex organ, the clitoris never ages. Once it matures, it maintains its sexual peak for the rest of a woman's life. And that's just a fraction of the things I didn't know about the clitoris before I started writing this book.

Sex is much easier to write about than to talk about. The most direct discussions I've had with women about the sexual act were in southern Africa, where women have learned to talk specifics in response to the spread of AIDS. South African women told me shocking details, such as how men put washing powder into women's vaginas to increase friction when they penetrate and thereby their pleasure. On a never-to-be-forgotten occasion in Maputo, when we were talking about how to educate women so they could get men to wear condoms, our interpreter said, 'I can't do that.' Her husband travelled for his work but she couldn't ask him to wear a condom as that would imply he was being unfaithful. At that moment all of us realised we were in the same place when it came to talking about sex with our partners. We need to learn more about how to talk about sex.

In the future, after we've been to our new consciousness raising groups, we'll be better able to express what we want, armed with role models like Rose and Bertha and what we've learned. If I'm widowed, I will try a clitoral vibrator and other sex toys— they sound like fun. And I'm very happy to have learned about outercourse and my sexual fluidity. As in all other aspects of our life as we age, what's important is to keep learning, and stay flexible and open to new experiences.

HOT TIPS For sex and remarriage

➤ Talk openly to other women and your partners about sex. Do not talk to your children—no matter how old they get your children will not want to know.

➤ Remember, where there's a will there's a way.

➤ Knowing what you want is the key and, if you don't know, experiment with some of the options so you can make an informed decision.

➤ Give it up if you have no interest in sex. It is perfectly fine not to want or need sex.

➤ Before you give up sex, read about the clitoris and give self-pleasuring a go. No one need ever know.

➤ It could be true that if you don't use it, you lose it—another reason for some experimentation before you make your final decision.

➤ If you feel that you want to want sex more, you might try Lybrido should it be available and proved safe and effective.

➤ If you have a partner there is no age at which you need to stop having sex, although at some stage you might need to move to outercourse.

➤ If you want to find a partner, make a list of the qualities you're looking for.

➤ For those seeking male companionship, be clear with any prospects that you are not interested in a sexual relationship if that's the case.

➤ Try online sites and make sure you do your research. What's important to you—a hot night of sex every now and again, a younger man or shared interests? Choose a dating site that will work for you. And don't lie, well not too wildly.

➤ If you want a long-term relationship that combines sexual pleasure and emotional commitment, and you are over seventy, you are more likely to find the right woman than a man.

➤ Learn more about your own body.

➤ You can be a sexual being without being in a relationship.

➤ Buy a cliterol vibrator and see how you like it.

➤ Always insist that your new man wears a condom. Buy a packet and keep them somewhere handy—in your handbag and the drawer of your bedside table are two good spots.

➤ Building and sustaining any new relationship involves attention, time and effort, compromise and cooperation. Ask yourself if you care enough about this person to put in the hard yards?

➤ How important is your independence to you? How much of it are you prepared to give up for a new relationship? You are both fully formed beings with your own habits and likes and dislikes.

➤ Be wary about moving in with a new love. Always keep your own home in case it doesn't work out.

➤ Talk to your children and grandchildren before you shack up with anyone. They need to know why you've made this decision.

➤ Decide carefully how much you want to blend your lives. Whatever you decide, keep your finances separate.

➤ Make sure you have a will. You can leave your money to anyone you like. Let your family and partner know what's in the will. If you are wealthy you may need to do more than a will to ensure your money goes where and to whom you want it to.

Acknowledgements

Everyone I've spoken with, and everything I've read, seen and done over the last four years, has fed into this book. It's been great fun trying out ideas and heartening to hear the positive responses—especially from women—when I told them what I was writing. 'I can't wait to read your book,' is what most said.

For connecting me to such wonderful women to interview I am grateful to my friends Barbara Fiorito, Ilana Abramovitch and Carole Kunstadt in New York, and Beth Thyer, Helen Light, Jeannie Shorland, Helen Vorrath, Judy Turner and Glenyys Romanes in Melbourne. Thank you also to Dr Rodney Syme, Sandy Grant of HardieGrant Publishing, Jane Peck, president of the Lyceum Club, and especially to Susan Ryan, Australia's first Age Discrimination Commissioner.

Among the many experts and researchers I contacted to confirm facts and interpretations, only one chose not to assist me. I appreciate these busy people making the time and effort to answer my queries and extend my knowledge.

How lucky I've been with my publisher, Melbourne University Publishing. Thank you Louise Adler for immediately giving the book an enthusiastic thumbs up, and to Sally Heath for your guidance and encouragement. I've never had an editor while writing a book before and now I'll never be able to do without one. Thank you Yael Cohn for typing all the transcripts and to Monica Svarc, Cathryn Smith and everyone else at MUP—you've been a delight to work with.

My beloved family and friends are probably breathing a sigh a
relief that they won't be bombarded with factoids about growing
older and anecdotes about this or that wonderful old woman I've
met. Perhaps they are also dreading what I'll take up next. Watch
this space.

Apologies if you've helped along the way and I've forgotten
to thank you. Put it down to anomia, and that my brain is so full
of information that I can't always retrieve everything on demand.
To all who've been part of this book, a heartfelt thank you. I hope
you are pleased with the result.

Notes

Introduction

1. E Wilder, 'An Afternoon With Bel Kaufman', viewed at www. advancedstyle.blogspot.com.
2. 'Life Expectancy Trends—Australia', 4192.0, Australian Social Trends, Australian Bureau of Statistics, viewed at www.abs.gov.au.
3. 'Life Expectancy: Data by Country', 2012, Global Health Observatory Data Repository, World Health Organization, viewed at http://apps.who. int/gho/data/node.main.
4. ibid.
5. 'Life Expectancy Trends', op cit.
6. P Hetherington, 'Research dispels old myths about ageing', *The Guardian*, 29 May 2012, quoting Professor Kirkwood, Head of the Biomedical Research Centre in Ageing at Newcastle University: 'UN forecasts of 1980 predicted it was going to bump into a ceiling and stop increasing next week, but it didn't happen; [it] carried on increasing pretty much as before.'
7. Media Release, 'Population Projections Australia 2012 (base) to 2101', 3222.0, Australian Bureau of Statistics, viewed at www.abs.gov.au. Much is written about eighty-five plus being the fastest-growing age group in Australia, the United Kingdom and the United States. The reality is that although the number of people over eighty-five is predicted to triple, or even quadruple, by 2040, the increase in Australia is from 2 per cent of the population in 2012 to just 4 per cent in 2040—'Life Expectancy Trends—Australia', 4102.0, Australian Social Trends, March 2011, Australian Bureau of Statistics at www.abs.gov.au. The data is similar for the United Kingdom and the United States: see, respectively, J Bingham, 'Golden girls' era passing as men close longevity gap on women', *The Telegraph*, 17 February 2014, and W He and MN Muenchrath, US Census Bureau, American Community Survey Reports, ACS-17, '90+

in the United States: 2006–2008', US Government Printing Office, Washington, DC, 2011.

8. Dr MM Merzenich, 'Change minds for the better', *The Journal on Active Aging*, November/December 2005, pp. 22–30.

1 A Working Life

1. T Colebatch, 'Working longer, retiring stronger', *The Sydney Morning Herald*, 9 February 2012.

2. M Toosi, 'Employment Outlook 2006–16, Labor Force Projections to 2016: more workers in their golden years', *Bureau of Labor Statistics Monthly Review*, US, November 2007, pp. 33–50.

3. A Ellin, 'For Some, Retirement is Out of Reach. For Others, Boring', *The New York Times*, 31 January 2014.

4. *Australian Biography Series 6: Margaret Fulton,* directed and produced by Robin Hughes and Linda Kruger, Film Australia, Sydney, 1997.

5. Quoted in L Turner, 'Work Longer, Live Healthier? How retirement can seriously damage your health', *The Independent*, 16 May 2013, using data from GH Sahlgren, 'Work Longer, Live Healthier: The relationship between economic activity, health and government policy', Institute of Economic Affairs Discussion Paper no. 46, May 2013, London.

6. E Calvo, 'Does Working Longer Make People Healthier and Happier?', Center for Retirement Research at Boston University, February 2006, viewed at http://crr.bc.edu/briefs/.

7. Quoted in I Cowrie, 'Delay Retirement and Live Longer Experts Say but Dead Comedian Disagreed', *The Telegraph*, 3 November 2014. See also H Friedman and L Martin, *The Longevity Project: Surprising discoveries for health and long life from the eight-decade study*, Hudson Street Press, New York, 2011.

8. N Bita, 'Baby Boomers to Work into 80s', 26 November 2013, viewed at www.news.com.au.

9. Quoted in 'It's the Same Old Story for Australian Women', 31 July 2004, viewed at www.theage.com.au.

10. S Cote and LM Miller, 'A Longitudinal Analysis of the Association Between Emotion Regulation, Job Satisfaction, and Intentions to Quit', *Journal of Organizational Behavior*, vol. 23, no. 8, December 2002, pp. 947–62.

11. Skill Shortages, Employment Research and Statistics, Department of Employment, Australian Government, viewed at https://employment.gov.au/skill-shortages.

12. 'Dame Scott Dances Again in Nutcracker', transcript of *7.30 Report*, ABC Television, 24 February 2000, viewed at www.abc.net.au/7.30/stories/s103130.htm.

13. T Colebatch, 'Working Longer, Retiring Stronger', *The Sydney Morning Herald*, 9 February 2012.

14. F Norris, 'The Number of Those Working Past 65 is at a Record High', *The New York Times,* 18 May 2012; and P McDonald, 'Employment at Older Ages in Australia: Determinants and trends' in T Griffin and F Beddie (eds), *Older Workers: Research readings*, National Centre for Vocational Education Research, Department of Education, Employment and Workplace Relations, Adelaide, 2011, pp. 25–41.

15. M Miller, 'Older Unemployed Workers Half as Likely to Get Hired', 14 January 2011, viewed at http://blogs.reuters.com; based on data from RW Johnson and J Park, 'Can Unemployed Older Workers Find Work?' Urban Institute, Washington DC, 12 January 2011, viewed at www.urban.org/publications/.

16. E Gringart and E Helmes, 'Age Discrimination in Hiring Practices Against Older Adults in Western Australia: the Case of Accounting Assistants', *Australasian Journal of Ageing*, vol. 20, no. 1, March 2001, pp. 23–28.

17. Australian Human Rights Commission, 'Fact or Fiction? Stereotypes of Older Australians', Research Report, Canberra, 2013.

18. Miller, 'Older Unemployed Workers Half as Likely to Get Hired', op. cit.

19. Buttonwood, 'Keep on Trucking: Why the old should not make way for the young', *The Economist*, 11 February 2012.

20. D Fastenberg, 'Worker Debra Moreno Wins $193,000 in Age Discrimination Lawsuit', 25 July 2012, viewed at www.huffingtonpost.com.

21. S Rice, 'Why My Age is My Concern, Not Yours: Ageism, law and human rights', paper presented at COTA Australia National Policy Forum, Melbourne, July 2013.

22. 'Staying Ahead of the Curve 2013: The AARP work and career study—older workers in an uneasy job market', AARP Research, Washington DC, January 2014.

23. D Fastenberg, 'Employer Vita Needle Seeks Elderly Workers', 6 September 2012, viewed at http://jobs.aol.com.

24. 'Working Past our 60s: Reforming laws and policies for the older worker', Heading 132, Australian Human Rights Commission, Canberra, June 2012.

25. Australian Bureau of Statistics, Voluntary Work, cat. no. 4441.0, ABS, Canberra, 2006.
26. 'Realising the Economic Potential of Senior Australians: Turning grey into gold', Final Report of the Advisory Panel on the Economic Potential of Senior Australians, Canberra, December 2011.
27. Email from B Howe, member of The Advisory Panel on the Economic Potential of Senior Australians, 27 February 2014.

2 Love and Loss

1. 'Life Expectancy Trends-Australia', 4102.0, Australian Social Trends, Australian Bureau of Statistics, March 2011, viewed at www.abs.gov.au/AUSSTATS.
2. 'Widowhood: Demography of the widowed', The Marriage and Family Encyclopaedia, viewed at www.family.jrank.org.
3. 'Widows Better Off on Wellbeing Index: Survey', Business Standard, 26 December 2013, reporting on data from the annual NAB Wellbeing Index that surveyed 2100 Australians, viewed at www.business-standard.com.
4. *Australian Biography Series 3: Flo Bjelke-Petersen*, directed and produced by Frank Heimanns, Film Australia, Sydney, 1994.
5. AR Rey, 'Global Poll: Most Believe in God, Afterlife', *The Christian Post*, 26 April 2011, reporting on a global survey of 18,000 people conducted by Ipsos Social Research, London.
6. D Marr, 'Faith: What Australians believe in', *The Age*, 19 December 2009.
7. D Cole, 'Study Finds Grieving Men Retreat, While Women Reach Out for Help: Psychology: Coping styles of women and men may be linked to socialization. By learning about the differences, we can help one another to suffer less, researchers say', *Los Angeles Times,* 18 November 1989.
8. R Davis Konigsberg, '5 Surprising Truths About Grief', 14 March 2011, viewed at www.aarp.org.
9. T Rando PhD, 'Sudden Death', 1 June 2008, viewed at www.legacy.com.
10. 'April Hamer Enjoys Darebin's University of the Third Age', *Preston Leader*, 4 April 2012.
11. Dr S Jain, 'Lifetime Marriage and Divorce Trends', 4102.0, Australian Social Trends, 2007, 7 August 2007, viewed at www.abs.gov.au.
12. D Carr, 'The desire to date and remarry among older widows and widowers', *Journal of Marriage and Family*, vol. 66, no. 4, November 2004, pp. 1051–68.
13. ibid.

14. K Davidson, 'Gender differences in new partnership choices and constraints for older widows and widowers', *Ageing International*, vol. 27, no. 4, Fall 2002, pp. 43–60.

15. D Schneider, P Sledge, S Shuchter and S Zisook, 'Dating and Remarriage Over the First Two Years of Widowhood', *Annals of Clinical Psychiatry*, vol. 8, 1996, pp. 51–57.

16. J Bingham, 'Silver Sinners? How decline of taboos about sex is transforming life for the over-85s', *The Telegraph*, 6 December 2013.

17. M Bury and A Holme, *Life After 90*, Routledge, London, p. 23, 1991.

18. Jain, 'Lifetime Marriage and Divorce Trends', op. cit.

19. M Healy, 'Adult Orphans: When parents die', *Los Angeles Times*, 5 May 2008.

20. D Umberson, *Death of a Parent: Transition to a new adult identity*, Cambridge University Press, New York, 2003, cited by Healy, 'Adult Orphans', op. cit.

21. LA Schreiber, 'When a Parent Dies', *O, The Oprah Magazine*, November 2004, p. 6.

22. D Athel, *Somewhere Towards the End: A memoir*, WW Norton & Company, New York, 2009.

23. *Australian Biography Series 6: Margaret Fulton,* directed and produced by Robin Hughes and Linda Kruger, Film Australia, Sydney, 1997.

24. 'When a Child Dies', A Survey of Bereaved Parents Conducted by NFO Research Inc. on behalf of The Compassionate Friends Inc., Chicago, June 1999, viewed at www.compassionatefriends.org.

25. 'Sibling Relationships Across the Life Span', Marriage and Family Encyclopaedia, viewed at www.family.jrank.org; and Wikipedia at http://en.wikipedia.org/wiki/Sibling_relationship.

26. Viewed at http://family.jrank.org/pages/1564/Sibling-Relationships-Sibling-Relationships-across-Life-Span.html. There is a lack of comparative data in Australia.

27. 'Sibling Relationships Across the Life Span', op. cit.

28. CA Price, 'Aging Families—Series Bulletin #1: Sibling Relations in Later Life', Ohio State University, undated, viewed at www.osu.edu.

29. 'Britons lose friends as they age', *The Guardian*, 25 July 2001.

30. RG Adams, 'Patterns of Network Change: A Longitudinal Study of Friendships of Elderly Women', *The Gerontologist*, vol. 27, no. 2, 1987, pp 222–27.

31. D Shmotkin, 'Affective bonds of adult children with living versus deceased parents', *Psychology and Aging*, vol. 14, no. 3, September 1999, pp. 473–82.

3 Being Well

1. 'Healthy Ageing', Achievement Report, The Australian Longitudinal Study on Women's Health, March 2005. Other studies confirm that older Australians 'overwhelmingly' say they have good, very good or excellent health: COTA NSW 50+ Report, Council of the Ageing NSW, Sydney, February 2014.

2. 'Lady Flo Turns 90!' *Woman's Day*, 9 August 2010.

3. P Hetherington, 'Research dispels old myths about ageing', *The Guardian*, 29 May 2012.

4. 'The U-bend of life', *The Economist*, 16 December 2010.

5. Laura Carstensen, 'Older People are Happier', TedxWomen 2011, viewed at www.ted.com/talks/laura-carstensen_older_people_are_happier? language=en.

6. Michael Bury and Anthea Holme, *Life After 90*, Routledge, London, 1991, p. 64.

7. J Medew, 'Rational suicide: Why Beverley Broadbent chose to die', *The Age*, 2 April 2013.

8. ibid.

9. J McCarthy, 'Seven in 10 Americans Back Euthanasia', 18 June 2014, viewed at www.gallup.com.

10. 'Majority of Brits want assisted suicide legalised as new poll reveals strong support for change in the law across Europe', *Mail Online*, 30 November 2012, viewed at www.mailonline.co.uk.

11. Abdul Lateef, 'Euthanasia in Canada: Survey Shows Overwhelming Support For Assisted Dying', *The Canadian Press*, 8 October 2014, viewed at www.huffingtonpost.ca.

12. B Carey, 'The Older Mind May Just Be a Fuller Mind', *The New York Times*, 27 January, 2014.

13. 'Older Adult Drivers: Get the facts', Motor Vehicle Safety, Centers for Disease Control and Prevention, viewed at www.cdc.gov.

14. P Tariot, Banner Alzheimer's Institute, 'A New Era of Alzheimer's Research: Focusing on prevention', 12 March 2013, viewed at www. huffingtonpost.com.

15. D Snowden, 'Aging with Grace: What the Nun Study teaches us about leading longer, healthier and more meaningful lives', Bantam Paperback, New York, 2002, p. 3.

16. M Bury and A Holme, *Life After 90*, Routledge, London, 1991, p. 77.

17. '90-year-olds mentally sharper than recent generations', 11 July 2013, viewed at www.cbs.news.

18. Snowden, Aging with Grace', op. cit., p. 99.

19. E Innes, 'Could a Laser Zap Away Alzheimer's, Parkinson's and even CJD?' *Mail Online*, 4 November 2013, viewed at www.dailymail.co.uk.

20. K Jagger, 'Breast cancer mammograms: Overrated and over-diagnosing women', 28 April 2014, viewed at www.theguardian.com, quoting results of studies of nearly 90,000 Canadian women over a 25-year period in *The British Medical Journal,* February 2014, and N Biller-Andorno and P Juni, 'Abolishing Mammography Screening Programs? A view from the Swiss Medical Board', *New England Journal of Medicine*, vol. 370, no. 21, 22 May 2014, pp. 1965–67.

21. A Hill, 'Elderly "Live Longer if They are Overweight"', 13 February 2010, viewed at www.theguardian.com.

22. M Sollitto, 'Exercise for the Elderly', viewed at www.agingcare.com.

23. J-M Kvamme, J Holmen, et al., 'Body Mass Index and Mortality in Elderly Men and Women: the Tromsø and HUNT studies', *Journal of Epidemiology & Community Health*, early 2011, viewed at www.jech. bmj.com; L Flicker, KA McCaul, et al., 'Body Mass Index and Survival in Men and Women Aged 70 to 75', *Journal of the American Geriatrics Society*, vol. 58, no. 2, viewed at onlinelibrary.wiley.com/doi: 10.1111/j.1532-5415.2009.02677.x/abstract.

24. Hill, 'Elderly "Live Longer if They are Overweight"', op. cit.

25. JGZ van Uffelen, J Berecki-Gisolf, et al., 'What Is a Healthy Body Mass Index for Women in Their Seventies?' results from the Australian Longitudinal Study on Women's Health, *The Journals of Gerontology*, vol.65a, no. 8, April 2010, pp. 847–53.

26. A Sifferlin, 'Eat More Mediterranean Foods Now: Your later self will thank you', *Time*, 4 November 2013.

27. M Castillo, 'Meat, Dairy May be as Detrimental to Your Health as Smoking Cigarettes, Study Says,' 4 March 2014, viewed at www.cbs. news.com.

28. M Bittman, 'Butter is Back', *The New York Times*, 25 March 2014.

29. H Villarica, 'The Secrets to Long Life: Worry, worry hard and marry well (if you're a man)', *Time*, 17 March 2011.

4 Money Matters

1. K Betts, 'The ageing of the Australian population: triumph or disaster?' Australian Policy Online, 24 April 2014, viewed at www.apo.org.au.

2. 'Healthy Ageing', Achievement Report, The Australian Longitudinal Study on Women's Health, March 2005.

3. Interview with Roslyn Odgers and Larke Reimer, April 2014. Odgers is a director of Westpac Private Bank and has held a wide range of positions in banking, and specialises in advising women about money. Reimer is the director of Women's Markets for Westpac. In 2009, she was appointed chair of the Global Banking Alliance for Women in Banking. She is a world-recognised expert on women and money.

4. D Olsberg, 'Women and Superannuation: Still MS ... ing Out', *Journal of Australian Political Economy*, no. 53, June 2004, pp. 161–78.

5. *Australian Biography Series 3: Flo Bjelke-Petersen*, directed and produced by Frank Heimanns, Film Australia, Canberra, 1994.

6. *Australian Biography Series 6: Margaret Fulton*, directed and produced by Robin Hughes and Linda Kruger, Film Australia, Sydney, 1997.

7. ibid.

8. 'Home equity release', ASIC MoneySmart, viewed at www.moneysmart.gov.au.

9. RA Cummins, J Woerner, et al., 'Household Income', The Wellbeing of Australians: Social media, personal achievement, and work, Deakin University, Geelong, 2013, pp. 85–87.

10. M Bury and A Holme, *Life After 90*, Routledge, London, 1991, p. 32.

11. Household, Income and Labour Dynamics in Australia (HILDA) Survey, 2010, Melbourne Institute of Applied Economic and Social Research, University of Melbourne, 2011.

12. D Kadlec, 'Sizing Up the Big Question: How much money do you need to retire', *Time*, 11 February 2013, viewed at www.business.time.com.

13. 'How Much Super Will I Need?' SuperGuru, viewed at www.superguru.com.au.

14. Interview with Larke Reimer, Director, Westpac Women's Markets, Melbourne, May 2014.

15. D Hood, 'Retirement: A Number You'll Love', MoneySense, 14 April 2008, viewed at www.moneysense.ca.

16. C O'Hara, '10 Myths That Could Ruin Your Retirement', *The Week*, 23 January 2014, viewed at www.theweek.com.

17. Hood, 'Retirement: A Number You'll Love', op. cit.

18. ibid.

19. A Horin, 'Pet Ownership linked to Depression', *The Sydney Morning Herald*, 24 April 2004, viewed at www.smh.com.

20. 'Trends in Superannuation Coverage', Australian Social Trends, Australian Bureau of Statistics, 25 March 2009, viewed at www.abs.gov.au.

21. 'Women Must Work 25 Years More to Retire with the Same Amount of Super as Men', Westpac Media Release, The Westpac Women & Retirement Readiness Report conducted by Sweeney Research August 2013, 4 November 2013.
22. 'Who manages the money in your family?' Fidelity Viewpoints, 23 September 2013, viewed at www.fidelity.com.
23. J de Silva and A Harnath, 'Super-Poor but Surviving: Experiences of Australian women in retirement', Australian Institute of Superannuation Trustees, Melbourne, 2011, viewed at www.aist.asn.au.

5 Keeping Up Appearances

1. T Kiisel, 'You Are Judged by Your Appearance', *Forbes*, 20 March 2013, viewed at www.forbes.com.
2. S Tantleff-Dunn, 'Biggest Isn't Always Best: The effect of breast size on perceptions of women', *Journal of Applied Social Psychology*, vol. 32, no. 11, 2002, pp. 2253–65.
3. J Willis and A Todorov, 'First Impressions: Making up your mind after a 100-Ms exposure to faces', *Psychological Science*, vol. 17, no. 7, July 2007, pp. 592–98.
4. A Glennie, 'I Dye My Grey Hair Because Age is an Issue For Women on TV, says Fiona Bruce', *Mail Online*, 17 September 2012, viewed at www.dailymail.co.uk.
5. P Dunbar, 'Why Britain's Next Top Models are Over SIXTY: As retailers chase the grey pound as never before, older women are topping up their pensions with £2,000 modelling jobs', *Mail Online*, 13 July 2014, viewed at www.dailymail.co.uk.
6. A Kreamer, 'Looking For a Job When You're No Longer Young', *Harvard Business Review*, 12 March 2012, viewed at www.hbs.org.
7. D Solomon, 'Cutup', *The New York Times Magazine*, 31 December 2008.
8. J Wong, 'Hillary Clinton Doesn't Care If You See Her Without Make-up', *Today Style*, 9 May 2012, viewed at www.today.com.
9. N Johnson, 'Dame Helen Mirren Admits that Photo of Her in the Red Bikini Will Haunt Her for the Rest of Her Days', *HeraldSun*, 4 July 2014.
10. B Talarico, 'Helen Mirren Works Out for 12 Minutes a Day, Says She's Retired Her Bikini', *People*, 24 July 2014, viewed at www.people.com.
11. Karen Kay, 'Elderly Struck by "Epidemic" of Body Image and Eating Disorders', *The Observer*, 9 June 2012, viewed at www.theguardian.com.

12. J McCarthy, 'Older Americans Feel Best About Their Physical Appearance', Gallup, viewed at www/gallup.com.

13. L Abbit, 'In the Flesh: Aleah Chapin's Aunties Project', *Senior Planet*, 15 December 2013, viewed at www.seniorplanet.org.

14. Mary Beard, 'Too Ugly for TV? No, I'm too brainy for men who fear clever women', *Mail Online*, 23 April 2012, viewed at www.dailymail.co.uk.

15. B Dowell, 'Mary Beard Suffers "Truly Vile" Abuse after *Question Time*', *The Guardian*, 21 January 2013, viewed at www.theguardian.com.

16. Article from Hoopla quoted in J Davies, 'The Mysterious Case of the Disappearing Women', *The Sydney Morning Herald*, 19 January 2013.

17. 'Women Feel "Invisible" by the Age of 51: Confidence plummets after hitting 50, says new study', *Mail Online*, 25 March 2014, viewed at www.dailymail.co.uk.

18. ibid.

6 Home or a Home?

1. K McGarry and R Schoeni, 'Social Security, Economic Growth, and the Rise in Independence of Elderly Widows in the 20th Century', National Bureau of Economic Research, Working Paper no. 6511, April 1998, viewed at www.nber.org.

2. J Bryant Quinn, 'When Parents Move in with Kids', AARP Bulletin, 6 September 2012, viewed at www.aarp.org.

3. C Kahn, '10 Best States for Retirement', Bankrate, undated, viewed at www.bankrate.com.

4. LE Troll, 'Family Connectedness of Old Women: Attachments in later life' in B Formaniak Turner and LE Troll (eds), *Women Growing Older: Psychological perspectives*, Sage Publications, Thousand Oaks, CA, 1994, pp. 169–201.

5. M Bury and A Holme, *Life After 90*, Routledge, London, 1991, p. 106.

6. B Friedan, *The Fountain of Age*, Simon and Schuster, New York, 2006.

7. Y Davydov, 'Kensett at Hoyt and Wakemore Opens', *Darien Times*, 2 October 2012, viewed at www.darientimes.com.

8. D Athill, 'Why I Moved into an Old People's Home', *The Guardian*, 17 April 2010.

9. 'Caring for Older Australians', Report no. 53, Final Inquiry Report, Productivity Commission, Canberra, 2011.

10. G Vaillant, *Triumphs of Experience: The men of the Harvard Grant Study*, Belknap Press, 2012, data from JW Rowe and RL Kahn, *Successful Aging*, Dell, New York, 1999.

11. Athill, 'Why I Moved into an Old People's Home', op. cit.

12. Friedan, *The Fountain of Age*, op. cit., p. 378.
13. ibid., p. 526.

7 Technology

1. K McKinney, 'Ignore Age—Define generations by the tech they use', *Vox*, 20 April 2014, viewed at www.vox.com.
2. Communication Report 2012–2013, Australian Communication and Media Authority, Melbourne, December 2013, viewed at www.acma.gov.au.
3. J Chesters, C Ryan and M Sinning, *Older Australians and the Take-up of New Technologies*, NCVER, Adelaide, 2013.
4. K Jones, 'Women Fight to Break into Nerd World of IT', *The Age*, 13 October 2013.
5. 'Women in Computing', Wikipedia, viewed at www.en.wikipedia.org, citing data from TJ Misa, ed., *Gender Codes: Why women are leaving computing*, Wiley/IEEE Computer Society Press, 2010, pp. 32–34.
6. H Seybert, 'Gender Differences in the Use of Computers and the Internet', Eurostat, European Communities, Luxembourg, 2007, viewed at www.bibsonomy.org.
7. Chesters et al., '*Older Australians and the Take-up of New Technologies*', op. cit., p. 38.
8. A Smith, 'Older Adults and Technology Use', Pew Research Internet Project Report, 3 April 2014, viewed at www.pewinternet.org.
9. A Qureshi, 'German Researchers Develop Assistant Robot FRIEND for People with Disabilities', *Global Accessibility News*, 6 March 2012, viewed at www.globalaccessibilitynews.com.
10. Australian Mobile Phone Lifestyle Index 2013, Australian Interactive Media Industry Association, 1 October 2013, viewed at www.aimia.com.au.
11. Chesters et al., *Older Australians and the Take-up of New Technologies*, op. cit., p. 11.
12. S Gibbs, 'Driverless Cars Get Green Light for Testing on Public Roads in UK', *The Guardian*, 30 July 2014.
13. H Hodson, 'Sensor-laden Smart Bandages to Monitor Vital Signs', *New Scientist*, 17 July 2014.
14. E Strickland, 'We Will End Disability by Becoming Cyborgs', *IEEE Spectrum*, 27 May 2014, viewed at www.spectrum.ieee.org.
15. R Wallace, 'Robots to the rescue in aging Japan', *The Australian*, 13 October 2012.

8 Sex and Remarriage

1. R Spencer, 'Libidos, Vibrators and Men, Oh My! This is what your ageing sex drive looks like', *The Guardian*, 25 March 2014.

2. S Tessler Lindau, LP Schumm, et al., 'A Study of Sexuality and Health among Older Adults in the United States', *New England Journal of Medicine*, 23 August 2007, pp. 762–74, viewed at www.nejm.org.

3. 'Summary of results from the Third National Survey of Sexual Attitudes and Lifestyles', *The Lancet*, 26 November 2013, viewed at www.thelancet.com.

4. YK Fulbright, 'FOXSexpert: Senior Sex—Use It or Lose It', *Fox News*, 23 October 2008, viewed at www.foxnews.com. This article quotes from The University of Gothenburg Study, 'Sexuality at MidLife and Beyond', 2004 Update of Attitudes and Behaviors, AARP, Washington, May 2005; and S Hite, *The Shere Hite Reader*, Seven Stories, New York, 2006.

5. I Krasnow, *Sex After ... Women share how intimacy changes as life changes*, Gotham Books, New York, 2014.

6. S Barness, '91 Year-Old With 31 Year-Old Boyfriend Says Sometimes He Feels Like a Son, Until They're in Bed', *The Huffington Post*, 5 June 2014, viewed at www.huffingtonpost.com.

7. V Minichiello, S Rahman, et al., 'STI Epidemiology in the Global Older Population: Emerging challenges', *Perspectives in Public Health*, vol, 132, no. 4, July 2012, pp. 178–81.

8. J Power, 'STI Rates Soar Among the Over-50s', *The Sydney Morning Herald*, 9 June 2013.

9. C Rosenblatt, 'Dating Adventures of Alice, At 89', *Forbes*, 8 August 2012, viewed at www.forbes.com.

10. K Munro and R Browne, 'Over 50s Leap into Online Dating', Stuff. co.nz, 15 September 2009, viewed at www.stuff.co.nz.

11. M De Lacey, 'Meet the Foxy Fifties! Silver surfers give internet sites a boost as it is revealed more over-50s than ever before are finding love online', *Daily Mail*, 3 October 2012, viewed at www.dailymail.com.

12. A Smith and M Duggan, 'Online Dating and Relationships', Pew Research Center Report, Washington DC, 21 October 2013, pp. 12–13, viewed at www.pewresearch.org.

13. 'Baby Boomers and the Senior Dating Boom', *Dating Sites Reviews*, 10 July 2013, viewed at www.datingsitesreviews.com.

14. S Choney, '90-Year-old Weds Beau Met on Match.com', *Today*, 21 June 2011, viewed at www.today.com.

15. Smith and Duggan, 'Online Dating and Relationships', op. cit.
16. R Fisher, 'Where Are All The Older Single Men?' *Huffington Post*, 16 December 2013, viewed at www.huffingtonpost.com.
17. LM Diamond, *Sexual Fluidity: Understanding women's love and desire*, Harvard University Press, Boston, 2008.
18. 'Study Suggests Difference Between Female and Male Sexuality', *Science Daily*, 13 June 2003, viewed at www.sciencedaily.com.
19. Krasnow, *Sex After . . .: Women share how intimacy changes as life changes*, op. cit.
20. LT Coffey, 'On 100th Birthday He Married the Woman of his Dreams', *Today*, 5 June 2011, viewed at www.today.com.
21. 'Cradle Snatcher! Indian man who says he's 120, ties the knot with bride half his age (she's a mere 60 years old)', *Mail Online*, 27 October 2011, viewed at www.dailymail.co.uk.
22. 'Dana Jackson, 100-Year-Old Bride, Gets Married at Nursing Home', *Huffington Post*, 9 June 2012, viewed at www.huffingtonpost.com.
23. 'Britain's Oldest Bride and Groom, 84 and 93, Tie the Knot', *Mail Online*, 20 November 2011, viewed at www.dailymail.co.uk.
24. S Jain, 'Lifetime Marriage and Divorce Trends', Australian Social Trends 2007, Australian Bureau of Statistics, 7 August 2007, viewed at www.abs.gov.au.